me with it all. This book is a charming history, written with affection and wit by Anna and Jane, and now everyone can share in the story of their lives and lineage. It is a love story really, of a time, a place and a remarkable sisterhood that has given the world some of its most unique and stunningly beautiful music." **Emmylou Harris**

"Be it family history, beautiful snapshots from the early lives of three remarkable women or significant slices of Canadian history from the last two centuries, this book stacks up to at least be a triple threat. Add music and humour, well, now that's positively formidable. Thanks for keeping the bar raised, ladies." **Rufus Wainwright**

"Not many public figures become part of our 'family album.' In Canada, the McGarrigle sisters have. We grew up alongside them, went to their concerts, bought their albums, and then got to listen to the amazing next generation. We heard the sisters talk on the radio about 'harmony'—it made you feel you were living on a much more civilized planet. Their songs—in English and French—became part of our dialogue, our thought processes." **Michael Ondaatje**

"A detailed, intimate portrait of one of Canada's great musical families. Vivid with stories of a changing country, a transforming Quebec, all its real-life to-and-fro ringing with vibrant music." **Sean Michaels**, author of *Us Conductors*

MOUNTAIN CITY GIRLS

Mountain City Girls

The McGarrigle Family Album

Anna & Jane McGarrigle

RANDOM HOUSE CANADA

PUBLISHED BY RANDOM HOUSE CANADA

Copyright © 2015 Anna McGarrigle and Jane McGarrigle

www.penguinrandomhouse.ca

Random House Canada and colophon are registered trademarks.

Library and Archives Canada Cataloguing in Publication

McGarrigle, Anna, author
Mountain city girls : the McGarrigle family album / Anna McGarrigle, Jane
McGarrigle.

Issued in print and electronic formats.

ISBN 978-0-345-81402-9
eBook ISBN 978-0-345-81404-3

1. McGarrigle, Anna. 2. McGarrigle, Jane. 3. McGarrigle, Kate. 4. Singers—
Canada—Biography. 5. Composers—Canada—Biography. I. McGarrigle, Jane, author
II. Title. III. Title: McGarrigle family album.

ML420.M145A3 2015   782.42164092'2   C2015-902682-2

Text and cover design by Five Seventeen
Cover photo © Randy Saharuni
Interior images: (palm-lined avenue) courtesy of DeGolyer Library, Southern
Methodist University; (vinyl record) © Image01 / Dreamstime.com

Printed and bound in the United States of America

2 4 6 8 9 7 5 3 1

CONTENTS

PREFACE: I AM A DIAMOND . . . 1

PART ONE: ANCESTORS . . . 5
Saint John, New Brunswick and Montreal, Quebec

PART TWO: LIFE IN THE COUNTRY . . . 25
Saint-Sauveur, Quebec

PART THREE: RETURN TO MONTREAL . . . 153
Montreal, Fredericton, San Francisco, Saratoga Springs,
London, New York City

EPILOGUE . . . 321

Acknowledgements . . . 323
Image Credits . . . 325
Text Credits . . . 327

LATRÉMOUILLES

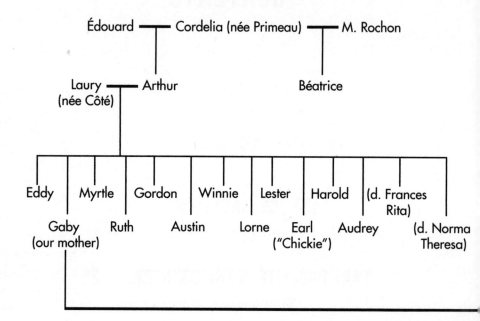

Édouard ——— Cordelia (née Primeau) ———— M. Rochon

Laury ——— Arthur   Béatrice
(née Côté)

Eddy   Myrtle   Gordon   Winnie   Lester   Harold   (d. Frances
                                                                Rita)
  Gaby   Ruth   Austin   Lorne   Earl   Audrey   (d. Norma
(our mother)   ("Chickie")   Theresa)

McGARRIGLES

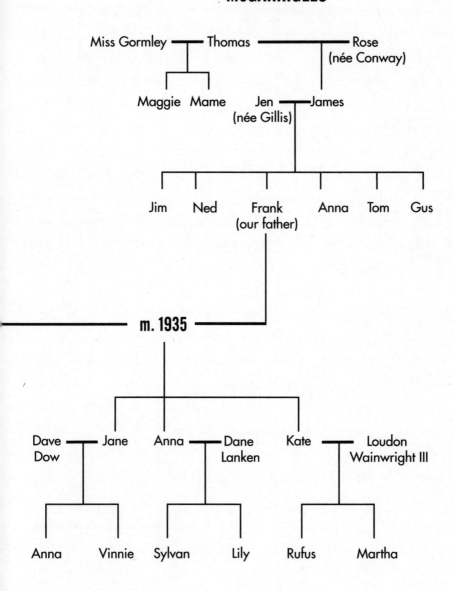

PREFACE: I AM A DIAMOND

In June 2012, two years after our sister Kate's untimely death from cancer, Toronto's Luminato Festival paid homage to her with a concert at Massey Hall. Upwards of thirty people, special guests, musicians and family were brought together by producer Joe Boyd, assisted by Catherine Steinman, to honour Kate and her music. Joe produced the first two Kate and Anna recordings for Warners, *Kate & Anna McGarrigle* (co-produced with Greg Prestopino in 1975) and *Dancer with Bruised Knees* (1977), and had curated two previous tributes to Kate, one in London, the other in New York.

ANNA: The Kate McGarrigle Tribute Concert at Massey Hall was a resounding success. The only thing that could have made it better would have been if Kate had floated onto the stage, picked up a banjo and led us in "Red Rocking Chair," an Appalachian complaint that highlighted her driving frailing-style. With her perfect timing she was the coxswain on the McGarrigle *chasse-galerie*.*
Kate's kids, Rufus Wainwright and Martha Wainwright, were the charming hosts and the musicians that made up the band had all worked with Kate and me at some point, some of them for many years, as in the case of Chaim Tannenbaum, Joel Zifkin, Michel Pépin and my husband, Dane Lanken. As each successive guest took up one of her songs, another facet of the brilliant diamond that was Kate was revealed, from the light-hearted "NaCl (Sodium Chloride)," a song about the love pairing of two atoms to make salt, to the bleak "I Eat Dinner," an elegy mourning the death of desire,

---

* The allusion is to *"La chasse-galerie"* or "The Bewitched Canoe" illustration by Henri Julien, based on the fable by Honoré Beaugrand.

with the haunting refrain *When the hunger's gone.* That night, my daughter, Lily Lanken, and I did "Jacques et Gilles," a song Kate wrote about the one million French Canadians who left Quebec over a span of a hundred years to work in the textile mills of New England. It's a powerful history lesson in the form of a children's rhyme, with a conversation between a mother and her young daughter weaving throughout, and a prequel to a musical Kate was writing about Jack Kerouac.

Earlier in the week, I was invited by Jörn Weisbrodt, Luminato's Artistic Director, to participate in a lunchtime "Illumination," a chat format that had "creativity" as the topic, with a special focus on Kate. I shared the stage with two old friends, author Michael Ondaatje and pianist Tom Mennier, and surprise guest Lily on vocals. The talk was interspersed with passages from Kate's songs, played by Tom.

At one point, Michael O. and I got onto the subject of eccentric relatives and how they unwittingly contribute to the creative process. We both had our share of these characters. Michael had written about some of his in *Running in the Family*. I told the audience about our maternal grandfather Arthur Latrémouille, who rode around on a city bus with a pig's head in an old valise. The head was for the headcheese he made for himself (nobody else would eat it). There's more about Arthur and the pig's head further in the book.

Tom Mennier, himself a rather eccentric character, ended the Illumination with the "Gardencourt Waltz," a piece in the romantic style he composed to celebrate the marriage of Martha and Brad Albetta, which took place on the family property in St. Sauveur in September 2007. It was a stunning performance, the first time Tom had played it in public, and the audience at David Pecaut Square gave him a standing ovation. We all basked in it.

Louise Dennys, Michael O.'s Canadian editor, was in the audience. She came up to me afterwards and told me how much people love stories, stories like the one I'd just recounted about our grandfather. Had I ever thought of writing them down?

From there a book idea was proposed (I guess we can thank old Arthur, in part, for that). I told Louise I would want to do it with my sister Jane, whose turn of phrase I've always admired. In a way I was carrying on what Kate had done when she'd asked me to join her in a musical career. She'd said to me, "Anna, I don't want to do this alone."

Thanks, Jane! And thank you, Kate, for being such an inspiration.

JANE: I've always been a closet writer and could not believe my good luck when Anna invited me to join her on this memoir project. Here was a chance to retrace our family's story and write it up for a larger audience than the people close to us, who were well acquainted with the fables and foibles of our clan.

Before there were Kate, Anna and Jane, there were Frank and Gaby, our parents, and before them, an assortment of memorable characters who created a powerful narrative that affected us in a very personal way. We experienced history as it touched our family. World War I, the most documented event of its time, is defined for us by the death of our mother's Uncle Percy on the killing fields of Passchendaele, leaving a widow and four children, two of them taken a year later by the Spanish flu. Uncle Percy's death broke the heart of his sister, our grandmother Laury Latrémouille, and she never got over it. Neither did we, and though we never knew him, we cried for Uncle Percy and his orphaned children. The Great Depression, to our minds, was a continuous game of bridge at the Latrémouille family table that went on for years, as people came and went to whatever jobs they could get, leaving the most recent arrivals to pick up their unplayed hands.

Show business, before we were in it ourselves, was Grandfather James McGarrigle, a pioneer film exhibitor who toured Eastern Canada and the Caribbean with his films at the beginning of the twentieth century. According to family lore, he was associated at one time with Louis B. Mayer, who left Saint John, New Brunswick, for Massachusetts and later established himself in Hollywood, and the rest is history.

Kate and Anna had long been intrigued by our uncle Jimmy McGarrigle after coming across a box of his letters written in New York *circa* 1930. He appeared to have led a dual life, publicist for CBS by day and emitter, pseudonymously, of testy cultural critiques by night. Uncle Jimmy's life would be explored in the course of our project and become part of our father's family history.

We always meant to record our mother's recollections, and did collect a few things late in her life, but never got the whole canon, and one day she was gone. Kate had almost total recall of McGarrigle/Latrémouille lore, and though it seemed she would always be there to remind us of some details we mangled, one day she too was gone, her razor sharp wit and wry perceptions much missed during the building of our story.

It was typical of Anna's generosity to include me in this project. I knew it would be a gas working together but there were emotional dividends I hadn't reckoned on. Because of the age difference when we were growing up, and Kate and Anna's close involvement with each other as creative and business partners, not to mention best friends, I've always been a little apart from my sisters. Kate's death left our sister dynamic on an uncertain footing. Who were we to each other now? Going back through many decades of memories recast our relationship to each other, and drew us closer as sisters and friends. That was to be the true wish fulfillment, though I didn't know it when we started. Thanks, Anna.

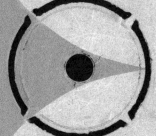

ANCESTORS

PART ONE

Saint John, New Brunswick
and Montreal, Quebec

Broken Blossoms . . . 7

Mad Hatter . . . 10

A Streetcar Named Desire . . . 13

The Courtship of Frank and Gaby . . . 17

Daddy and the Bolsheviks . . . 18

BROKEN BLOSSOMS

Our paternal grandfather, James E. McGarrigle, was the only son of Thomas McGarrigle, a ship's blacksmith working in the Saint John, New Brunswick, shipyard, and his second wife, Rose Conway. Thomas's first wife had died, leaving him with two adolescent daughters, Maggie and Mame, half-sisters to James. Maggie worked as a cobbler, and when James was old enough, he was sent to barber's college to learn a trade. Mame was a milliner who specialized in that confection worn by Catholic priests, the black biretta. One gets the feeling that Mame may have been one of those parish spinsters who spent most of her spare time in and around the church "praying down the statues," to quote James. Maggie adored her half-brother, but there was no love lost between James and Mame. James was the apple of his mother's eye and it's safe to assume he was a spoiled boy, which would have caused some resentment.

Our paternal grandmother, Jen Gillis, was the youngest child of Donald Gillis and his wife, Catherine O'Connor. Just as Jen was coming into this world, her father was killed by a runaway horse. She had two sisters, Teresa and Annie, and four brothers, John, Edward, Thomas and William. The Gillis family lived in Fairville, once a farming community across the river from Saint John.

In 1895, nineteen-year-old James McGarrigle married seventeen-year-old Jen Gillis. His doting mother, Rose, never forgave Jen for stealing away her only son. They had six children in quick succession, beginning with Jim in 1896, then Ned, Frank (our father), Anna, Tom and Gus. It was said, somewhat disparagingly, that the boys were named after the horses at the fire hall.

In the early 1900s, James was drawn to the newly emerging film industry and saw this as an opportunity to break with the humdrum barber's life he had been leading. He became a motion picture exhibitor, perhaps the first in Canada. After striking a deal with a film distributor, the exhibitor would set up in a hall or vacant storefront and the exhibitor would stay there for the run, which could be months at a time. James's first "nickel" was in the Market Hall in Charlottetown. To underscore the onscreen drama of these silent films, James hired a piano player, a young woman named Ethel Blanchard.

Needless to say, James was rarely home in those days, leaving Jen to take care of the young brood. He sent money back to his family, though, and a 1907 letter to him signed "Your ever-loving Jen" shows her enduring affection for him. But his fascination with the itinerant life and contempt for the respectable are clearly stated in his poem "Songs of the Midway":

Not the merchants for me but the grifters
The boys with the wheels
Who'll take a sucker for plenty
Then laugh at his frantic squeals
The barkers, the shills and the pitchmen
Those modern buccaneers bold
Of them shall my songs be written
Of them my tales be told.

In 1910, at thirty-three, Jen died of a lung ailment, most likely consumption. James was not by his dying wife's side. He was either on the road with his theatrical equipment, or on an extended drinking bout that broke months of sobriety, as had become his pattern.

Six-month-old Gus was sent to live with his mother's sister, Teresa Purcell, in Boston. The remaining five children, aged two to thirteen, were cared for by their beloved Grandma Gillis and maiden aunt Annie, a little hunchback. Both women moved into the family flat on Main Street in Saint John. Aunt Maggie, the cobbler, lent both financial and moral support to the children. Our aunt Anna McGarrigle, eight at the time of her mother's death, recalled visiting her dear aunt Maggie at the cobbler shop on her school lunch hours, where she would sit amidst the smells from the hides and the dyes.

Despite the loss of their mother and the frequent absences of their father, the McGarrigle children were well cared for by their loving relatives. Their apparent musical gifts were encouraged at home, and in the church productions of musicals and operettas in which they regularly appeared. Jim and Anna, both formally trained to some extent, were particularly well remembered by contemporaries.

A hundred years on, it's hard to forgive James McGarrigle his benign neglect, and indeed his half-sister Mame and his oldest son, Jim, both distanced themselves from him over time. Jim, who to all appearances was on the straight and narrow, strongly disapproved of his father's drinking habits, as did Aunt Mame. It was said that if Jim saw the old man approaching from the other direction, he would cross the street to avoid him.

The McGarrigles were dreamers, people of wit and charm. They were musically gifted and quite literate, loved to laugh and were excellent company. They were also a family touched by darkness; dispersed early on, they never really reunited.

Our father, Frank, the third McGarrigle child, was imaginative, generous, sentimental. He was immensely personable, well liked and something of a looker—enough to have done collar-and-tie ads of the day, according to admiring friends. He was musically talented to a rare degree. He tried his hand at many things, did well at some of them, and probably had more success at enjoying life than anything else.

MAD HATTER:
PORTRAIT OF JIM McGARRIGLE

Frank and his siblings stood in awe of their big brother Jim. It is generally accepted, and not just by the other McGarrigles, that Jim was a man of exceptional talents and a bit of a snob who yearned for the finer things in life. Who could blame him for wanting to lift himself above his humble beginnings? Had the family been on a more solid footing, he would have gone on to higher learning, but coming from a working-class Irish background in the British colonial outpost of Saint John, he became a milliner, a choice likely influenced by his aunt Mame. For a time he was a commercial traveller for the firm of Golding's, and this was probably considered a good job for a young man.

Aunt Mame was a fairy godmother to him, and when she passed, she bequeathed him one thousand dollars. His inheritance in hand, Jim immediately abandoned the hatter trade and moved to New York City in an attempt to reinvent himself. He sought out work more suited to what he felt were his real talents, and worked for a while as a publicist for CBS Radio News. In letters to friends he wrote terse and sometimes scathing commentary about the goings-on in the glamorous New York arts community, entitled "Pests in the News."

> Countess von Haughwitz und Reventlow—Another eye-sore back in town. She has composed some songs (God help us!) collaborating with, above all people, Elsa Maxwell.

Continuing with his reinvention of self, he composed short pieces of the magazine variety and signed them Kevin Talbot, a more noble-sounding name than Jim McGarrigle, he who was named after a horse at the fire hall and had a last name sounding like an amusement park ride. One story concerns Oscar Wilde's impromptu visit to Baron Thomas Talbot de Malahide's Canadian family seat in Port Talbot, Ontario. Another recounts a road trip he took (or it may be total fabrication—perhaps concocted from travel brochures) to the lower Saint Lawrence and Gaspé Peninsula, replete with a colourful cast. We have the original drafts, and it is not clear if any of them were ever published, but it is unlikely. His prose can be described as prissy, but his letters are truer to his character, if a bit boastful. In January 1939, Jim reminisced to a friend, a touring player installed at the Stanley Theatre in Pittsburgh:

> I was practically brought up in show business, as I told you my father was the first motion picture exhibitor in Canada, the British West Indies and Venezuela, back in the days when there were no American producers at all, and we had to rely on the Italian and French films until [D.W.] Griffith, [Jesse] Lasky and [Adolph] Zukor started in. I used to go down to Montreal East after school and run the machine in his first nickelodeon, turning out miles of [Sarah] Bernhardt, Réjane, [Eleanor] Duse, and Mimi Aguglia, before I fell in love with Mary Pickford (no one knew her name), Edith Storey, Florence Lawrence, the Gishes and so on. The old man stood to make a million dollars, but he was not smart enough for the booze. Guess the road has not changed much since then, and I knew all the old troupers.

On October 7, 1939, his forty-third birthday, his five-year sojourn in New York came to an abrupt and tragic end. Jim drowned in the East River after jumping or falling off a boat, an apparent suicide. Our mother, Gaby, used to say snidely, "I think he was pushed." By way of explaining her statement, she told us that women were crazy for Jim, implying there might have been a jealous husband, but she herself believed him to be homosexual. Jim's good friend Frederick Ryan, an artist living in Boston with his wife, Bea, a doll maker, was the first person contacted by Jim's landlady when his body was pulled from the river. Our father went to New York to identify his brother's body and had him buried in the Catholic cemetery in Hastings-on-Hudson, in a plot our father paid for. There is no grave marker, just as there are no markers on the graves of the McGarrigle anteced-ents in the Catholic cemetery in Saint John where they rest, except for Aunt Mame and Aunt Maggie, who both have simple stone ground plaques that they likely bought and paid for in advance. Fred Ryan wrote to the landlady, "My wife, who stayed at your home during August [1939], joins me in my deep regret at the passing of Mr. McGarrigle, whom I have greatly respected for many years as a man of brilliant intellect and extreme kindness."

Sometime around the year 2000, on one of her many back-and-forth trips between Montreal and New York, our sister Kate took old Route 9 out of NYC in search of Uncle Jim's grave at Mount Hope Cemetery, Hastings-on-Hudson. It was almost closing time when she stopped at the gatehouse for directions. The boozy, red-faced custodian was not happy about having to go way back in his dusty old burial records to 1939. She apologized for her lateness, explaining she was just passing through. He told her that our father Frank McGarrigle owned the double plot. She was surprised, even a bit pleased, to find out she owned real estate in New York, albeit a grave. The custodian became flirtatious and, flashing her a ghoul-ish smile, said, "There's room for another in there." She hightailed it up the hill where Jim's marker-less grave was, and then got the hell out of there.

A STREETCAR NAMED DESIRE

Our maternal grandfather, Arthur Latrémouille,[*] was the only son of Édouard Latrémouille and his wife, Cordelia Primeau. Arthur was born in Montreal and lost his father at four. Soon after, his mother married a M. Rochon, an ogre-type who forbid Arthur to live with them. Arthur was orphaned, for all practical purposes, and handed off to uncaring paternal relatives in Embrun, Ontario, who stuck him with the moniker *pensionnaire* (boarder), treated him as an unwanted visitor and sent him to bed hungry. His cousin Laura, his senior by a few years, watched over him and would sneak food to the diminutive *pensionnaire*. Cordelia and the ogre Rochon begat one child that we're aware of, Béatrice, a half-sister to Arthur, known not too affectionately as "Béatrice La Crisse."

As a young adult, Arthur returned to Montreal, where he began work as a streetcar conductor in the waning days of horse-drawn conveyances. These horse-drawn streetcars were soon replaced by electric trams that ran on tracks, and the transit authority was known as the Montreal Street Railway. Driving a tram was a good way for a young man to meet young ladies.

Laury Côté, a lithe, auburn-haired beauty, was the middle daughter of Édouard Côté, a Montreal tailor, and his wife, Catherine Bannon. Catherine was from the Irish settlement of Sainte-Marthe, a farming community on the south side of Mont-Rigaud. Like many Irish arrivals, they didn't stay long on the land, gravitating to the city, where there was work. Laury's older sister Dora died in childbirth at seventeen and her infant daughter, Dolly, was raised by her Côté grandparents. Dora's husband, forever to be

---

[*] The original French spelling for this noble name is de la Trémoille. In Québec it became the phonetic Latrémouille.

referred to as That Bastard Vaillancourt, was missing in action from his child's life.

Arthur was twenty-seven when he married seventeen-year-old Laury. They were to have twelve children who would survive into adulthood, and a few more who didn't, for a total of fifteen: Eddy, Gaby (our mother), Myrtle, Ruth, Gordon, Austin, Winnie, Lorne, Lester, Earl (Chick), Harold and Audrey. Two died in infancy, France Rita and Norma Theresa, and one was stillborn. Apart from Eddy, probably named for his grandfather Côté, the provenance of the children's names is unknown, with the exception of Winnie. The story goes that Arthur brought his newborn daughter to a nearby church for baptism while Laury stayed home after her confinement, as was the custom. He was given strict orders from Laury to call the baby Phyllis. When the moment came, neither the priest nor the father could spell "Phyllis," so the priest offered the name Winnifred, another English name he knew from a previous christening. Arthur agreed and they got on with it, but when he returned home with the baby and the baptismal certificate, it was discovered that the poor little girl had been christened Wilfred.

Laury's beloved brother Percy was killed in 1917 at Passchendaele, the longest and bloodiest of World War I's battles. Our mother, Gaby, always said Percy had no business signing up, leaving his wife and four young children, but it was hard to resist the battle cry of the recruiters, who literally picked the men off the streets. There was much anti-British feeling in our mother's household. She herself had a soft spot for the Scots.

Arthur leaned to the left and helped to found the first union for tramway employees. He was promptly fired and thereafter was a small-time usurer, lending money to his former colleagues. Unlike today, the street railway company was operated as a franchise, where drivers had to buy their weekly allotment of tickets in advance. Many of them didn't have the ready cash. Along the way, Arthur acquired some modest rental properties down east in the working-class district of Montreal, below the escarpment that our mother always called Le Faubourg, an area that now encompasses Montreal's Gay Village. A Madame So-and-So was often months late with the rent, and when Arthur would ring her up to announce he was on his way down there, she would reply, "Why don't you send Gordie?" Gaby used to crack about her handsome brother Gordon, "I think he collected more than the rent."

Arthur was fond of get-rich-quick schemes, but Lady Luck rarely smiled on him. We know of two such ventures: an attempt to corner the sugar market, and the manufacture and distribution of the Vin Rita, a tonic wine with salubrious properties, named after one of his deceased infant daughters. Both businesses ended badly, particularly in the case of the Vin Rita, which turned out to be a laxative. It had been sold as house wine to a wedding party.

Arthur was the first cousin of Urgel Bourgie, founder of Montreal's biggest undertaking concern and the first we know of, locally anyway, to institute the hugely successful practice of layaway funerals. Urgel's daughter Mignonne was the first wife of Montreal's most famous mayor, Camillien Houde, whom Arthur always referred to as *mon petit cousin.** Arthur is said to have given Camillien the deposit he required to present himself as a candidate for the Quebec National Assembly, his start in politics. Our mother loved to recall the lively political evenings around the Latrémouille table, where Grandpa was joined by Houde and R.L. Calder, the noted jurist who had once debated US politician and pacifist William Jennings Bryan and was a staunch defender of Quebec's rights within Canada. Arthur, the barefoot orphan and latter-day union organizer, had become quite politicized and could hold his own. He never ran for office himself but retained a lifelong passion for politics that rubbed off on his children and inevitably their children, all political junkies to this day.

The Latrémouilles were tribal, patriarchal, industrious and resilient. Humorous, irreverent and generally upbeat people, they were united as a family.

---

* According to our mother, Camillien was a partner of Arthur's in the Vin Rita scheme.

Gabrielle, the third Latrémouille child and eldest girl, was smart, spunky and hard-working and could do a lot with a little. She spoke her mind and enjoyed a wonderful sense of the ridiculous. Lacking confidence but gutsy, she resented and resisted male authority. She didn't believe in her own attractiveness, but to quote her sister-in-law Anna McGarrigle Miller, "When Gaby walked into a room, everyone noticed her." She wanted to be a dancer.

With his eye for quality and good design, Frank McGarrigle liked what he saw of Gaby Latrémouille.

THE COURTSHIP OF FRANK AND GABY

(Anna)

Sometime in the 1990s, I met an old woman who, like my dad, was a native of Saint John, New Brunswick. She confessed to me that all the girls in this hilly city used to wait at the foot of King Street hoping to catch a glimpse of my seventeen-year-old father as he came down the hill. This was a revelation to me, as I'd never thought of my wheezy old man as an object of desire, but I accepted it as the truth. He was a handsome dude, a bit on the short side, but there's no denying he was a charmer. The only person he seems not to have charmed was my mother. She was on the rebound when she grudgingly asked Frank, a mere acquaintance, to a company picnic back in the 1930s, ignoring him throughout, as she tells it. It was only when a curious co-worker came up to her and said, "So, Gaby, who's the good-looking fella with your sister Myrt?" that she reacted. "He's not with Myrt! He's with me!" She liked to say, "I took a second look at him." This part happened in Montreal. By the early 1930s, my father and his five siblings had all left Saint John for Central Canada and the northeastern United States.

DADDY AND THE BOLSHEVIKS

ANNA: In spring 1916, as the Great War raged on, Frank enlisted in the Canadian army. He was sixteen years old, but the conscripting officer's handwritten remarks on the form read: "looks nineteen." As a resident of Saint John, he likely did his training in his home province before finally shipping out with the Canadian Siberian Expeditionary Force in early winter 1918 to Vladivostok in the far eastern reaches of Russia.

At the outset of the Great War in 1914, Imperial Russia was allied with Britain and France against Germany, the common enemy. The United States would come into the war in 1917. The Russian Revolution occurred in 1917 and, soon after, the newly elected Soviet government was to make a separate peace with Germany. This truce in the spring of 1918 came months before agreements were reached between Germany and the other countries in the original alliance. The situation on the eastern front continued to worry some Allies, including the Americans, who still had a lot of military equipment on the ground in Russia and feared it could fall into either Bolshevik or German hands. As a dominion of Great Britain, Canada had been involved in the war since 1914, and in 1918 the Canadian government sent forces to the eastern front to support the White Russians against their Red Russian foes, already well entrenched in the eastern port of Vladivostok. There was much national opposition to this venture, which was seen as prolonging an unpopular and brutal war, but our father was lock-step with the government and used to brag when we asked him what he did in Vladivostok: "We went there to put down the Bolsheviks." In truth, the Canadian troops saw little action. Vladivostok was like the Wild West, with booze and brothels, and lots of soldiers with not much else to do but work on their Russian.

We grew up with reminders of our father's short stint in Vladivostok: a couple of old army-issue bayonets that would have been fastened to the end of an infantry rifle; an incendiary bomb stored in a box with old paper in the basement; and a *Hugo's Russian Grammar* with a faded yellow cover. Unlike Janie, who was taught Russian by a genteel baroness, Kate and I learned ours phonetically from our father. We could count to ten—*adeen, dva, tree, chyterry, pyat, shest, siem, voseim, dievat, diaset*; say the salutations—good day and good night, *dasvidaniya* and *dobre noches*; and say "gentleman"—*gaspadeen*—and "cigarette"—*paparushka*. It occurs to me now that what we were speaking was brothel Russian.

One of our father's friends in Saint-Sauveur was Canadian army major Guy Boyer, a large, imposing man maybe fifteen or twenty years older than Frank. He and my father were among the war vets who marched sombrely through the village every Remembrance Day, in their berets, to the foot of Hill 70, a ski hill named after an allied position in World War I. There, a commemorative wreath of red poppies was placed on a big rock halfway up the mountain. In the early 1950s, the Major lived in a nice white clapboard house up behind the church. I had gone there a couple of times with my father, just tagging along as we kids often did. I don't recall a Mme Boyer, but he may have had a housekeeper, who led us into a book-lined study where the Major sat in a winged armchair. The customary shots of whisky were poured and the two former soldiers conversed in low, manly tones about the affairs of the day. I would also have a drink, ginger ale with a maraschino cherry.

The last time we were at the Major's, he was in bed and clearly very ill. An ambulance was called and my father and I rode with him to the hospital in Saint-Jérôme. I have a dim recollection of holding the old warrior's hand as he lay on the stretcher for the half-hour drive, though it would have been a faster trip with the siren and flashing light going. After leaving the hospital my father took me to Castonguay's department store in Saint-Jérôme, where he bought me a floppy Dutchman's cap in maroon corduroy, maybe as a reward for being a little trooper. Sometime later he announced grimly that the Major had died.

Fast-forward to the present. While researching what the Canadian Siberian Expeditionary Force was up to in Vladivostok, I came across a mention of a Major Guy Boyer who was on the ground in Victoria, BC, in early winter 1918 with Company D of the 259th and 260th battalions. Our father was one of the four thousand soldiers in these battalions, who had travelled across Canada by train to Vancouver and were in the process of being shipped out from Victoria to Russia's eastern front. While they were dockside, a group of French-Canadian troops staged a mutiny, refusing to board the ship (SS *Teesta*) bound for Vladivostok. Many of the rebelling soldiers had just recovered from the Spanish flu epidemic of 1918; they'd contracted the virus after landing in Victoria, so they must have been a ragged, unhappy bunch. The mutineers were rounded up at bayonet point by soldiers from other regiments and forced to board the ship, where they spent the voyage shackled together in the hold. Could my father have been one of the soldiers rounding up the mutineers with his bayonet? One of the bayonets in our house?

Earlier in fall 1918, the Great War had ended, the peace treaty with Germany having been signed by the rest of the Allies. Canadian prime minister Robert Borden's ill-advised last stand on the eastern front was eventually abandoned, and in June 1919 the remaining Canadian troops in Vladivostok, including our father, were sent home.

Upon their return, the organizers of the rebellion would stand trial in a military court, where a Major Guy Boyer testified that he'd heard Onil Boisvert, a twenty-two-year-old farmer from Drummondville and leader of the mutiny, say repeatedly, "*On y va pas en Sibérie*" ("We're not going to Siberia," reminiscent of the later anti–Vietnam War slogan "Hell no, we won't go"). Boisvert did two years' hard labour for his part in the mutiny.

Was this the same Major Boyer whose hand I had held in the ambulance?

Had my father and the Major known each other in Vladivostok? I can't imagine someone with the rank of major fraternizing with a teenaged conscript, so it must have been during World War II that they met, when my father worked at the Ferry Command in Montreal, or maybe even at the Canadian Legion Hall in Saint-Sauveur, where their shared memories of the eastern front would have formed the basis for a warm friendship.

In the early 1960s, when Kate and I were involved with the left-leaning folk movement in Montreal, I went with friends to a political rally. Dissent and folk music—it went with the territory. The event was held at a workers' hall on Saint-Laurent Boulevard near Saint-Viateur. We climbed the poorly lit stairs to the second floor and filed into the room, taking our places at long tables set up for the occasion. Before the proceedings began, a woman stood up on a chair to reach the portrait of the Queen, back then a fixture on the wall in all public spaces, and with real disdain turned the monarch's face to the wall. I can admit now that this development made me nervous, but I pretended I was used to this kind of thing. A succession of speakers stood up and railed against the government's position on such-and-such, and there was much banging of fists on tables. Motions were passed, committees were formed, and people vowed to continue the fight for whatever it was they were fighting for (and then—I may have imagined this part—the crowd began waving little red flags). One thing for sure, the din in the room was deafening, but I don't remember any rousing protest songs being sung.

When I arrived home later that evening, our father, who had a habit of snoozing on the couch while he waited up for his daughters, asked me groggily where I had been and with whom, using his old standby line, "Did you meet anyone you liked better than yourself?" This always made me laugh, so while my guard was down, I told him about the rally I had attended and casually dropped the bomb about the portrait of the Queen being turned to face the wall. If my father had been half asleep before, he sure wasn't now. He jumped to his feet, his face purple with rage, and in a pinched scream, so as not to wake the neighbours, he went on about how "these kinds of places" were under surveillance, that my name could end up on "some list" and before long the RCMP would be at the door, my reputation "ruined" forever.

Then he told me about Raymond Boyer, the son of his old friend the Major. In the early 1940s, Dr. Raymond Boyer was a distinguished chemistry professor at McGill as well as a card-carrying member of the Communist Party. During the Gouzenko Affair in postwar Ottawa, when Soviet cipher clerk Igor Gouzenko defected to Canada in 1945 with state documents, Dr. Boyer was arrested and tried for passing secrets to the Soviets, information regarding a new and deadly explosive Boyer thought people should be warned about. He did two years in prison.

For a decorated military man such as the Major, and in particular one who had gone to quash the Bolsheviks in eastern Russia, the disgrace of having one's son working for the other side must have been heartbreaking. I should point out that to this day Dr. Raymond Boyer has many sympathetic supporters.

JANE: I met Raymond Boyer on a visit to the Major's house with my dad in the summer of 1952, when I was eleven. My impression is that Dr. Boyer was slowly adjusting to being back in society and hadn't seen many people. I say this because my father was in the habit of prepping me if we were going into a sensitive situation, and he had let me know that Dr. Boyer had been having a bad time of it, without of course telling me why. The Boyers were exquisitely polite and went out of their way to draw me into the conversation, not that I needed much encouragement. I don't know quite how we got to the subject of little girls and their entertainments, but I was telling them how much I enjoyed listening to the radio. My father must have seen this coming, but it was too late. Dr. Boyer asked me about my favourite show and I blurted out, "*I Was a Communist for the FBI*! It's about spies." My father was terribly embarrassed, but it became one of his favourite stories and he got plenty of mileage out of it for a long time after.

ANNA: Music venues come and go in Montreal, and sometime around 2005, Kate's daughter, Martha Wainwright, did a show in the short-lived Main Hall on Saint-Laurent Boulevard in the Mile End district of the city. That night Kate and I stood with the long line of fans stretched down the street, waiting to climb the narrow stairs to the second floor to hear Martha, performing that evening with pianist Tom Mennier and my daughter Lily on backups. When we got to the top of the stairs and I saw the room, I said to Kate, "This may be the hall where that socialist rally took place back in 1963, the one Daddy flipped out over."

It was standing room only that night, and one of the best shows I've seen Martha do. Sadly, the building was torn down last year. A real pity, as the acoustics were great in that place.

LIFE IN THE COUNTRY

PART TWO

Saint-Sauveur, Quebec

Why Are We Here? . . . 27

Life in the Country . . . 31

École Marie-Rose . . . 36

Visiting the Dead . . . 41

Au village . . . 44

Gaby . . . 45

Daddy's Postwar Career . . . 50

Mrs. Pagé . . . 52

The Crackpot Club . . . 56

Our Friends in Saint-Sauveur . . . 59

Turcot's Lake . . . 69

Home Life . . . 71

Daddy: Domestic Artist, Lover of All Things Maritime . . . 72

Talent Show . . . 74

Reading . . . 82

Frankenflynn . . . 89

Rebus . . . 94

The Camps . . . 101

Tenants . . . 103

The Baroness . . . 105

NIMBY . . . 109

Saint-Sauveur Today . . . 112

Good Times . . . 116

Strangers in Ste. Angèle . . . 118

St. Mary's School, Combermere . . . 121

Organ Grinder . . . 131

My Year of Living Dangerously . . . 137

Friar's Balsam . . . 142

Juvies . . . 145

WHY ARE WE HERE?

In the early 1990s, toward the end of her life, our mother, Gaby, spent most of her time sitting on the sofa in the sunroom of our Saint-Sauveur home. She would stare out the bay windows at ever-mounting snow berms left by the plough and say, with some asperity, "Can someone please tell me why we're here?"

JANE: In the summer of 1947, our family pulled up stakes and moved out of Montreal up to Saint-Sauveur, a picturesque village in the lower Laurentians of Quebec. Though mostly populated by succeeding generations of the original French-Canadian settlers, Saint-Sauveur has always had a sprinkling of outsiders, some living there year-round and others visiting seasonally. First came Scandinavians attracted by the skiing, then city people in the summer for the cool mountain air. A dozen or so wealthy Anglo-Quebec families acquired properties on riverbanks and mountaintops.

Our father had bought an acre of land in Saint-Sauveur back in 1933. He first came to the Laurentians in 1929 or 1930 for a year-long stay at the Royal Edward Sanitarium in Sainte-Agathe, where he was being treated for tuberculosis. He met Victor Nymark while doing publicity for the Seignory Club while it was being built in Montebello. Nymark was a Finnish master builder who was overseeing construction of the project and later built many other log structures throughout the Laurentians, including Nymark's Lodge, his hundred-room resort hotel in Saint-Sauveur.

Before our parents married in 1935, Daddy had already begun building a house on his lot and when we moved there more than ten years later, it was still a work in progress. We doubt he had planned it to be a full-time residence—if he had planned it at all. But over time our circumstances changed, as they do, and there it was, a place to land. Mountain air was thought to be better for our father's chronic lung problems, and country living was cheap. On the downside, our mother was a city girl who didn't care for the country or country people, and would probably not have agreed to move there had she known that it would be forever.

The move took place over the summer, a refrigerator finding its way to the country in the back of a pickup truck, other odds and ends in an open trailer hitched to our father's car. It must have been a bit of a comedown for our parents, who up until then had been in high cotton, relatively speaking.

During the war years, when we lived in Montreal, Daddy held what people referred to as "a big job." He was ranked a Civilian Specialist IV and worked for the Ferry Command, a special branch of the RAF that delivered thousands of planes built in North America, mostly bombers, to England for the war effort. The idea of the Ferry Command is credited to Lord Beaverbrook, the Canadian press baron who worked closely with Churchill. In our world, Daddy's purchasing agent job meant steady money, plenty of ration coupons for sugar and butter and bacon, and the newest car available, a 1942 Chevrolet, the last model GM manufactured for the civilian population until it resumed production in 1946. Daddy reported to a Colonel Orlady, a man I remember as gruff, with bright red eyes.

We had lived in a nice flat on Saint-Joseph Street, a boulevard that borders Lac Saint-Louis in Lachine, not a huge space but big enough that the war housing agency would billet someone with us from time to time. Our parents had friends with names like Kiki and Piff and entertained a lot. There was ample food, thanks to pooled ration coupons; the liquor flowed freely, thanks to grateful defense suppliers; and always music. When Gaby and Frank married, the first pieces they bought were a rug, a sofa and a harmonium, all acquired from the Sally Ann and all still in the living room of our family home in Saint-Sauveur. Frank had come into the marriage with a Gibson arch-top guitar, and not long after, they acquired a

Chickering piano. Our father was a natural musician, untrained but blessed with a golden ear, and could play almost anything on the piano. It's a familiar scene in drawing-room comedies of the 1930s and '40s: in the middle of a party, a man is seated at the piano banging out a song, surrounded by people waving drinks and singing along—that was our dad at the keys.

A merry time, despite the war, until two things occurred, possibly at the same time, but certainly fused in my recollection of events: demobilization when the war ended, and a terrible accident after one of our parents' parties. My father loaned his car to a guest who crashed it into a tree a few hundred feet from our flat, totalling the car and killing himself instantly. The police came to the house late in the night, when no one was left but a few stragglers. Our mother was frantic when she first heard what happened, and paced the floor long after our father had left with the police to go to the scene of the accident to identify his friend, then to the police station. The car was replaced soon after with a similar model, and very little was ever said about it. Years later, we three daughters speculated about the accident. Was it really an accident? Was it a hit? Who was supposed to get whacked, the driver or our dad?

We McGarrigles love a good conspiracy theory but it's more likely the friend had too much to drink and should not have been driving. It was a very boozy era. Whatever the cause, the event cast a long shadow and marks our move to the country. I was six, Anna three, Kate a year and a half.

At the time of our arrival in Saint-Sauveur, the most recent newcomers were veterans or displaced persons of World War II who came to the Laurentians looking for a new life after the chaos of the war. For whatever reason, many of the outsiders who migrated to Saint-Sauveur before and after the war were artistic in temperament or decidedly eccentric, or both. In no time at all, Frank found his inner bohemian and gravitated right to them, and Gaby followed him.

Almost seventy years later, the question could be asked, "Why are we *still* here?" For we are still very much in the old family homestead, with its ghosts and memories that have infected our children and their children. We're clearly here because we need to be.

LIFE IN THE COUNTRY

JANE: We were still settling in when I started grade one in September 1947, at École Marie-Rose, the village convent school. Later in life, people complimented our parents for being enlightened Anglo-Quebecers who had the foresight to put their children straight into French schooling. The truth is, it made their daily lives a lot easier. The nearest English school was a few miles away, and was governed by the Protestant school board, as most English schools in Quebec were at that time. It would have meant getting me a dispensation from the Catholic diocese, and organizing transport five days a week. It seems like a no-brainer now, but at the time it was a trail-blazing decision that paved the way for Anna and Kate and other anglo kids who were recent to the village.

The abrupt change of language didn't throw me, as I was used to hearing my mother speak French, and I was a quick learner. The greater challenge was trying to fit in with the other kids with my unpronounceable English name and my embarrassing parents. Frank and Gaby had a natural disinclination toward the herd mentality, to put it mildly, and didn't take my social anxiety very seriously. They enjoyed being slightly offbeat, some would say they gloried in it, and they expected the same of us. The most sympathy I could expect was my mother's standard advice: "Just rise above it, dear."

École Marie-Rose was an attractive red-brick building with a gabled roof and a small bell tower topped by a cross. A set of stairs led to a neoclassical portico at the main entry on the first floor; that was the visitors' entrance, where notables such as the school inspector or the parish priest, Monsieur le Curé, entered. The students assembled in the playground and entered through a rear door at ground level, then descended stairs to the cloakroom and lunchroom. We assembled by grade and formed a line when the bell rang.

My first day was one of the few times in my years at Marie-Rose that I got there ahead of the bell; we McGarrigles tended to be late for school, for church, for almost everything. Mummy hadn't considered uniforms and sent me off to school in a short-sleeved smocked cotton dress (it was a very warm day) and long black stockings (a gesture to the convent setting). The older girl who walked me there was wearing the school uniform, a long-sleeved black wool dress with a celluloid clerical collar and beige lisle stockings. Soon after, the uniforms changed to black dresses with white Peter Pan collars and cuffs, at first made out of cotton, then replaced with plastic. Anna remembers scrubbing the cuffs to get rid of the stains from the Waterman's washable blue ink, the only ink the nuns allowed us to use. Despite our efforts to keep them sparkling white, the cuffs darkened more with each passing month, progressing to a deep cream colour by the time the dress code changed again a few years later, to navy-blue box-pleated jumpers and blouses. We all welcomed this change, and Gaby saw a chance to recycle Daddy's old business shirts. She cut them down to fit us, the only students at École Marie-Rose, or possibly anywhere, to wear Tooke pinstriped shirts under their school jumpers. I objected to this, mostly because of the outsized collars and cuffs, but my mother's mantra was "You'll wear it and like it." And so I did.

As the weather grew colder, my mother insisted we wear thick knee-length bloomers under our dresses, embarrassing and impossible to conceal, and I would sneak out of the house without them whenever I could. One very cold morning, my mother discovered the discarded bloomers and called the convent to let the sisters know that my father would be delivering them in his car. The Soeur Supérieure came into class and whispered this information to my grade four teacher, Soeur Gilles. Something got lost in the translation, and Soeur Gilles, who was both nasty and crazy, announced to the class that Laury Jane McGarrigle had left home without her *culottes* (underpants), and that her father was bringing them to her. Anything to do with underpants is comedy gold to fourth-graders, as Soeur Gilles knew only too well. I cursed that wretched nun and my parents, but of course I never again tried to ditch the bloomers. There was no sympathy from my mother; she told me to rise above it and remember to wear them next time.

The sisters could be of uneven temperament, but Soeur Gilles was in a class by herself. She had poor impulse control and would fly into terrifying rages with little provocation. Kate first crossed swords with her when she was about five. On a show-and-tell day in my grade four class, my mother hadn't planned anything, and at the last minute she sent Kate to school with me as my *objet d'intérêt*. Kate was a hyperactive child, always in motion, so much so that some of the sisters thought her afflicted with St. Vitus's dance. She was supposed to sit at the back of the class with me until it was my turn, but within minutes she had jumped off the bench and run to the front of the room and was scooting around under the desks and climbing over the fourth-graders in their seats. Soeur Gilles was chasing after her and screaming, her false teeth clattering as they did when she got excited, until we corralled Kate and I took her home. This unfortunate episode with Soeur Gilles was soon followed by another when I was rehearsing in church to be received as a Croisillon, a sort of religious Brownie, the lowest tier of a movement known as La Croisade.

ANNA: La Croisade Eucharistique was an ultra-Catholic lay movement that fostered prayer, self-denial, regular Mass attendance, and frequent confession and Communion. The only thing missing was the hair shirt. The main in-school activities of La Croisade were to huddle in groups of four or five girls to outline the good deeds they would perform that week, to recite the rosary in the kneeling position, and to buy the inevitable religious medals or holy cards from the nun who would have laid out a display of these on her desk. So while the rest of the school was outside in the yard enjoying games of skip-rope and marbles, the Croisées (the next level above Croisillon), stayed inside and practised self-denial. I was intrigued by the accoutrements of La Croisade after seeing a fascinating item the nun was flogging that week to the older Croisées. It was a scapular, but not the little tin medal most of us Catholic kids wore to protect us from eternal damnation. This big scapular was a narrow band of white felt with blue piping that had two-inch-square pictures of Jesus and Mary sewn onto the ends of it and left dangling. It was worn around the neck like a stole but under one's clothing, against the skin—a pity, as it was so attractive, with straps that went under the arms to secure it and keep it from falling off. This religious harness offered the wearer extra protection, or so Soeur Gilles claimed. I was so tempted by this talisman that I joined La Croisade just to get my hands on one, forgetting, in my ardour, about the three to four years of self-denial that lay ahead. Not surprisingly, after a week of the joyless life that is the Croisée's, it was clear I was not made of the right stuff, so I bailed. My parents didn't balk; my father wasn't keen on zealots anyway.

JANE: I was new to the game and quite willing to be a zealot if it meant making a few friends, and had gladly presented myself as a prospective Croisillon. There were preparations ahead of the actual induction ceremony to make sure we would be solid in the movement, and eventually a dress rehearsal in the church. Gaby sent Kate with me to the rehearsal, probably to get herself a few hours of peace and quiet. As fate would have it, the Croisillons were led by Kate's old nemesis, Soeur Gilles. Kate tore up and down the main aisle, ran in and out of the pews, and disrupted Soeur Gilles's carefully arranged proceedings. It didn't blow my chances, as I feared, but Soeur Gilles blackballed Kate right then and there, saying to her, "Kate McGarrigle, *tu ne seras* jamais *Croisillon*." She carried on the vendetta when Kate was in her grade four and five classes, and Kate never forgot those miserable years. Decades later, when Kate and Anna performed on a Québécois TV variety show, Soeur Gilles caught the programme and must have had some pang of conscience. She phoned me, the only McGarrigle in the phone book, to invite Kate up to the nuns' retirement home for tea. I passed the invitation on to Kate. Her response: "Tell the old bitch to go fuck herself." Kate McGarrigle took no prisoners.

We were taught in no-frills classrooms—desks, a blackboard, a roll-down map, a bare light bulb hanging from the ceiling. The walls were decorated with colour prints of the Blessed Virgin Mary and the Sacred Heart—our Lord Jesus in his robes, his flaming heart in a circlet of thorns—and a photograph of the solemn Pope Pius XII giving his papal benediction. There was another piece of furniture tucked into a corner, roughly the size of a dresser, covered with a green floor-length slipcover. There were books neatly arranged between bookends on it, and a bud vase holding a single plastic flower. We never thought about it much until Anna arrived in class early one morning—an exceptional occurrence—and found the sister scrambling to fold up her bed and get the green slipcover over it. The sisters slept in their classrooms! There were no rooms for them at the convent, not even a dorm.

Our father was dismayed to see a bare light bulb in the classroom when he entered it one day. We spent seven or eight hours a day in those classrooms, and he feared it would damage our eyes. He was also surprised and unhappy to see that British Columbia had been renamed "Colombie Canadienne" on the roll-down map of Canada. "What business do they have renaming Canadian provinces?" he wanted to know. Nor did he care much for the version of Canadian history we were taught, with its emphasis on French victories and Jesuit martyrs, and grudging acknowledgement of the Plains of Abraham battle and its disappointing outcome. Daddy was from New Brunswick, United Empire Loyalist country, and his Canadian history had a different slant.

ÉCOLE MARIE-ROSE

(Anna)

Music Room and the Cabinet de Curiosités

The music room was at the front of the school building and the first room on the right if you were coming in the front entrance. Across from it, on the far wall of a wide corridor, was something known as a *cabinet de curiosités*, a floor-to-ceiling display case of varnished wood and glass, with stuffed birds and unidentifiable life forms floating in jars of formaldehyde resting on its shelves. This cabinet was the first thing a visitor to the school would have seen.

If we had taken life science classes, the specimens in this case might have been useful as teaching aids. But these subjects were not taught at the school, the nuns showing little interest in the living world. Their purview was the afterlife and ensuring we got there in a spotless state, and at this they excelled.

As piano students, we spent a lot of time across from the cabinet, waiting for our lesson to begin, staring cross-eyed at the lifeless forms, hoping one would start moving, while some kid in the other room *pioched* the upright piano. A *pioche* is a pickaxe, a tool used to break through bedrock before the invention of the jackhammer, and it was the usual insult levelled by the music teacher at a piano student who had "too heavy" a touch.

Lunchroom

Students who didn't go home for lunch ate in the school's basement. Everything in this high-traffic lunchroom was painted medium-grey glossy, from the cement floors to the long wooden tables we sat at to eat our sandwiches.

The kitchen and lunchroom were the preserve of Soeur Agnès, a tall, gaunt woman with a big smile who wore a long striped apron over her habit. Her sleeves were always rolled up, exposing her white forearms, and because of this she always seemed more human to us than the other nuns—that and the fact she was called Agnès, a woman's name, and not a man's like the "teaching" nuns had chosen for themselves when they took their vows.* For just five cents, you could augment your sandwich diet with a bowl of this nun's excellent soup, something the three of us always did: *tomates vermicelles, soupe aux pois et lard salé*, and Kate's favourite, *tomates, choux et riz.* Jane and I remember Kate trying to re-create the *tomates, choux et riz* soup in her Outremont kitchen. She would get in character and, like Agnès, always wore a long apron and rolled up her sleeves when cooking.

Soeur Agnès wasn't just a good cook but also a model of selflessness and compassion. One winter, two very neglected children, a girl and boy with red hair, turned up at Marie-Rose. They were from a small settlement in the mountains east of the village, still a wild and inaccessible place, and only loosely connected to civilization by bad roads. I'd overheard some older girls on the staircase say that the children's mother had died in a home birth after being delivered of a stillborn baby with only one leg. The girl, who was about nine, was placed in my class. The nuns had dressed her in a tunic and white blouse, and put barrettes in her wavy hair so she would fit in. But these efforts by the nuns to ease the child into her new surroundings could not make the look of abject terror on her face go away.

Soeur Agnès doted on this strange girl and her brother, and always hugged them as she served them up second helpings of her hearty soup. The children may have lived at the school that winter while the parish hierarchy figured out the next step. This sad episode brought out the best in the nuns, and I'm sure they would have kept the children indefinitely if they'd had a say. But by the end of the year, the girl and her brother were gone.

---

* The nuns were a big question mark for a six-year-old. They didn't appear to eat or use toilets and most had men's names. For a long time I thought they were a separate species, somewhere between a human and an angel.

Reports and Medals

ANNA: At the end of every month, report cards were given out along with medals for excellence in the four main subjects taught at Marie-Rose: *catéchisme, lecture, histoire, calcul.* The medals were of sterling silver and kept in dark blue, velvet-lined boxes, the hallmark of Birks jewellers in Montreal, where they may have come from. The most impressive, a large, ornate star hanging on a chain of oversized silver links, was for best all-round student, similar to a piece of ceremonial jewellery the Lord Mayor of an important city might wear. The medals were an incentive to do well, and during our careers at Marie-Rose all three of us were recipients of the star on more than one occasion. Janie remembers coming first for eight of the nine school months when she was in grade one, but being in second place at the end of the year and missing out on the *médaille de très grande distinction.*

JANE: This didn't sit well with Daddy, who had a strong sense of justice and suspected a political fix: they couldn't have a little English kid beating out the rest of the class for that coveted star. There were some phone calls and a meeting with the Soeur Supérieure, one of the few times my parents took up for one of us against the nuns, but the ranking stayed. He was later vindicated when all three of us girls came first in the provincial exams at the end of grade seven, with marks in the nineties.

Skits and Flicks

ANNA: Adjoining the lunchroom was a more formal area with a highly polished hardwood floor, and this was where a skit would be put on or where a talented student might treat the student body to a performance of *danse à claquettes.* Back then, tap dancing was popular in the country and it seemed that everyone from the grocer's delivery boy to the blacksmith could break into a spontaneous clog at the sound of a harmonica. Kate, Jane and I tried to get that rollicking feel in our cover of the Balfa Brothers' song "Parlez-nous à boire" on our *ODDiTTiES* album.

There was a lot of group singing at school but very little acting, except for the time our class staged the saga of the Duke of Marlborough, an English nobleman and soldier who had waged a fierce battle against the French foe under Louis XIV. The story, told in song form, was sung to the tune of Beethoven's "Wellington's Victory" (or "The Battle of Vitoria," better known as "The Bear Went Over the Mountain"), and it ended badly for Marlborough. I'm guessing that the mock sympathy for the embattled duke as expressed in this song was intended to be delivered tongue-in-cheek—after all, the English were the enemy—but we didn't know that back then. So when the hero Malborough gets killed in the end, we were heartbroken, the nuns included. Some of us even wept.

> *Marlb'rough s'en va-t-en guerre,*
> *Mironton, mironton, mirontaine.*
> *Ne sait quand reviendra.*

The tallest girl in the class was cast as Marlborough, and I was one of three small *mirontons* singing and waving pine boughs that were folded over the body of the slain duke as he expired on one of the grey lunch tables at the song's conclusion.

As mentioned, les Soeurs des saints noms de Jesus et de Marie (Sisters of the Holy Names) were famous for their music instruction. In early fall, before it got cold, the school would celebrate something called *la semaine musicale*, essentially a week of singing. One of the composer-nuns at the mother house of Vincent d'Indy would have written a chorale, there was a new one every year, that the whole school body would then learn (and presumably all the other schools in which this order of nuns taught). I remember the songs as being musically interesting, if a bit on the flowery side, but we would have liked that. The lyrics were inspirational but not necessarily religious.

The girls who could sing or read harmony were assigned to those parts while the rest sang the melody line. As long as it didn't rain, the rehearsals were held outside in the schoolyard with the individual classes standing single file in rows while the music teacher who directed us walked up and down through the rows, listening to make sure everybody was singing the right notes. She used a diapason, a tiny harmonica, to give us the starting tone. By the Friday, the last day in *la semaine musicale*, we knew the song well enough to perform it for our parents. It's one of the nicest memories I have of École Marie-Rose when the voices of all us young girls rose and floated above the village.

Very occasionally a movie was shown. I can recall only one, Hollywood's *Joan of Arc* from 1948, with Ingrid Bergman as the fetching martyr in a suit of armour and a short blond wig. All French Catholics revere the God-fearing French patriot who was burnt at the stake on a trumped-up charge of heresy. One of Joan's powerful detractors was the Sieur de la Trémoille, an adviser to the French king, the patron she had fought for and helped put back on the throne but who now ordered Joan's *auto-da-fé*, on the recommendation of the Sieur. Latrémoille also happened to be our mother's maiden name. It may have been our collective imagination, but we three girls always felt the nuns held this against us. Back then at the École Marie-Rose, having the surname of Latrémoille was akin to being a bin Laden today. After attempts by a succession of uncles and cousins to prove kinship with the noble Maison de la Trémoille, it turns out we weren't even related to this guy. I'm just as happy with this outcome. The Sieur was a despicable opportunist with lots of blood on his hands, and not just Joan's.

VISITING THE DEAD

ANNA: It was customary in those days for schoolchildren to pray *in situ* for the recently dead of the village. The funeral parlour was across the street from both the church and the school, and it was a busy place. If the close relative of a schoolmate had passed away, our class would always go to pay its respects to the grieving family, and with everybody in this small village related to everybody else, we were there a lot. The makeshift parlour was in a rambling old boarding house, the formal living room of which converted quickly to a viewing room. The parish *bedeau* lived in this house owned by the morticians, and he would drape the long windows with old purple velvet shades to shut out the daylight, and light the six big kerosene candles in tall stands that were placed around the bier, along with the floral tributes. It was into this grim scene that our class would traipse to take our places kneeling on prie-dieux set up in rows before the casket. Because I was one of the shorter girls, I had a front-row view of the deceased, and of course the box was always open. Usually it was an old grandparent, now tarted up, and that was bad enough. But once, sadly, the unfortunate occupant was the nine-year-old brother of a classmate, who was killed in a bike accident. Seeing this lifeless boy produced an added frisson on this visit.

I remember another time, as the nun led the class in reciting the mantra-like Litany for the Dead ("Lord have mercy on us, Christ have mercy on us"), an old woman roomer, still in her dressing gown and slippers, emerged from behind a creaking door, making an unintentionally terrifying entrance into the "parlour"; her bedroom was directly off the viewing room and she was likely headed for the bathroom in another part of the house. In the dim light, I recognized her as one of a clutch of older ladies, habitués of The Pub, that Kate and I often saw strolling on rue Principale as we walked home from school. The poor thing was deeply embarrassed, apologizing in her broken French for the commotion she had caused. But the surprise apparition of this flustered old dame added some levity to the gloom, especially after she turned out to be alive and not some ghost.

JANE: Sometimes the deceased were laid out in their own homes, and if a visit was warranted, a couple of nuns would walk the class, double file, from the school to the home and back again—all part of our school day. As a rule, the front door of these houses opened right into the kitchen, the main room of the house, where relatives and friends would be gathered around the table, eating and drinking in a continuous wake that went on for days. Off the kitchen was a small, narrow parlour reserved for formal occasions, and known as *le beau côté* ("the nice side"). The *mise en scène* was similar to Anna's description of the funeral home, windows draped in black or purple, the open casket placed at the far end of the room and lit by candles. It was all very gothic and frightening, and I would enter the house, my eyes looking straight ahead till I got past the little room at the left. I'd linger in the kitchen for as long as possible, chatting up the other mourners, but sooner or later it would be my turn to brave the shadows and kneel on the prie-dieu to say a prayer for the soul of the departed.

ANNA: I doubt I was the only kid who didn't look forward to these visitations, but thinking back, I suppose that seeing our fresh young faces gave some solace to the grieving family, the way household pets when brought to rest homes are said to cheer up the old folks. Some kids couldn't get enough of it, though. Like Kate and her friend Nina. The purple wreath had no sooner appeared on the front door of the parlour, the sign that someone was "in repose," than those two were in there paying their respects. I always admired their sang-froid, but I never joined them on their extracurricular visits.

All this talk of death puts me in mind of my father and this bois-terous song he played at parties, singing and laughing in the face of the inevitable:

Look at old Grandma, stiff in her coffin,
Ain't it grand to be bloody well dead.
Let's have a snifter, let's have a bloody good cry,
And always remember the longer you live,
The sooner you're going to die.

AU VILLAGE
(Jane)

Saint-Sauveur of the 1940s and '50s would be unrecognizable today. Not only was it much smaller than it is now, but it had a much larger proportion of English-speaking people, and few of them bothered to learn French. They didn't need to, since the town's administrators, merchants, car mechanics, doctors, notaries, cab drivers, waitresses, cops, bartenders, almost everyone, could speak enough English to interact with the anglo population, the convent sisters being a notable exception.

In some ignorant anglo circles, it was considered a little déclassé to speak French, as though it were the language of lesser mortals—"speak White" was one of the uglier slurs of the time—but I like to think that in Saint-Sauveur it was more a case of benign neglect than contempt for the language.

Our mother spoke French. Despite her maiden name of Latrémouille, she had been schooled in English and it was her first language. Our father, Frank, spoke a sort of pidgin French, with a lot of hand gestures to make his point.

Of the two parents, he was the stronger advocate of us learning French early on, and tried to pass on a trick he thought would improve our accent: we should speak as though we had a mouthful of walnuts. He was earnest about this, and tried again and again to demonstrate the technique, but we couldn't take him seriously; we were too busy laughing at his terrible French which, sad to say, improved very little over time.

GABY

(Jane)

Qui prend mari, prend pays ("Who takes a husband, follows him"), goes the old French saying, and when Gaby was transplanted to Saint-Sauveur, and in reduced circumstances at that, she played it by the book. You could say she applied her mantras to herself: "You'll live it and like it *and* rise above it."

She threw herself into her cooking, scribbling down recipes for new dishes she heard about on daytime radio shows. We still have her scraps of paper in a tin box in Saint-Sauveur, her faded Pitman shorthand impossible to decipher, but we remember the dishes: baked green rice, curried eggs, Harvard beets, creamed finnan haddie, various organ meats in sauce (which my father couldn't stomach, although we had to—"You'll eat it and like it"), a good steak or roast on Sunday. I went through her old recipe box recently and came across directions for a pork liver and eggplant casserole. I doubt she ever put that in front of us—I think I would remember the *en masse* flight from the dinner table.

There was an old Singer sewing machine in the house, which Anna remembers as having belonged to Gaby's mother. It was set up in front of the picture window in our sunny upstairs dayroom. Gaby patched our play clothes, mended seams, made us costumes and cut down cast-off clothes to fit us. Occasionally she made us clothes from scratch, memorably three beautiful silk dresses in the summer of 1949. She'd found a bolt of raw silk my father had rescued from somewhere, and she used some of it to make us matching dresses, painstakingly hand-smocked, and three little Dutch hats. They were sweet outfits and inspired Daddy to take the rest of the bolt to his tailor Sam Ogulnik in Montreal, who fashioned him a smart jacket out of it. Only Gaby was not dressed in raw silk for Sunday Masses that summer; she never sewed for herself.

As a business-girl-about-town in Montreal, she had enjoyed good clothes and wore them well with her nice figure and good posture. A girlfriend had put her on to Percy Green, an Old World tailor who was able to translate her magazine photos of designer fashions into dresses and suits she could afford. She loved to tell us about Percy working up a drawing and adding the finishing touches—"a little flurry here, a little flurry there" (in an approximation of Percy's Russian Jewish accent)—until they were both happy with it. Thanks to Percy's custom knock-offs, Gaby was fashionably turned out and known for it. Once we moved to Saint-Sauveur, she took less interest in clothes but still picked up the odd nice outfit on trips to the city. When she dressed up, Daddy used to tell her, "Gaby, you look like a million dollars!" Daddy would sometimes buy something that he thought would look nice on her, but more often than not she would make him return it because she found it too expensive.

At one point she became interested in weaving and had a loom moved into the dayroom. It became a passion, and for a while it seemed everything in the house was handwoven: curtains, stair coverings, placemats, rugs. She progressed from strips of rags in her shuttle that produced nubby pieces, such as the placemats, to a very fine wool she wove into her own cloth. When I was about fifteen, she made me a beautiful skirt cut from a piece she had woven. It was black wool, with a gold and multicoloured thread pattern a few inches above the hemline, and had a matching stole. I wore it for a few years, then lost track of it. I wish I had it today. It should have been a family heirloom but was probably lost to the moths.

There were several boarding houses in Saint-Sauveur in those years, one of them run by Mr. and Mrs. Fred Bratberg, Norwegian émigrés whom my father had known early on. Gaby had become friends with Mrs. Bratberg, who had a little pastry shop on the main street where she sold homemade pies and cakes. Gaby was a good baker in her own right. My father enjoyed dessert with his meals and there was usually a sweet with dinner—once in a while honey-butter tarts or cream puffs, in summer a fruit tart or Nesselrode pie.

Inspired by Mrs. Bratberg, Mummy took her baking up a notch and started experimenting with yeasted breads. She was working on her Danish pastries around the time, winter 1949, that Daddy suffered a recurrence of the TB he had first been treated for in the 1930s. He was admitted to the Veterans' Hospital in Saint-Hyacinthe, a town on the Yamaska River, east of Montreal, some 130 kilometres from Saint-Sauveur. Gaby was left to cope alone with three young children in an unfinished house. Her morning would start at around four or five o'clock, when she went outside to where the basement access was, often in temperatures of minus-thirty degrees, and got the coal furnace started. Then back up to the kitchen, where her Moffat stove, an electric-wood hybrid, was waiting to be fired up. She'd have left the pastry dough to rise before going to bed, and once she'd gotten the heat going in the morning, she shaped the pastries on the basket of an inverted ski pole, probably a tip from Mrs. Bratberg, and put them in the oven to bake. The house and the pastries were warm when we came down to breakfast.

Gaby took good and loving care of us, but she was not an indulgent mother. My father had a favourite story he liked to tell, about her sending us off to school one extraordinarily cold morning, something like forty below zero. His car wouldn't start and he had heard on the radio that it was too cold for the Montreal mounted police to take their horses out. He wanted to keep us home, but she bundled us up and off we went to school on foot, a mile or so away. He fretted at her all day about it, and when I got home, he was still at it. She asked me: "Who was missing from school today?" My answer: "No one." We Laurentian kids were a hardy lot.

Depending on where the family was in its mercurial finances, at any given time Gaby's homemaking may have been about creative fulfillment or there may have been an economic imperative, but we never knew the difference. She had lived through the Great Depression; recycling, reusing and making do to postpone an expense were second nature to her. When we couldn't or wouldn't wear our father's cut-down shirts anymore, they were ripped into strips that were sewn together into a long tail and loaded onto her shuttle to be woven into a rug. Our father was more expansive about money, profligate in some ways, though he enjoyed getting a good buy when he could, probably his background as a purchasing agent and the joy of discovering a treasure someone else had overlooked.

She decided one day to try making her own soap, with animal fat and lye. She made a big batch of it—economy of scale—but it was a disaster. The product didn't smell very good and burned the skin ever so slightly. We howled, and the bathroom was restocked with Palmolive.

Gaby had opened a charge account at Marche Réal Chartier when we first moved to Saint-Sauveur, and did all her grocery shopping there. Réal's parents and nine siblings lived up the street from us on Lanning, close to the store's location on rue Principale. Although we always had a car, Mummy didn't drive and usually phoned in her order to be delivered later in the day. Money was thin at the time of my father's illness in 1950, and my mother later told me that Réal carried us for many months. After we got back on our feet, she settled with him and rarely ever shopped anywhere else afterwards. She still had the charge account in 1994 when she died, and Kate took it over from her.

It was a long time before Gaby had her own set of friends, and initially she must have found life in Saint-Sauveur very lonely. I think of her as being solitary in those early years, except for when family and old friends came to visit. I have a recurring memory of coming home from school some winter afternoons and seeing her through the living room window, sitting at the piano, my father's usual place. She read from a book of popular songs, singing and using the music notation to accompany herself. It's an oddly poignant recollection, because as far as I know, she never did it in front of anyone else—unlike my father, who could, and did, play practically anything by ear on piano and guitar, for himself and anyone who cared to listen or sing along.

I think the first person in Saint-Sauveur to befriend my mother was Mme Lavigueur, an elderly widow who lived next door with her maiden sister Mlle Côté. They were great gardeners and gave Gaby fresh vegetables from a big patch behind their house. Mrs. Lavigueur sewed beautifully and helped my mother when she was having trouble sorting out dress patterns or was struggling with fitting sleeves and other tailoring challenges. They were the first people we knew to have a television set, and invited us over a couple of times a week to enjoy the marvel that was early TV. We watched *The Honeymooners* and NHL hockey games on Saturday night, and on Wednesday nights *La Lutte*, pro wrestling matches televised by Radio-Canada, often featuring Anna's favourite, Gorgeous George.

ANNA: Between programmes, Mlle Côté, or Hedwidge as she was known, a small, spry woman with white hair in a chignon and wire-rimmed glasses, would race to the kitchen and return with a tray of refreshments for our family. If Daddy was along, he got a glass of beer while the rest of us were served orange juice and grenadine in a highball glass with a swizzle stick. Mme Lavigueur's son-in-law owned a Montreal nightclub with a tropical theme, and though the two old ladies didn't take a drink, they knew how to serve one. We loved going there. They were most gracious, letting us watch English TV, foregoing their own enjoyment. For some reason, I loved Milton Berle. But if I know Kate, she was probably inspecting the many pink moles on Hedwidge's face as she bent forward to collect our empty glasses.

DADDY'S POSTWAR CAREER

(Jane)

I'm not sure what we lived on after Daddy left the Ferry Command. He may have done some work for Uncle Austin, Gaby's brother, who had by then acquired the Noorduyn Company, famed for their Norseman bush plane. This was a bit of a turnabout. Before the war, Uncle Austin had worked for Daddy at Noorduyn's while the Norseman prototype was being built. He was a gofer, fetching screws and whatnot. Now he owned the company.

During summer 1949, Daddy shared space with some old friends, Don and Jim Stafford, who kept an office on St. James Street in Montreal, where they were representatives for Fuller Brush. He had been friends with the boys' father, Stuart Stafford. I remember the office being small, a couple of rooms, with a definite bachelor feel to it—a lot of stuff around, brush samples and unfiled paperwork. I don't remember there being a secretary. It was quite far west of the fashionable part of St. James Street where the country's major financial institutions were located, another universe where the rents would have been a few multiples of what the Staffords were paying and, knowing my father, where he would have liked to be; it was part of his expansive nature to see himself in grander surroundings. Still, the Stafford boys gave or rented him a desk and a telephone and a place to spread out and make his calls in a business-like atmosphere, and he was grateful for it. I think he was probably developing the idea of brokering aircraft parts, a business he would launch a few years later.

He often took me to town with him, and if there were children on the street when we arrived, he would send me out to play with them. Mostly the kids were little black girls who lived in the neighbourhood, Little Burgundy, and jumped rope on the sidewalk. They may have been children of porters who worked for CP Rail at

Windsor Station, or of men who worked in the rail yards a little west of there.

On the way back to the country, we sometimes stopped at a roadhouse for a meal. I was seven at the time, and loved these dinners out with my father, but they annoyed my mother, who was stuck at home holding dinner for us.

In the fall of 1949, Daddy took a job with the Sicard Company, manufacturers of snow blowers and other heavy equipment. I have no idea what he did for them, but the job was in Thetford Mines, Quebec, a five- or six-hour drive in those days. He would stay for the week and return to us on Friday night. I picture him in one of those second- or third-rate small-town hotels that Alice Munro brings to life in her stories, where salesmen and other itinerant workers put up. I expect he was very lonely for his family. Then again, the hotel might have had a friendly bar, and the bar might even have had a piano. At all events, six months into it, his health gave out again, and he had to leave the job for his three-month stay at the sanatorium.

MRS. PAGÉ

JANE: I was in grade three the winter my father went into hospital, and it was around that time that I developed a fear of death that became truly phobic. The village's older citizens tended to make their passage in winter, and they seemed to be dying like flies that season. I became fixated on death and was terrified by its rituals and trappings. I began having nightmares, and whenever news came of someone having died, I would walk the long way around to avoid the house with its dreaded purple wreath on the door. As chance would have it, while I was avoiding one problematic house on my way home from school, I walked past the home of a Mrs. Pagé, the grandmother of a classmate, only to see a black hearse in her driveway, rear doors open, and morticians carrying a coffin out of the house. They dropped it in the snow and I became hysterical. I ran home into my mother's arms and refused to let any of us go to sleep for a few nights, convinced we wouldn't wake up. My mother must have phoned my father that night, because I was excused from attending the funeral, and received a beautiful and comforting letter from him. The letter and the arrival of spring, with its lower attrition rate, helped me pull myself together, and we all went back to sleeping nights again.

ANNA: Back in early 1950, when my father was hospitalized for a recurrence of TB, I couldn't yet read or write, so to communicate my longing for him I would draw a picture of a clown that my mother would send along with her weekly letter to him. He acknowledged these in his return letters to my mother like this, as I recall: "Please thank Anna Ruth for the clown. It really cheered me up." I kept the happy clowns coming for the three months he was confined.

Then one grey day in May, my mother's brother Austin, now also living in Saint-Sauveur, came to get our mother, Kate and myself, and while Jane stayed behind in school, we four set out for Saint-Hyacinthe in his big grey Plymouth. Daddy was getting out of hospital. This was a change to Kate's and my daily routine of just running around the house and getting in my mother's way, so I remember this trip vividly. Kate and I sat in the deep back seat of the old car with its rough woollen-weave upholstery and windows set too high for us to see out of, and as often happened when I found myself in a moving car, I promptly threw up. We stopped while my poor mother, cursing me all the while, cleaned up the mess. (Thereafter, when I travelled any distance in a car, it was sitting on my mother's lap with my head out the window, like a dog.)

We drove south, through Montreal, crossing over the St. Lawrence River on the big Jacques-Cartier Bridge, and then east to Saint-Hyacinthe, a town on the flat south shore, featureless but for the strange Monteregian Hills that Kate and I couldn't yet appreciate. We were hungry as we reached Saint-Hyacinthe, so my uncle bought some cheese sandwiches from somebody, and before going on to the hospital we ate these on a cheerless stone embankment above the brown, frothy Rivière Yamaska. The sight of the plain mid-century sandwich, still with the crust on (my mother always cut off the crust), and the bright orange cheese, lingers on in my memory like Rosebud for Charles Foster Kane.

Kate and I waited in the car with Austin while my mother went in to help my father with his departure. Back then, children were not allowed in hospitals, especially not in the TB wards. Among the personal effects he brought with him was the little bundle of letters from home and my clown drawings. I don't remember the trip back, except that my father sat up front with my uncle while Gaby joined Kate and me in the deep back seat. I imagine Kate and I fell asleep, lulled by the reassuring sound of grown-up voices, relieved to finally have our father back with us, and waking as the Plymouth made the familiar turn into our driveway in Saint-Sauveur. For a long time after his return, our mother was on high alert, terrified the TB would resurface. If she so much as heard a cough from one of us, we were rushed off to the Royal Edward Chest Hospital for a TB patch test, which happily always came back negative.

A little later, I remember searching the house for my clowns to show to a friend, but they were gone. None of our parents' three-month-long back-and-forth letters to each other ever turned up, either, and I wonder now if my mother burnt them as a precaution. Or maybe they just got lost in the morass of my father's stuff.

The only document that survives from that time is our father's comforting letter to eight-year-old Janie, who kept it with her all these years.

Friday, April 14/'50

Dear Janie,

How are you? I can't wait to see you. I thought you were going to write me and tell me everything that goes on.

Mummy said you came first last month—Was I glad!

Mummy also told me about Mrs. Pagé and the funeral. I hear you have a difficult time going to sleep at night thinking about these things.

I can realize, Janie, how anything in connection with death, or the thought of it, has a terrifying effect on a child-ish mind. I used to be that way when I was a little boy about your age. But of course I did not know the things then that I know now.

I have learned that there is really no such thing as death—the way you think about it. It is true that when God wants to call any of us, he just does so and our souls are then sepa-rated from our bodies, and once the soul leaves the body, why then the old body is of no further use and it is disposed of into the ground.

We pay a lot of respect by giving it a nice funeral and everybody dresses in black, but only because it had, for a time, been the dwelling place of one of God's souls. So if you are a good little girl, you should have no fear whatever of God calling you, because he is going to call every one of us in His own good time.

All of life, Janie, everything living, is just one big succession of being born—living for a while—and then going back to Mother Earth.

You see all the wild flowers and the plants in the gardens? They all die in the Autumn and other ones come up in the Spring and Summer, growing from the seed that the dead ones left behind.

So just don't let things like old people dying worry you. You just go ahead and be as good as you know how—be good to Mummy, and be kind to your little sisters and your friends, and you won't have to worry about going to sleep at night—and be sure to say your prayers to your Guardian Angel, and then nothing—just nothing—can happen to you while you sleep—and you see that Anna and Kitty Kate say their prayers too.

Now if you have anything you are worrying about, just write and tell me. I'll understand it and explain it to you.

Yours affectionately,
Daddy

JANE: About a month after the funeral crisis, I came home from school and there was Daddy, waiting for me in our living room. He was weak and thin, and a clumsy bronchoscopy had knocked out some of his lower teeth, but he was back with us. I literally jumped for joy, trying to climb all over him, but I was restrained by my mother because he was frail, and I think, too, because of her ever-present worry that he might not be entirely cured.

THE CRACKPOT CLUB

JANE: There was a pub in the middle of the village, called, in fact, The Pub, which Frank first frequented in the 1930s on his ski trips to the Laurentians. I don't know how much actual skiing he did (I never saw him on skis in all the years we lived there), but he spent a lot of evenings at The Pub playing the piano, before and after we moved to Saint-Sauveur. On weekends, the place filled up with skiers who had come up on the train from Montreal to ski and party. Mid-week, it was the watering hole for a certain set of local anglos whose numbers grew after World War II with the arrival of new people who ended up in Saint-Sauveur, refugees from another life. My father found kindred spirits among them, and began to gather regularly with a few of them and some locals to form the Crackpot Club. My mother was not a fan. I think she was a little embarrassed that my father would publicly self-identify as a Crackpot (privately was bad enough) and she objected to him "making a public spectacle of himself," as she put it, when he followed through with some of their odder rituals, for example the Crackpot Salute.

I was riding in the car with my father on rue Principale one afternoon when he suddenly stopped the vehicle, opened the door and stepped out into the street. He lifted his leg at a right angle, knee bent like a flamingo's, and stood there for a couple of seconds. A man on the opposite sidewalk stopped and lifted his leg at a right angle and held it for a few seconds. They were exchanging the Crackpot Salute. The man on the sidewalk was Shaky Brown, a photographer and early member of the club, not a favourite of my mother's, I'm afraid. She had a better opinion of Louis Rotenberg, a first-class violinist and another early member of the club. Louis was an occasional visitor to our house and I remember him telling us that he was the uncle of Percy Faith, a popular entertainer at the time. I'm sure that boosted him in my mother's estimation.

ANNA: Burton Bidwell was the main guy. He was from a well-off Montreal family and had gone to McGill. I remember hearing chat around the house that Bidwell had come into some money from his recently deceased mother. He quickly proceeded to burn through his inheritance with the purchase of a Scandinavian-style log house with a grass roof, built by Mamen, a Norwegian. The house and property were at the end of a long lane off Montée St-Gabriel near the crossroads for Christieville, a hamlet a few miles west of Saint-Sauveur. There was at least one outbuilding, a log shed also with a grass roof, which Kate and I remembered as having goats grazing on it. The movie *Heidi* had just played in the village at the Nordic Theatre, so we were thrilled to see these little creatures, and with being allowed to climb a ladder to touch one.

As we entered the kitchen area, a dark-haired gentleman named Rudi was just taking a loaf of freshly baked challah from the oven, and he served us some with butter. Rudi had a thick Austrian accent and, we learned later, was a DP (displaced person). It really was beginning to feel like *Heidi*. Had we imagined the whole thing?

There were other men about, including Mr. Bidwell, whom we knew, but certainly no women, and it was unclear to Kate and me just what it was they did there. Our impression was that it was a kind of boys' club (GIRLS KEEP OUT!) for old guys.

JANE: The Crackpot Club was a free-form organization with no rules, no officers, no dues and no agenda. The Crackpots enjoyed good talk about music, art, literature, current affairs. I think what they did was talk and drink, and escape the womenfolk. And eat Rudi's bread.

ANNA: Almost fifty years later, Kate and I were looking for a studio near Saint-Sauveur to begin recording our 2003 release, *La vache qui pleure*. As it turned out, our producer-musician friend Borza Ghomeshi, already based in the Laurentians, had just bought the old Mamen-built house and had converted the shed to a studio. What better place to record a song about a crying cow than in a shed where goats had once grazed on the roof? We told him about coming to this place as children, and described the house when it was called Crackpot Castle. When Eloi Painchaud, a Madelinot musician/producer, and his wife, the performance artist Jorane, bought the property from their friend Borza a few years ago, he filled them in on the history of Crackpot, and the place now goes by its original name, Studio Crackpot.

I was last at Crackpot in the spring of 2012 to do an accordion overdub for Angèle Arsenault, the brilliant Acadian songstress whom Kate and I had worked with on and off over the years. She was leaving PEI for good and moving to Saint-Sauveur. We talked of getting together. I didn't know it at the time but she was sick with cancer and died in 2014.

JANE: Over the years, there's been speculation in the village that Mamen's log house in the mountains was an espionage centre of some kind during World War II, and that the grass roofs were camouflage to blend it into the surrounding scenery, making it undetectable to aircraft. Maybe the goats were ringers to give it a realistic touch.

OUR FRIENDS IN SAINT-SAUVEUR

ANNA: Kate's and my best friends in Saint-Sauveur were Nina and Judy Hinds, two pretty sisters who lived a few doors away from us on rue Lanning. Petite, dark-haired Nina was the same age as Kate; fair, lithe Judy was a couple of years younger. The Hinds family settled in Saint-Sauveur not long after we did, and one of my earliest memories is of walking up the street hand in hand with my mother and meeting Mrs. Hinds, who was pushing Judy, still a baby, in a big grey pram. The girls' German-born father, Gerry, worked in Sainte-Thérèse, about halfway from Saint-Sauveur to Montreal, and was one of our uncle Austin's passengers. Austin commuted to Montreal five days a week (to his company Noordyun-Norseman Aircraft, which he now co-owned) and provided an informal shuttle service for a number of people in the village who worked in or near the city. Betty, Nina and Judy's tall, willowy mother, had travelled the world as a nineteen-year-old, some of it astride a motorcycle, even visiting far-off Tahiti. I remember her as a keen renovator and builder of houses, who always kept a stack of *House Beautiful* magazines for inspiration by her chintz-upholstered armchair in their cozy living room. Compared with our place, the Hinds' house always felt serene.

The girls were well behaved and I never heard either parent raise their voice. Kate, by contrast, could be strident and often found herself at odds with Mrs. Hinds. After Kate had called the girls' mother an insulting name, she was banned from their home and, more importantly, from riding in Mrs. Hinds's Hillman station wagon, a real hardship for Kate as this was how we got to the swimming hole in Christieville, a few miles away. The standoff went on for a couple of weeks before Kate eventually capitulated and apologized. Over the years she grew very fond of Mrs. Hinds, and I think Kate's later love for real estate and renovations originated with Betty.

On rainy or very cold days, we mostly congregated at their place. The girls had the large set of Prismacolor pencils, perfectly sharpened using their wall-mounted sharpener, so there were enough pencils to go around four ways. While a recording of a Tahitian chant played in the background, *Hiro e, Hiro e,* Mrs. Hinds made rhubarb compote in the kitchen and we girls huddled around their maple colonial dining room table, illustrating homemade versions of favourite fairy tales, such as Rapunzel, the princess locked in the tower who could let down her ridiculously long hair so her prince could climb up it, or poor Sleeping Beauty, who spent one hundred years on her back waiting for her prince to show up and wake her with a kiss. It has occurred to me that the actions of these princes mimic what some birds, bees, butterflies and moths have to do in the natural world just to fertilize some finicky flowers.

When it was just the two of us at home, Kate and I sat at "a corner" of the long pine table in our living room and played with cut-out dolls, sometimes making the dolls out of our father's shirt cardboards, and of course all their clothes and accessories. I emphasize "a corner" because the rest of the table was usually covered with my father's papers in the open-style vertical filing system he favoured. This way, he knew where everything was, like Harold "Biss-on-ay," the W.C. Fields character in *It's a Gift,* who kept a similar "filing" system on his rolltop desk and when asked for a particular document could stick his hand into the middle of the two-foot pile of papers and pull out the exact one.

On our free corner, Kate and I constructed elaborate split-level apartments for our paper ladies from stacks of soft leather-bound books with gilt-edged pages, incorporating old brass and marble bookends for the doorways that made them look like the entrances to Egyptian tombs. Our mother's motley collection of porcelain figurines also found their way into our dolls' dream homes, behaving as free-standing sculptures that we would move the dolls around as they went about their very busy social lives, visiting each other in their respective apartments. Kate and I spoke for the dolls: "Would you like a cup of tea, missus?" "Oh yes, thank you, missus. That was lovely!" Our genteel banter was superimposed over our mother cursing the Bendix washer in the kitchen, which had a habit of overflowing.

But mostly Kate, Nina, Judy and I played outdoors. Behind all our houses on the west side of Lanning was a dense swamp with a stream running through it. The stream flowed out of a small lake to the north and drained into a culvert under chemin du Lac Millette to the south before joining Le Grand Ruisseau, the sandy-bottomed river at the base of the ski hills. Village boys fished for speckled trout in the river's golden waters, and where the creek went under the road, there stood an old Quebec farmhouse, a white board-and-batten, and beside it a very large willow, its big branches hanging out over the water. In early May a profusion of bright yellow marsh marigolds magically appeared on the banks of the creek just in time for us girls to pick Mother's Day bouquets.

Our immediate neighbours to the north, the Booth boys, all good Scouts, cut trails through this swamp and named the paths according to their topography: the Green was leafy and tame, easily negotiated; the Skeleton dense and treacherous. The trails were accessed from the backyards of our homes and went down into the swamp, over the creek and up an embankment to an overgrown meadow where there stood a rustic, varnished log cabin with an overhanging porch belonging to a man with the intriguing name of "Swiss" Renaud. It was like something from the set of a Hollywood Western and just having it there greatly enhanced our field of play. Beside the cabin was a grove of mature white pines the four of us spent hours climbing, hanging by our knees from the thick branches. Kate usually got highest up the tree, and standing precariously on her lofty perch, she would dare the rest of us to join her.

There was a trail directly behind our house that didn't have a name, but it's where Gaby would send us girls with a shovel and pail to collect the black mud from the creek bottom to enrich the sandy soil of her perennial garden. The Booths, often in the company of the two McDowell boys who lived on the other side of the Lavigueurs, built forts along the trails using strong branches for the frames and covering them with pine boughs. The building of forts was more the boys' pastime, but when the boys weren't there, we girls snuck in and played house. We likely had a doll or two in tow. "The babies" who now travelled in Judy's old grey pram would not have been safe with the boys around, armed as they usually were with bows and arrows, and bowie knives in leather sheaths worn around their waists.

The boys also owned BB guns and were famous for shooting birds, which always saddened us girls and angered Gaby, who loved her birds. Our job was to lay the poor things to rest in an Eddy matchbox (we'd empty all the matches out, to the annoyance of our mothers) lined with dandelion flowers, and marking the bird's grave with a cross made from Popsicle sticks.

There was another house in the meadow, a one-storey Laurentian-style shack lived in by the eccentric Buck Hughes and his old father. In winter, we girls played in the tall snowbanks bordering the street, which had been pushed up by the ploughs, just crawling around eating handfuls of snow. We saw Buck a lot. He was known as a ski bum, a guy who spent his days on the hills and his evenings in the bar. Always elegantly done up in corduroy knee-length plus-fours and hand-knit Scandinavian knee socks, hiking boots and a royal-blue boiled-wool jacket with a red and white polka-dot neckerchief, this deeply tanned Laurentian fashion plate would strut up rue Lanning every afternoon on his way to happy hour at The Pub. If Buck had been a bird, he'd have been a blue jay, at his showy best in a winter landscape against a background of white snow.

In summer, a number of families from the city rented village houses, boosting the kid population. The Aronsons' house, also on rue Lanning, was close to the CN railway tracks at the top of the street, where trains pulled by huge black steam locomotives origi-nating in Montreal travelled northwest to Montfort, Arundel and

Huberdeau and back again. What they transported did not concern us; those big, heavy trains were there to flatten the pennies we'd left on the tracks. The Aronsons had a screened-in porch and throughout the summer there was usually a Monopoly game in progress with a queue of restless young property speculators wanting in on the game. Mrs. Aronson, a vivacious brunette, was the piano accompanist for Les Grands Ballets Canadiens, founded in Montreal by Russian émigrée Mme Ludmilla Chiriaeff. Mrs. Aronson's father was a hat wholesaler, and I remember one summer everybody getting free straw hats. We McGarrigle girls wore ours to Sunday Mass; back then, women and girls had to cover their heads when they entered a Catholic church.

We were some of the few Catholics in our group of friends, the delineation of society being more along language lines, but not strictly. On Saturdays most kids went to the movies at the Nordic Theatre, a modern white stucco building on chemin de la Gare across from the train station. After the tragic Laurier Palace fire in Montreal in 1927, when seventy-eight children died, the city passed a bylaw prohibiting children under sixteen from entering movie houses. Happily, this was not the case in Saint-Sauveur, where all were welcome. Even if not all the films shown were suitable for children, we saw them anyway. For a while one of the cinema owners had a thing for Gina Lollobrigida, so we got to see most of her oeuvre, which in retrospect was pretty lightweight, like the flimsy blouses she wore.

It goes without saying that Kate, Nina, Judy and I were very close, not just in Saint-Sauveur but later in Montreal, when both Nina and Judy were at McGill at the same time as Kate. Tragically, while I was writing this chapter in early 2014, our friend Nina was murdered in Mexico with her boyfriend during a house robbery.

JANE: The Booth family arrived on Lanning Street sometime in the early 1940s. Ron and Gert Booth bought the house just to the north of ours and moved in with their family of boys. Ronnie, the oldest, was a year younger than me, and Sean and Wayne were about the ages of Anna and Kate. The Booths were weekenders at first, and made Saint-Sauveur their permanent home in 1950, around the time their fourth boy, Dean, was born.

Ronnie and I started playing together not long after they arrived and were best friends for the better part of ten years. I left my dolls behind and picked up a Roy Rogers six-shooter to play Cowboys and Indians. Ronnie was Roy and I was Dale Evans, Roy's real-life wife; we renamed our bikes Trigger and Buttermilk after Roy's and Dale's real-life horses.

On Ronnie's inspiration, we formed the Daredevil Club and held our meetings in a clubhouse Mr. Booth built for us in their backyard. Although our siblings and other kids on the street came and went in the Daredevil Club, Ronnie and I were the charter members—we ruled.

Ronnie was a youngster of imagination and ingenuity. Our bedrooms were directly across from each other in the second-storey gables of our houses, and the seven-year-old MacGyver rigged up pulleys outside our windows and a cord between them so we could send each other messages in a tin can. The messages might be updates on some spying we were doing, or clues to a mystery we were trying to solve. We devised a communications system using flashlights to beam signals at each other, often an alert that a message was on its way and an answer expected.

In summertime, we fished, rode our bikes, swam in a lake up the road, shot BB guns at tin cans up in the hills, made trinkets with the birchbark we peeled from trees. After supper we played hangman, with flashlights to read the maps we drew for each other in the earth. There was an overgrown, creepy swamp behind our properties, as irresistible as it was repulsive, full of snakes and toads and imagined horrors, and we were drawn to it like steel shavings to a magnet. In our games of hide-and-seek, Ronnie would make a point of hiding himself somewhere in the swamp, forcing me to go into it alone and show my true Daredevil colours.

Ronnie's kid brothers colonized it a few years later, but it was still pretty creepy.

Sometimes on rainy days we played in the Booths' garage. It had a sand floor on which we built play villages and a network of roads for our model cars and trucks. We could identify every make and model on the road. I was encouraged in this interest by my father, who was a car fancier himself. One of Daddy's first jobs as a young man was to teach prospective car buyers how to drive, a skill he may have learned in the army. Evidently, in those days, car buyers got their driver's licence from the dealer. They received instruction, and off they went in their new automobile.

It was on one of those rainy days that Ronnie told me the facts of life. I think it was while Mrs. Booth was carrying Dean, and these matters were much on our minds. This was Ronnie's version: The father is a car and the mother is a garage. The father drives into the garage and nine months later a baby car comes out of the garage. The miracle of birth, by General Motors.

I think the worst mischief we got up to was pranking neighbours after dark by tapping on windows with a bolt tied to a string. Tap-tap-tap, and sure enough, our victim would come to the window and look around to see where the noise was coming from. We'd wait just long enough for the poor soul to get comfortable again, and tap-tap-tap . . . In one case, we pranked a crabby old lady who was in the habit of yelling at us when we took a shortcut across her property. She died not long after, and for years I wondered if we had hastened her demise.

We played outside till suppertime most afternoons, and one winter's day Ronnie hit on the idea of collecting that day's lift tickets from passing skiers. In those days, ski equipment was more forgiving than it is now—light leather boots, and harnesses that could be set for either downhill or cross-country skiing—and most people skied back and forth from the village to the slopes. A plan was born. We thought if we could figure out the system, we might be able to reuse the tickets. We even had an idea about reselling them.

The sturdy paper bands, about one inch by eight inches, and looped through the skier's pole strap, were a different colour for each hill and day of the week. The pattern never varied from one week to the next, and it didn't take us long to master the system. Hill 69 was red on Tuesday, Hill 70 was yellow on Thursday, and so on.

After the sun had gone down, and we saw that the rope tows were still, we stationed ourselves in a snowbank and waited for our prospects. Traffic was thin mid-week but picked up on weekends, when little platoons of three or four skiers piled up and waited for us to take their tickets. They were remarkably good-natured people and got into the spirit of things as far as giving us their used tickets, but they were a hard sell about buying them back, so we dropped that part of the operation. We looked forward to seeing our regulars, and I think they liked seeing us. We'd get an update on snow conditions, commiserate if it was icy—no artificial snow in those days—and pass a bit of time before they continued on their way, no doubt to some après-ski grog. It was a magical variation on the lemonade stand, two little kids in a snow fort under an ever-darkening Laurentian sky.

I was very fond of Ronnie's parents, and slightly in awe of them. They were classy, good-looking people, and lived in a graceful style. I can't remember either of them ever raising their voice to their own kids or their playmates. The Booths' house was properly finished and painted a nice maroon colour, all the windows trimmed with white shutters that had Christmas tree cut-outs—a most Laurentian motif. They had planted a honeysuckle hedge along the property line, but even if they hadn't, there was no mistaking where their neat lawn ended and our shaggy yard started. The front of the house had a wide verandah where we sometimes played, and in good weather Mr. Booth would sit out on the verandah at sundown, wearing a summer jacket and a shirt with an ascot tucked into it. Mrs. Booth would appear in a pretty dress, a cardigan over her shoulders, carrying a tray with a couple of tall glasses on it, probably Tom Collinses, the summer drink of the era. Mr. Booth was in the appliance business, and Mrs. Booth had the latest household equipment, including a machine in her kitchen that washed both clothes and dishes (though not at the same time). We marvelled at this invention. At home we took turns washing and drying the dishes, and Gaby struggled with the old Bendix washing machine that never worked properly. In a couple of years Daddy would pull our place together, but for a time I was quite envious of our elegant neighbours.

When Ronnie and I were ten and eleven, Gert and Gaby had a secret project of their own. There were a few hushed telephone conversations, and one summer day my father drove Mummy and me to Castonguay's department store in Saint-Jérôme to buy me a dress— unusual, as there was no big occasion in the offing that I knew of. Daddy left Mummy and the saleslady to confer while I tried things on, and we ended up choosing a pretty shirtwaist of polished cotton, with horizontal stripes in the colours of Neapolitan ice cream, vanilla, strawberry and chocolate. My mother had me twirl around in front of the mirror a few times and nodded her approval. She gave me one of her best secretive smiles, and said, "You'll be *tripping the light fantastic*, my dear."

The two mothers had conspired to arrange a "date" for Ronnie and me, the last thing we would have thought of doing. They would have us tripping the light fantastic at a golf club dance at Nymark's Lodge the following Saturday night.

On the day of the party, Ronnie came to call for me at the front door after supper, all dressed up in long pants and a dress shirt and jacket. A friend of the Booths who happened to be visiting that day drove us to the dance. He was a private detective (of course, the Booths *would* have a cool friend who was a private eye) named Bill. He drove a big grey car equipped with a siren. I think Bill may have been enjoying a few of Gert's Tom Collinses earlier in the day, because when it came time to deliver us to the dance, he drove very fast and ran his siren full blast all the way there. It was a thrilling experience, somewhere between a police escort and a high-speed chase, and the crowd on the patio stopped dead in their tracks while Ronnie and I made our entrance. Someone got us Shirley Temples and we sat at a table in the lounge with grown-ups, listening to the band and staring at each other. This was new territory for the Daredevils. We had a few awkward dances and drifted outdoors, no doubt to plot some future mischief. As I remember, our favourite part of the evening was the transportation.

Gaby and Gert's seed didn't take. Ronnie and I were the best of companions until I reached adolescence. I got there a little ahead of him, as girls do, and then everything changed. I started making more friends at school, and I think an older boy had caught my eye. I last saw Ronnie ten years ago at a big party the Booth brothers organized at Mont Habitant, a ski resort in Saint-Sauveur where Dean is the leaseholder and general manager of the facilities. The older boys came from the west coast with their families, and we had a great reunion. We saw people we hadn't seen in decades, and Ronnie and I were able to spend a few hours together catching up and reliving our childhood memories. The first thing he said to me while we were hugging was, "Remember how we used to go into the swamp and scare ourselves to death?"

TURCOT'S LAKE

(Anna)

Our mother taught us to swim in the small lake behind our house by cupping her hand under our chins to keep our heads out of the water while we moved our arms and legs, until we got the hang of it. She was never happier than when she was in or near the water, but our father, who grew up on the Bay of Fundy, never learned to swim and had a fear of water, not just for himself but for us too. He did, however, own a bathing suit, a grey satiny thing he wore only when he came to the beach with us, just to be social, revealing the big puffy varicose veins on his left leg, a source of great embarrassment to us.

The local swimming hole, the swamp and the land on the other side of it was all owned by a M. Turcot. A big light-blue pavilion, a rickety affair on tall stilts, stood high on the shore of his small lake. From behind the counter in his pleasure dome, M. Turcot collected the five-cent admission and sold pink popcorn and other cheap treats to the kids. The pavilion had a hardwood dance floor and a jukebox that teens and some adults jitterbugged to. The place was a gold mine, with no lifeguards and no water-quality standards in place. This was post-colonial Canada in the early 1950s, just pre–Salk polio vaccine, and I've got to say, life was pretty sweet (apart from the polio). Until one fateful afternoon a young boy, enrolled in the village day-camp programme, drowned in the lake. After this tragic accident, the town ordered the swimming hole closed and the pond emptied. A backhoe was brought in to dredge and widen the creek so the water would drain out of it quickly.

The creek was a lot wider now, and the bigger boys began calling it the Congo River. The Congo must have been in the news, though I doubt any of us had a clue as to what was going on there. It was just another post-colonial outpost where bad stuff was happening. The boys didn't waste any valuable summertime and started right in building a narrow raft they hoped to float down the mighty Congo. We all pitched in, so we'd be allowed aboard the vessel, if you could call it that, when it was finished. It was no more than a few boards nailed together, and there may have been a mast, but to us it was equal to anything coming off the assembly line of Harland and Wolff.

One summer when Mrs. Hinds was renovating another house to rent out, a large pile of scrap lumber began to form behind their garage. In it were lots of end pieces of boards of varying widths. These boards suggested "shoes" to us. We matched the scrap pieces by length, then wrote the size numbers on them with a pencil: 1, 2, 3, 4. Sometimes we drew a bow on them or a curved line across the top, indicating an open-toe model. We were both sellers and buyers, and played happily at our "shoe store" for a couple of weeks.

Another time we four girls spent many days running trying to find a cure for cancer using discarded spices from Mrs. Hinds's kitchen. She gave us pots and spoons and turned on the garden hose so we could mix up different combinations. Her fifty-one-year-old mother had recently died from the disease. I remember taking the challenge seriously and testing our potions on the dolls and on ourselves.

HOME LIFE
(Jane)

Frank and Gaby were conscientious parents in their own way, but supremely unconventional. They were great believers in self-expression and personal responsibility, and for a period of about six or seven years I was on a long leash for a little kid, roaming the landscape and experiencing life on my own terms. Earlier on, before we left the city, my mother had a lot of fears about my well-being, documented in snapshots of her leaning anxiously over my playpen wearing a medical face mask, and stories of me being rushed to the Children's Memorial Hospital to be X-rayed for missing buttons and bobby pins.

Here, I must contrast this with my own mothering. I once left my six-month-old daughter with an attendant in the San Francisco Trader Vic's ladies' room while lunching with a friend. There were extenuating circumstances, and my dear daughter Anna is none the worse for it, though she herself, maybe not surprisingly, grew up to be the very definition of a helicopter parent.

Everyday living loosened up when we moved to the country. My father was around all the time now and shared in the child rearing and its consequences. He and I had struck an arrangement in which I would be rewarded once in a while for good behaviour or high marks in school by being allowed to "have my own mind," the idea being that I would develop a sense of responsibility and make good choices. Having my own mind usually involved some privilege such as staying up later, or playing outdoors longer in the evening, or skipping a piano practice. It dovetailed with the Catholic belief system that children reached the age of reason by about age seven and thereafter knew right from wrong, if not good from bad. I was launched across that threshold when I made my First Communion at age six, within our first year in Saint-Sauveur. By the time I reached adolescence, my father had smartened up and started following me around in his car.

DADDY:
DOMESTIC ARTIST,
LOVER OF ALL THINGS MARITIME
(Anna)

Even as I dreamed of having long hair like Princess Rapunzel, for years my mother made me wear my straight, unmanageable hair in a short shingle cut given to me by my father. My prince had good barbering skills. After all, his father was a barber before he became a film exhibitor.

There was no end of things our father was good at. He sewed beautifully, in a tiny, regular hand-stitch, better than any of us women, reversing the collars and cuffs on his shirts when they became frayed. A good draftsman familiar with the laws of perspective, he illustrated building plans tidily in pencil and precisely enough for a carpenter to follow.

As a proud Maritimer, a lot of the foods he liked were staples in that part of the country and not available locally. In the fall he'd have a case of canned clams and boxes of salt cod shipped up from Saint John. This Atlantic bounty he'd confect into various chowders and fish cakes that kept us going all winter and were usually served with flat, flaky sea biscuits from Marven's, also a New Brunswick company. Frank was a tea drinker, but not of any old tea. It had to be Red Rose brand, another New Brunswick company before it was sold to Lipton in the seventies. But he was no teetotaler—his tea more often than not being laced with a jigger of Demerara rum, a sailor's ration on the mothership Earth. "It's what keeps me alive," he'd say, and we believed him. When he was alone, he survived on cheese and crackers, local aged cheddar or Bleu Ermite from the Benedictine abbey in Saint-Benoît-du-Lac on unsalted Christie's soda crackers, which he'd eat standing at the kitchen counter.

If Daddy made breakfast for us, it was soft-boiled eggs served in egg cups with a dollop of butter and lots of pepper, with a slice of toast he'd cut into thin strips he called fingers. These we dipped in the runny, peppery egg. To this day I over-pepper everything, especially the fish chowder that I make on a weekly basis, and the only tea consumed in our house is King Cole orange pekoe from Barbour's in Sussex, New Brunswick.

TALENT SHOW

JANE: Music was our father's abiding passion. Only someone who lived with him could grasp how completely it engaged him. Our uncle Earl "Chick" Latrémouille, who lived in the flat below ours in the 1940s in Montreal, shared his recollections with Kate, sixty years later, about life at one remove from the McGarrigle household. From notes Kate kept:

> You see, he had to be at the Ferry Command by nine, and right up until five minutes before nine, I could hear him playing the piano. And after work, at five o'clock when he got home, on to the piano, and didn't stop till everybody was in bed. At midnight, I'd hear the piano stop. Then a shoe would drop, then the other, and it was all over until the next morning! Day after day after day, and on the weekends, well, let me tell you, Kitty Kate, on the weekends . . .

Talk about waiting for the other shoe to drop. If we can believe Uncle Chick—and there's no reason not to—Daddy was on the piano *every waking hour* in those days. In notes Kate kept on this conversation, she wasn't sure if Uncle Chick and Auntie Helen liked it or if it drove them crazy. One hopes it was the former. Chick himself enjoyed music and was a keen singer at parties, but Frank's relentless (Kate's word) piano playing over their heads may have been a bit much even for music lovers.

Daddy didn't read music, so he played songs he knew, worked out new ones, and improvised melodies. I think music was a solace for my father and helped fill a lifelong hole created by his raggedy family situation. I think my mother understood this; she complained about a lot of things, but never about Frank's music.

Our long-suffering relatives soon had more music coming their way. My parents got me a little toy piano when I was two or three, but I showed more interest in my father's instrument. He was delighted, and hired a Polish émigrée named Mme Landoska to come to our home in Lachine and give me lessons. I don't remember much besides her amazing flame-coloured hair and the encouragement she gave me to make up songs. "Up Jump the Pigs" was one of my early compositions. My parents thought it a work of genius.

Kate and Anna and I took music lessons at École Marie-Rose from grade one on. The nuns who taught us piano and *solfège* (how to sing on pitch) were a cut above the other teachers, all of them pretty decent to us, and probably happy to have students with some aptitude, and parents who made them practise. The lessons were extracurricular and offered by the Holy Names* Order for four dollars a month. There were two lessons a week, making fifty cents the effective cost of a one-hour private lesson from a Conservatory-trained professional. The Holy Names Order was known for its superior musical education, and we took our yearly music exams at École Vincent-d'Indy in Montreal, a distinguished school of music operated by the Order and linked to their mother house in Outremont, now the Department of Music at the Université de Montréal.

The house in Saint-Sauveur took on more instruments. When I was about seven, my father arrived one day with a ukulele and taught me to play and sing "In My Castle on the River Nile." I was expected to perform it for company, as I was expected to perform piano pieces I had learned at school or picked up on my own. People always made a big fuss and I enjoyed the attention and looked forward to more opportunities to show off. In 1955, when "Let Me Go, Lover!" was all over the airwaves, I picked it up and added it to my repertoire.

Picture a chubby fourteen-year-old belting out "You made me weep, cut me deep/I can't sleep, lover" to a captive audience of my

---

* Sisters of the Holy Names of Jesus and Mary.

parents' friends. It always got a good hand and I don't remember anyone laughing, at least not in my presence.

ANNA: In lieu of a family bible we had our father's old Gibson arch-top guitar, the body of which was inscribed with the names of his and Gaby's friends. Sometimes an important milestone was noted, as in "Bill and Betty Green, Fort William (now Thunder Bay)," where this couple, close friends of our parents, had gone on their honeymoon. Later, Janie continued the tradition of scratching the names of her friends into the soft spruce top, and enthusiastically recorded an important arrival on the scene by adding his name in two-inch-high block letters on its back: ELVIS. There wasn't much free space left on the guitar when it came time for Kate and me to add our friends or a favourite musician, but I did manage to gouge the name of guitarist Duane Eddy into the wood, spelling it phonetically in the French syllables I was familiar with: DOUANE. In French, *douane* means "customs," as in Canada Customs. I felt like an idiot when the mistake was pointed out to me, and I struck a line through the *O*, drawing even more attention to it, a reminder of a misspelt youth.

It was on this battered artifact that our father showed his three girls their first chords. The G was the first learned, made simple by placing just one finger on the high E-string at the third fret and strumming the four high strings. Our fingers weren't long enough to reach the two other strings you needed to depress to make a full G-chord, the low E-string on the third fret and the A-string on the second fret.

Somewhere along the way, our father picked up a "ban-uke," a cross between a banjo and a ukulele with a skin head and four strings. This compact, kid-friendly instrument disappeared from the house long ago. A lot of our father's more interesting stuff went missing over the years, but because of all the clutter, nobody noticed the pieces were gone till it was too late to do anything about it.

JANE: The Chickering piano that we had moved to Saint-Sauveur from Lachine was given by my father to the pastor of a poor parish somewhere in northern Quebec, a fellow TB sufferer he had met at the Veterans' Hospital in Saint-Hyacinthe. Daddy was a soft touch. It was replaced by an 1880s Steinway that, remarkably, still holds its A440 tuning unless it's really pounded (Rufus Wainwright, I'm looking at you!). To the Steinway, the harmonium, the guitar, the ukulele and the ban-uke, my father added a piano-accordion and a zither. The accordion belonged to a British guy named Alan whom my father met one evening at The Pub and brought home because he had nowhere to sleep. When I left for school, Alan was still sleeping, and when I got home, he was sitting in a chair, playing the accordion behind a cloud of smoke from the lit cigarette in his mouth. He was a romantic sort of character, a soft-spoken, skinny guy with shaggy red hair, completely lost in the music he was playing. My mother didn't want him there another night, so my father loaned him some money and drove him back into the village. Poor Alan—I think of him as having been driven by my father "to the edge of town, where he caught a bus to nowhere." He left the accordion behind and we never saw him again.

We acquired a zither a few years after the film *The Third Man* came out in 1949. "Harry Lime's Theme," composed and played on zither by Anton Karas, was an enormous hit, and may have caused a brief spike in amateur zither-playing, and a resulting oversupply of used zithers. This is only speculation, but if I know my father, he got a good deal on the zither and that's why he bought it.

ANNA: The first song our daddy taught us was "Stand Up and Sing for Your Father an Old-Time Tune."

Won't you stop all that nonsense you're singing
Morning, Night and Noon
For I'm tired of all your ditties of your Moon and spoon and June
Won't you stand up and sing for your Father, an old-time tune.

Kate and I stood on the long piano bench, on either side of him, belting it out as the song's lyrics ordered us to do.

But it was Janie who taught us to sing harmony. This was still pre-Elvis, when the hit parade was full of songs sung by trios of women, such as the Andrews and McGuire Sisters, and here we were, a trio of sisters. Our earliest effort in three-part harmony was "I Don't Wanna See You Crying," the B-side of "Mr. Sandman," a hit for the Chordettes in 1954.

JANE: Our father was a good singer and a superb harmonizer—he could put a part on any song—and the genes were passed on to his daughters, along with his golden ear. We can hear a song once and reproduce a recognizable version of it on any instrument we are familiar with, and like him, we are natural harmony singers. It's an odd little gene that can favour singers of moderate ability and bypass very fine singers. Of course, there are great singers who can also sing harmony, but the two gifts don't always go together. Harmony singers can be terrific snobs about their God-given ability. George Burns was fond of saying he didn't even speak to people who couldn't sing harmony.

I started having fun with music at boarding school in Combermere, where I discovered country music, a genre that lends itself particularly well to harmony singing. The convent had a recreation hall where we gathered after supper and on weekends. There was a gramophone at one end of the room and a piano at the other. One way or another, we came by 78s of recent or well-loved country hits and listened to them on the gramophone. Since the same group couldn't hog the record player all night, we'd move to the other end of the room and continue the music on the piano, where I would play the songs with three or four girls joining in on the singing.

There were two nuns who traded off supervision duties in the rec hall: Mother Bridget, a tall, bony Irish sister with the palest strawberry-blond eyebrows and lashes, and Mother Rita, a short, feisty pistol from New England. Unaccountably, they both loved country music and openly favoured our faction over the pop music fans when it came to control of the record player and piano. We listened to and sang the songs of Webb Pierce, Eddy Arnold, the Hanks (Thompson, Williams and Snow) and Porter Wagoner layering harmony upon harmony. Mother Bridget was very partial to Wilf Carter ("There's a Love Knot in My Lariat") and urged us to play more of his records. For years I thought Wilf Carter was part of the celebrated Carter Family from the southern United States, until I was set straight by some folk music friends in San Francisco in the sixties. Wilf was from Nova Scotia.

I continued my music activities at home during the school holidays, and got a few friends over to the house on rainy days to sing around the piano. My friends in Saint-Sauveur didn't care for hillbilly music, as they called it, and so the repertoire inclined more to pop songs than country. Kate and Anna and I had sung along with Daddy on Stephen Foster songs and hymns we knew from school, and one day I tried out my little sisters on a Patti Page song I'd been working out with some friends. Kate and Anna turned out to be faster studies and better singers, so I now had co-conspirators right in the house.

We worked up "I Don't Want to See You Crying" and "Cross Over the Bridge," a big hit for Patti Page in 1956. I think I tried to teach them "Blackboard of My Heart" and other tear-jerkers, but they were never the fans of country music that I was. Singing together was a great family pastime and friends were always welcome to join in.

My parents couldn't have been happier about these musical encounters, but there was one very awkward afternoon when my friend Lise Dagenais was visiting. She and I were at the piano working up "Cheveux au vent," which had been a radio hit for Les Soeurs Étienne from France in the late 1940s and was picked up again by radio in the 1950s. It was a most innocent, innocuous song, about the joys of being carefree. My father was out on the terrace and could hear us through the open windows. He stormed into the living room and ordered us to stop. He was very angry, so we didn't argue with him and moved on to another song. Later, when I pinned him down about it, the problem was not the song but his deficient French. We were singing *cheveux au vent* ("hair in the wind"), but he was hearing *je veux un bum* ("I want a bum"). They do sound alike if you say them fast enough, and the little percussive phrase POM-POM-POM-POM at the end of each chorus probably sounded to him like BUM-BUM-BUM-BUM and reinforced the misunderstanding. A comedy of errors, but he was miffed when I pointed it out and remained unconvinced.

One day our piano tuner, Mr. Menzies, brought his grandson Bobby Stefani over to the house to meet us. Bobby was very musical and was spending the summer in Saint-Sauveur. He started coming over on his own to join in our songfests. Bobby was my age and had an older brother, Eddie, who was a good piano player and singer. Eddie came over once in a while, but less often because of his summer job.

In midsummer 1958, Nymark's Lodge announced a talent contest *soirée*, with Valuable Prizes for the Winning Contestants. Without running it by anyone first, I entered Kate and Anna and myself in the contest. I was certain we would win no matter who the competition was. My parents objected at first, but when the Stefani brothers signed up too, they saw it differently. Game on!

Kate and Anna and I sifted through our repertoire and settled on "Bon Voyage," a hit on French radio that year for Gloria Lasso, which we sang in three-part harmony with me on the piano. It was Grandpapa Latrémouille's favourite of all our songs. Grandpapa was a man of the people, so how could we go wrong?

The night of the show, Bobby sang George Gershwin's "Summertime," accompanied by Eddie on piano, and we did our rendition of "Bon Voyage." It was close, but the applause favoured us over the Stefani brothers. The other contestants—an accordion player, a girl singer and a tap dancer—were left in the dust. Kate and Anna and I took home our prizes: a white bolero made out of something that was trying to be angora, and a string of dime-store pearls. Later, when my sisters were up there on the world stage, I took credit for launching them. And later still, in 1998, we recorded "Bon Voyage," just as we had performed it at Nymark's, on *The McGarrigle Hour* album, Kate and Anna's collection of favourites old and new.

READING

JANE: Our parents did a lot of improvised homework with us. We didn't need their help with assigned work, but they went to a lot of trouble to balance and expand on what we were taught in class. We had, and still have, a 1904 edition of the *Encyclopedia Americana* that my father had picked up on one of his rounds of second-hand stores, and we often referred to it for authoritative information on questions of geography or history, as long as the issues predated 1904. If a subject came up in conversation at dinner or while we were doing homework, Daddy would get out the right volume, and we would read it together to bone up on the subject. We used them so much through the years that reciting the volumes' headings from start to finish became a family parlour trick: *A-Ata, Ata-Bou, Bou-Con, Con-Doy, Doy-Fla,* etc. Anna thinks there might be the makings of a song in that string of unrelated syllables.

Some of our school textbooks were as out of date as our encyclopedia. The nuns taught from whatever they had at hand, and I remember learning how to trim a lamp wick at about the same time we were discovering television. It was in our ancient *Arts Ménagers* textbook and actually came in handy during the occasional power failure, when we had to break out the oil lamps.

Both of our parents were keen readers and they passed on the love of reading very early. Neither of them went to university, but they were well read and placed a great value on literacy and on being well informed. They made reading seem like fun, especially Daddy, who had a theatrical bent and liked to act out the various characters in a story when he read aloud.

My father enjoyed reading to us if he came across a newspaper article or a passage in a book he found interesting. He particularly liked to read from Cassell's *Illustrated Stories*, a bound Victorian publication that reprinted popular pieces of the time. It's still on our shelves, an armful of a book that's sixteen by ten inches and weighs about ten pounds. A favourite reading from Cassell's was the James Greenleaf Whittier poem about Barbara Frietchie, an American Civil War heroine who held off rebel soldiers in Frederick Town, Maryland, by waving the Union flag at them. There were two key stanzas that Daddy recited with his usual flair for the dramatic, taking on the characters' personae:

"Shoot if you must this old grey head
But spare your country's flag," she said.

A few more stanzas move the plot along, whereupon the commanding officer cries out:

"Who harms a hair on yon grey head
Dies like a dog. March on!" he said.

Stirring stuff, and we ate it up.

I've remained a dedicated reader and have lately, and reluctantly, been feeding my habit with e-books. It's a long way from Cassell's to Kindle, but I've finally turned the corner.

I have early memories of Daddy coming into my room after work, during the Ferry Command days in Montreal, still dressed in his suit, and turning the light on to get me caught up on the Teenie Weenies, a weekly comic strip. The Teenie Weenies were a colony of tiny folk who lived a secret life among regular people, always taking care not to be trampled as they went about their Teenie Weenie business. They lived in an old shoe under a rose bush, and provisioned their little world with castoffs from the real world. They were enterprising and resourceful in the use they made of an old tin can, a spoon, a jar lid, a teacup, a pencil. Almost any found object could be put to some ingenious use by the Teenie Weenies; you could say they were the original recyclers.

The strip's images were colour saturated and beautifully drawn, and each episode appeared as a single large illustration above a body of text. Some of the characters had names, but they were mostly known by their occupations or particularities: the Cook, the Sailor, the Doctor, the Old Soldier with a Wooden Leg. A few of the characters—the Dunce, the Chinaman, the Coloured Man—would now be judged politically incorrect at the very least, their appearance in a comic strip possibly actionable, but they were all strong, vivid characters who fired my imagination. There were nights when my father would turn up in my room very late, clearly post-party, but he rarely missed our Teenie Weenies reading date.

The first children's book that I really took to was called, I think, *Little Timmy Chick*. Timmy was a young barnyard creature who one day packed up some of his clothes in a bandana and ran away from home. I think I received the book as a third-birthday present from Mary Carroll, a woman who was billeted with us during the war. Mary read it to me a couple of times a day, her finger on each word as she spoke it so I could follow along. I either memorized the book or actually learned to read the simple words, I can't be sure which, but before long I was reading it myself and it quickly became my favourite book.

I identified strongly with Timmy Chick's sense of adventure, a cautionary tale as it turns out. My mother let me have an old scarf to play with. I liked to lay it out on the floor with some of my favourite clothes on it and then practise tying everything up into a bundle. I did this almost every day, and one day I took the bundle and walked out of the house onto Saint-Joseph Boulevard, headed for the corner trolley stop. I must have planned this very carefully, because Mummy and Mary generally kept a close eye on me, but, crafty child that I was, I evaded their surveillance. I had found the stub of a used tramway ticket at the bottom of an old purse and tried to board the streetcar when it stopped at 42nd Avenue. The driver got very angry and threatened to call the police. He shut the trolley doors on me and left me standing there, mystified and frightened. By this time, my mother was running up the street toward the corner and calling out to me. I think Mary was probably across the boulevard at the edge of Lac Saint-Louis, where a little boy had drowned the previous summer. I must have thrown a good scare into the two of them, because it was a long time before I was left to my own devices again.

Once I learned to read, I never stopped. Because we were being schooled in French, we were encouraged to read in English as much as we liked and whatever we liked. In my free time, I read a lot of English books. Some early titles I remember, *Robin Hollow* and *Anne of Green Gables*, were suitable for children. Others were less so, but I read them anyway, a big Webster's dictionary nearby to consult when I was stuck on a word, which was often. I read Gene Fowler's *Good Night, Sweet Prince*, a biography of John Barrymore. I was about eleven or twelve at the time, and I fell a little in love with its subject, a man of striking good looks and a terrible drinking habit that had done him in at fifty, ten years before. John Barrymore, his sister Ethel and brother Lionel were stage and screen royalty, a tradition that has been maintained by John's granddaughter Drew Barrymore. There were many photographs in the book, and I saw a strong resemblance between John and my father. I also saw a parallel in their bon vivant lifestyles, though my father never took it to the sad extreme Barrymore did. I was fascinated and horrified by the grip alcohol had on the great actor, and the ravages to his health and career. I read and reread the book, always wanting it to end differently, but it never did. I mourned John Barrymore.

Another favourite title was William Harrison Ainsworth's *Jack Sheppard*, in which Jack's poor gin-soaked mother ends up in the workhouse in eighteenth-century London. These and many others on the family bookshelves may have been discards from the Atwater Library in Montreal.

Not all my reading was about alcoholics. My mother put me on to Morley Callaghan's stories and Thomas B. Costain's novels, starting with *Son of a Hundred Kings*, which I especially enjoyed. Later she gave me *Brideshead Revisited* by Evelyn Waugh. It had been given to her by a friend who was a nun—the Catholic connection.

When the Reader's Digest Company came out with their Condensed Books series, Gaby signed us up. There was probably the usual book club giveaway at the front end, and my mother loved a bargain. Eventually the bill arrived and went disregarded, not thought to be too pressing a matter. Collection notices piled up and were ignored. One day my father answered the phone and had a heated conversation with someone about the unpaid bill. He hung up on the guy and fired off a telegram to the president of Reader's Digest. It started strong—"RESENT BEING PUSHED AROUND BY MINOR OFFICIAL NAMED BADGER"—and went on to chastise them about their "emasculated versions" of other people's work. I forget the rest, but I still love that the bill collector was called Badger. I don't know if the bill was ever paid; Reader's Digest may have found this deadbeat customer to be too much trouble and written him off. A note in passing: while writing this last bit, I wondered aloud to Anna, sitting across from me, whether I should explain what Condensed Books were.

Anna: "Add water."

ANNA: Kate and I were not natural readers like sister Jane, busily working her way through our father's stash of discarded library books. Unlike Jane, who learned to read English as a small child, I couldn't read at all when I started grade one at age five, so French was my first written language, and this was probably the case with Kate too. The two of us did have favourite books that our parents read to us over and over: the Comtesse de Ségur's *Old French Fairy Tales*, beautifully illustrated in the art nouveau style, and a couple of dog-eared Raggedy Ann and Andy books. When we were older and we sought out reading material from the shelves, three books come to mind. An old illustrated edition of George du Maurier's *Trilby* (also made into three early silent films), the story of a pretty young artist's model in Paris who is taught to sing by Svengali, an

evil manipulator and mind controller, though she shows no aptitude for music. Victor Hugo's *The Laughing Man*, the tale of a street
urchin whose mouth has been carved into a hideous smile by gyp-
sies, and the orphaned baby girl he finds suckling at the breast of
her dead mother, a girl who becomes his ward and later his love
interest. Finally, Jean Dutourd's *A Dog's Head*, a satire about a
young upper-class gentleman who has the misfortune to be born
with the head of a spaniel and the indignities he must suffer: his
cruel schoolmates train him to fetch newspapers, and he constantly
has to check a natural inclination to chase after female dogs.

At some point, it must have dawned on our mother that there was
a dearth of literature in our bookcases suitable for young ladies, so
she ordered a box of classics from the T. Eaton Company, among
them John Bunyan's *Pilgrim's Progress*, J.P. Hartley's *The Shrimp and
the Anemone* and Mark Twain's *Tom Sawyer*. Kate and I were thrilled
to get the books, but we hardly devoured them, preferring instead to
cover our new tomes with kraft paper, as we did our schoolbooks, and
assign them numbers, like they did in libraries, before placing them
on the shelves, where they sit today, still unread. It may have been too
late to encourage good reading habits in us. Besides, if our mother
had seen one of us curled up with a book, she likely would have said,
"Why are you inside?" We were outdoor kids now, and I don't remember any bookworms among our group of friends, at least not until we
were in our mid-teens and living in the city once again.

When Kate was about fourteen, a retired schoolteacher who
summered in one of our cottages gave her a copy of Thomas Hardy's
Tess of the d'Urbervilles. It took her a while to get through it, but this
novel had a profound influence on her. Later, when she was at
McGill, she told me she'd take Hardy any day over Dickens, whom
she'd had to read for a class. I would also become a fan of Thomas
Hardy's after Dane Lanken (who became my husband) gave me his
copy of *The Mayor of Casterbridge* to read on a long train trip, warning me that by page such-and-such I'd be a bawling idiot. I was.
Another favourite book of Kate's was Alain-Fournier's *Le Grand*

Meaulnes, read for a French lit class at McGill, and which she rec-
ommended to everyone.

As late teens and young adults, we made up for lost time. While
I was at the Beaux-arts, I was a member of the Bibliothèque de
Montréal, the lovely neoclassical building with white marble columns across from Parc La Fontaine, where I discovered Dostoevsky
and Gogol in their original English translations by Constance
Garnett. She's no longer considered the authority she once was.
I think it was Joseph Brodsky who said that when you read Garnett's
translations of Tolstoy and Dostoevsky you can't tell the difference
between them, because you're reading Constance Garnett. English-
speaking Montrealers were fortunate to have the wonderful Classics
Bookstore on Sainte-Catherine Street West, which stocked the
world's literary masterpieces, many of them in Penguin editions.

FRANKENFLYNN

(Anna)

People sometimes admire the house my sisters and I grew up in in Saint-Sauveur-des-Monts. It was designed by Frank and built by the carpenter Flynn, who, in the words of our mother, never drew a sober breath. It certainly looks as though they made it up as they went along, and I think this is what lends it its charm today. But it was not always so, and it was a long time coming.

At war's end, Frank owned a double lot in the village on what had formerly been a golf course. The house he chose to build for his family was in mock–Quebec farmhouse style, similar to those little village houses in the paintings of Clarence Gagnon or A.Y. Jackson. This type of cottage was very popular with the postwar settlers to these Laurentian climes.

Ours is a one-and-a-half-storey white board-and-batten, with red trim and a bellcast roof. Two three-quarter French windows flank a thick red door with a small wrought iron grille set in it, giving it the appearance of a confessional, and the door is intentionally off-centre and not a miscalculation given the habitually inebriated state of the builder. There's a large stone fireplace up the middle, and knotty pine walls in the living room, which is mostly furnished with antiques. Where my father saw an antique, my mother saw only junk.

As a small child, I couldn't yet appreciate the nascent charm of our house, with my mother complaining constantly about the location of this cupboard or the absence of counter space in the small galley kitchen, and asking herself over and over why it was that women didn't get to design their own kitchens as they were the ones who had to spend their lives in them. She was particularly disdainful of the black and brown dog of a linoleum on the kitchen floor, which she always referred to as "shit-brindle." When she'd say this word, we'd go into fits of laughter. The only two swear words she ever used were "Jesus" and "shit."

For many years the house was a work-in-progress. My earliest memories are of our backyard, blighted by the ghastly sight of several untidy piles of war-surplus stock, in the form of old windows and doors and scrap lumber, all of it discarded from demolished federal buildings. These heaps of war-surplus material were covered over with gloomy brown oilskin tarps to protect them from the elements, adding to the already dismal appearance of our property. Those forensic "body farms" come to mind.

What I didn't realize then was that my father was slowly incorporating this stuff into the house. A bit too slowly, as far as my mother was concerned. She tended to be impatient. Frank, who was perennially strapped for cash, was a recycler by necessity, long before the advent of Home Depot, which he would have loved.

Our backyard was a minefield where old boards with rusty nails were hidden from view by the long, unkempt grass. In summer, we kids and our mother always went around barefoot, and it was an almost daily occurrence for one of us to step down on a rusty spike then scream for our father to come pull the board from the sole of our foot. Once, a five-inch nail went right through my poor mother's foot and out the top. Invectives. Frank had been a medic in World War I and with these little mishaps happening on a daily basis, he had plenty of opportunities to practise his arcane knowledge of army field medicine. Usually this involved soaking the affected limb in freshly boiled water with salt, or Fyon's *eau de Javel* (bleach) if it looked really serious. But if he suspected an infection, a poultice was made from some old bread dipped in hot milk, which he applied to the puncture to draw out the "poison." A sort of holistic *pain perdu*. The wound was then doused with iodine, inflicting further agony on the patient. We used to beg for non-stinging mercurochrome, like our friends had, but Frank wouldn't have it in the house. To heal, it had to hurt. Life was a battle, after all. Growing up, my mother would often bark at us to "marry a doctor." Why did we need a doctor when we had Daddy? He never lost a patient, either, unlike his personal physician. The latter was arrested with the body of a woman in the trunk of his car. He had been performing illegal abortions to supplement his income. This was a pity all around, as he was a wonderful chest doctor.

A valuable show-and-tell item for us girls lay hidden under one of the tarps, and when pressed to trump either a new air gun or a Tahitian *pareo* (wraparound skirt) our friends were showing off, we could always fall back on this curiosity. "Wanna see our leopard?" we'd say, lifting the corner of the tarp. Even in its advanced state of decomposition, our mouldy old leopard skin rug still had the power to terrify small children with its ferocious pointed fangs and big round eyes of brilliant green glass. It had been left to my father by a friend who was stationed in Burma between the wars. Janie remembers it being in the flat in Lachine, but it never found its way into the new house and eventually disintegrated, leaving only the green eyes that Kate and I incorporated into our doll playing. Crystal balls for dolls, or for an eye transplant in our doll hospital. Our dolls, like our feet, were in pretty bad shape and could use all the help they could get. I remember having to bury one after its little sawdust head had rotted off.

My mother grew disheartened by all the piles of stuff and also by a large, unfinished shed that hung off the back of the house. And there was the matter of "the garage," which to my knowledge had never had a car in it. It was just another place for my father to keep his "smaller" stuff, like the thousands of unsorted screws and nuts, all spilling out of upturned jars and cans. Because the garage was built on the south side of the house, there were no south-facing windows in the living room, another gripe of my sun-worshipping mother. My clever father reiterated time and again how he had "planned it this way to ensure the sun would not fade the contents of the room," i.e., the old furniture from the Sally Ann.

The messy garage could be reached handily from the house by a small pine door in the south living room wall. It was about four

feet high, as in an Elizabethan half-timbered building, to accommo-
date the different floor heights of house and garage. People were
always asking where it led to. "Hell," would likely have been my
mother's answer. She hated it, but we kids loved this dwarf door and
were always scampering through it in endless games of hide-and-
seek. Kate's daughter Martha's very first song was about this curious little door.

There's a door
Handle's cold
Made of iron and brass
And this door it used to lead
Into what is now my past.
If you were to have opened this door
It would have led you onto a floor
Where my mother had played almost fifty years before.

When I was about nine, my mother's utter contempt for the
house began to rub off on me. I confess to a certain disloyalty to my
father when I say that I secretly wished to live in a building on the
next street over, a tall two-storey tenement (tall to me, who was
used to four-foot-high doors) clad in brown insulbrick. The world-
famous architect Frank Gehry also found this cartoonish brick
siding to be interesting stuff (maybe from seeing so much of it in
northern Ontario where he grew up) and used it to great effect on
some fancy Los Angeles houses he built in the 1990s.

I can't explain why I was drawn to this particular building, other
than that it seemed the antithesis of our neo-farmhouse with its
harvest of junk. I suppose I thought of it as urban, the closest thing
to a skyscraper in the village.

The second-storey flat was home to a girl in my class, a blond
cherub named Manon, whose homework was always beautifully
done, making everyone else's look amateurish. When she failed her
year at the end of grade three, it was discovered that her mother had

been doing her homework all along. I had once gone to Manon's house after school and been mightily impressed by the sheer variety of linoleum coverings on their floors, a different colour and pattern in every room and in the salon one that looked like a Wilton rug with a gold medallion in the middle. Apart from the sorry excuse for lino in our galley kitchen, we had boring old wood floors that had to be scoured with steel wool and then waxed.

REBUS
(Jane)

Once he was home and back on his feet, Daddy launched a company he called Resident Buyer Service (cable address: rebus) in partnership with a Mr. Sanderson, who was based in Santa Barbara, California. They were furnishing hydraulic aircraft jacks to the Canadian government. As I remember it, Mr. Sanderson lined up the equipment and Daddy made the deals, which involved sealed bids to the government, or tenders, as they were called. Our family life became about The Tenders and whether they would be submitted on time and be accepted. It was a cottage industry. Daddy worked out the specs and prices, and Gaby typed up the final version with its multiple carbon copies on a portable Remington typewriter. There were many false starts before the finished bid was ready to go, and I remember Gaby typing till all hours of the night before a Tender deadline. There would be finishing touches the next morning, and then Daddy would dress in his best suit, a crisp shirt and his customary bow tie, and drive The Tender to Ottawa to hand-deliver it. It was always a nerve-racking race against time. Would he make it? Would The Tender get into the right hands before 4 p.m., the official deadline? It mostly did, and we could all breathe a little easier until it was time for the next Tender, and the cycle would start again.

The little cottage industry started paying off and the family began to prosper again in 1951. Daddy turned in his old wartime Chevy for a nearly new 1949 Monarch, a sleek black torpedo-shaped beauty with an automatic transmission and a push-button starter.

There began an upgrade on the house, starting with the furnace. The old one, which had to be manually lit, its heat directed to one hopeful vent in the living room floor, was replaced with a modern oil furnace and thermostat for forced-air heating throughout the house.

When I think back on these renovations, I wonder why they didn't do something about the kitchen and the bathroom, the worst rooms in the house, in part because the weakest link in my father's chain of tradesmen was the plumber. The bathroom had a garden-variety toilet and sink, but the bathtub was a horror. It was forty inches square and made out of sheet metal welded together at the corners. I always thought the reason for this peculiar arrangement was a wartime shortage of materials, but Anna maintains it was a safety measure because she had cracked her head in the enamel tub in Lachine. Frank's custom tub, trimmed with a four-inch-wide knotty pine ledge, was awkward to sit in and never quite emptied because of a slight uphill slope at the drain. It was my job to clean it with SOS pads on Saturdays, and no matter how shiny I was able to get the sides, there was always a layer of suspect water on the bottom that, over time, left permanent stains. The hot water was sketchy, never quite enough of it, and though Anna remembers a shower, I remember having to rinse our long hair with pot after pot of tepid water; in fact, a kitchen pot was kept in the bathroom for just that purpose. It was a heartbreak all the way around, but what did it matter? The house was so charming . . .

The front yard was addressed. Truckfuls of earth were delivered to build up a terrace along the front and north side of the house at door level, about three feet high, and it extended outward from the house about ten feet before sloping down to the grade of the yard. The new terrace was covered with beautiful green velvety turf. Flagstones were set into the ground for a walkway and steps down the slope, and a retaining wall built to shore up the terrace. A hedge of cedar saplings was planted along the two-hundred-foot frontage of the property. My parents acquired some Adirondack chairs, painted white to match the house and placed on the terrace. They could now receive people in style.

Decorative improvements were made to the living room. The lateral beams that hold up the second floor were sheathed in one-by-six pine, stained black and trimmed with deep-pink architectural mouldings. The dropped ceiling of four-by-eight sheets of tentest that are the living room ceiling were panelled in the same materials, the tentest painted a very pale blue. An alcove was created on the north wall of the living room by building in my father's desk on one side and, on the other, a *circa*-1870s sideboard that had belonged to Gaby's mother. For some reason, we always refer to that piece as "the buffet." Father's craftsman-carpenter, M. Pilon, who did a lot of work in our house in the 1950s, did the ceiling details and built in the buffet and desk. He built shelves above the buffet and a recessed knick-knack cabinet above the desk. The interior of the desk had small compartments known as pigeonholes and small pullout drawers. M. Pilon incorporated the desk's hinged cover into the built-in design. To this day, when we're trying to find a rubber band or a pen that writes, the question is asked: "Did you look in the pigeonhole?"

The shelves above the buffet hold Gaby's china cups, which she used for the bridge parties she hosted once she had made some friends, and some vintage china serving plates that are too nice ever to be used. The shelves also hold six pewter beer steins, a wedding present to my father from his closest friends. Their names are engraved on the mugs, and whenever one of them died, my father put a little piece of red tape next to the name. It was a ritual that put him in a nostalgic mood, and if one of us was around, he would tell us stories about his old friend.

Below the desk is a cupboard where sheet music has been stored since the house first had a piano: Gaby's book of popular ballads and show tunes, all our books of Czerny and Mozart and Beethoven sonatas and Chopin preludes, some early photocopies of Daddy's sister Anna's compositions, the lyrics and musical arrangements to Kate's and Anna's songs, and the Christmas carols for the family holiday shows they organized. It's all still there, or whatever has survived the generations of mice who have been snacking on it over the years.

The original purpose of the alcove was to camouflage ductwork from the basement, but thanks to M. Pilon's artistry, it draws the eye agreeably to that end of the room, especially contrasted with the other three walls, which are finished in knotty pine. If only my father's plumbers and electricians had been as talented (and sober) as M. Pilon!

The walls behind the shelves were papered in a Wedgwood blue and white floral pattern. Over the years, squirrels got into the eaves of the house and chewed holes through that wall and parts of the ceiling. Some of our kids—my son Vinnie and Anna's daughter Lily—patched the holes and repainted the ceiling. We didn't want to change the wallpaper, so our friend Kathleen Weldon, who is a visual artist, went into the basement and mixed up exactly the faded blue of the sixty-year-old wallpaper from an assortment of discarded house paints, and did a perfect restoration. It's impossible to find the patch—I've tried.

The living room has seen a lot of history, and more than a few dramatic events for which the dining room table was the staging area. An early one that springs to mind took place at Christmas dinner, 1953. You could say it's burned into my head.

In our new prosperity, we had gotten a Westinghouse table-model radio for Christmas. It was about ten by twelve by sixteen inches, with a walnut console and a 78 rpm phonograph built into the top. The cover lifted back to get at the turntable to play a record. There were two knobs at the base, one to control volume and another to choose a station on the big round dial. I was just at that age when I couldn't be separated from popular music. I had the new radio playing all day, and insisted on sitting next to it at the end of the table so I could play it during Christmas dinner. My parents were annoyed about this. The table was beautifully set with Gaby's wedding silver, wine goblets for the parents, candles burning at either end. We were meant to reflect on the season and its blessings, and enjoy dinner *en famille*, but they decided not to fight me; it was Christmas after all. Gaby put the serving dishes on the table and we said grace.

Daddy was hacking away at the bird, and a song I liked began to play. I leaned over suddenly to turn up the volume, forgetting there was a candle between the radio and myself. The next thing I knew I was on fire, my long, curly hair going up in flames. We were all screaming and Gaby rushed into the kitchen for water. My father ran to where I was sitting, and by the time Gaby was back with a bucket of water, he had smothered the flames with his bare hands and put the fire out. She threw the water on me anyhow. I was so traumatized I can't remember how the evening ended, but I'm certain there was radio silence.

On New Year's Day 2010, a family drama was unfolding around us and the dining room table had another scene of its own. In exactly seventeen days, Kate would die of the cancer she had struggled with for five years. She wanted to spend her last Christmas season in Saint-Sauveur and I had driven her up to the country on December 18. Most of the family had come for all or part of the holidays, and we had Skyped those who weren't there. Kate was installed in her upstairs bedroom and we took turns sitting with her, bringing her cups of broth, plumping up pillows, keeping her posted on the household's activities. Except for the fact that Kate was dying, the family holiday in Saint-Sauveur was business as usual.

On New Year's Eve, we invited a few friends to join us at the house. Jack Nissenson, Peter Weldon and Michèle Forest, who had sung with Kate and Anna in the early days, and Carol Holland, Kate's best friend, rang in the New Year with family who were still in Saint-Sauveur: Anna, Dane, Lily, Vinnie, Vinnie's partner Kathleen, my daughter Anna, her husband Bob, their daughters Gigi and Islay, and me.

Kate made a brief appearance downstairs, hair pinned up and fully dressed with the help of the Annas. We sang some of the old songs while Kate sipped at a thimbleful of champagne. Michèle asked Jack to sing "Shenandoah," his signature song, and everyone joined in with harmonies. It was too much for Kate. She said, "You're making me cry," but by then we were all in tears.

On New Year's Day, she was feeling poorly and I called our friend Dr. Roger Tabah. Roger, a surgeon, had involved himself in

Kate's case when direction seemed to be lacking, and had more or less become her attending physician. He accompanied her to London for her last concert and made a point of stopping by her house a couple of times a week when she returned. I knew he was in the country for the holidays and asked if he could come by. In the meantime, Vinnie, Lily, Bob and Kathleen went out for a cross-country ski to clear their party heads. In happier times, Kate would have been leading the pack, but this time she could only send them off with her blessing. Daughter Anna stayed behind to pack up her little family for their flight back to San Francisco that night.

The doctor arrived just as the ski party was leaving. He stayed at Kate's side for about three-quarters of an hour, passing the time with whoever was coming and going from her room, and was about to take his leave when the house phone rang—Lily calling from her cell. "Is Roger still there?"

"Yes."

"Keep him there, we're on our way home. Bob has dislocated his shoulder."

Kate was following my end of the conversation with Lily and Roger, and said: "Ah, *A Death in the Family*, James Agee."

Roger and I went downstairs. Kate was too weak to sustain a conversation for very long, but there was nothing wrong with her hearing, and she was able to follow the action below through an old heating grate in her room.

It was now about 5 p.m. Bob was in terrible pain and we all knew the wait time at the clinic would be impossible. Roger took charge. Bob had two shots of Irish whiskey and some of Kate's Dilaudid. I fetched our biggest bedsheet from the linen closet and spread it on the dining room table. Bob, five foot eleven and two hundred solid pounds of Scottish stock, was helped on to the table and lay there supine, his face chalk white, while Roger fashioned a kind of sling for his body with the sheet. It could have been a field medicine scene from *Gone with the Wind*. Dane was stationed on one side of the table to pull the sling toward him, Vinnie on the other side to pull Bob's arm in the opposite direction, while Roger manipulated the shoulder.

Vinnie braced his foot against the table and *one, two, three*—POP! The shoulder was back in place. From Kate through the heating grate: "I heard that!" Bob called back, "It's a boy!" Everybody laughed and hugged and Roger said, "The last time I did this was twenty-five years ago." The thankful Californians rushed off to make their flight, and we tore down our little MASH unit to restore the living room to normal.

THE CAMPS
(Anna)

Over the years, after much hectoring from my mother, my father converted the back shed into a breakfast room that he affectedly called the "dinette" (he thought it Gallic-sounding). Adjoining it was a separate, self-contained apartment with bunks he leased to skiers, which went by the nickname the "Annex." These new rooms had separate locked entrances and my father labelled the keys with their corresponding tags, which he'd hand-printed neatly with his fountain pen, and hung them on a nail inside the house.

My mother loathed having strangers under the same roof, even if my father's tenants were always nice people. The walls were thin, and putting the Annex toilet up against the wall of the kitchen, where my mother spent a good part of her time, was a bad idea.

By the mid-fifties, the ski craze in Saint-Sauveur had begun in earnest and to cash in on it, my father hurried to build four Swiss-style cottages on our one-acre village lot. New keys were cut and tags printed for Camps 63, 67, 69 and 71 and went on the nail. Once again the piles of scrap were mined, and what didn't get used was thrown into an old septic pit on top of which my mother would later plant a perennial garden. This garden in turn inspired my father to name the property Gardencourt Cottages, even going so far as to make a hand-painted sign and erect it outside the hedge on the street. But we mean girls and our friends always called the place Garbagecourt.

I think my father missed all the junk. Sometime in the early sixties, he couldn't resist the graceful arched windows and neo-classical wood columns that had belonged to a mansard-roofed cottage torn down on the main street to make room for a common bungalow. Frank was intending to build another house, somewhere, using these elements, when he died suddenly in May 1965. The stuff of his dreams still lies there today, a moss-covered pile of punky wood and wavy glass being slowly reclaimed by nature. It comforts me to think that maybe he's building a house for us in heaven.

TENANTS
(Anna)

In summer, our father's tenants tended to be older people—a retired schoolteacher and his wife, both avid golfers, a United Church minister and his slightly batty wife, subbing in the local parishes for vacationing local ministers, a retired civil servant turned magic realist painter. But one year my father rented to a Mme Seda Zare, a ballet teacher with a nine-year-old son, Randy,* and her troupe of four dancers. Every morning the exotic, petite Seda exited the chalet wearing big shades and backless high heels. With cigarette in hand, she gathered the dancers around her in the empty field by the house and put them through their paces doing ballet warm-ups, calling out in her Armenian-tinged French, "*Jeté, plié, arabesque! Tendu, dégagé, battement.*" The two young women, Milenka and Lucie, were in sleeveless black leotards, sometimes with colourful scarves tied around their hips and ratty hand-knit leg warmers. Michel and Tommy, the two very buff men, wore only the skimpiest of bikinis, leaving nothing to the imagination, as my mother would have said.

The cedar hedge along the front of the property that our father kept trimmed was only about four feet high back then, and curious villagers who had suddenly found reasons to come to Lanning stood on the road, gawking at Seda's spectacle. Later, we let the hedge go, our collective memories secure behind its now-twenty-five-foot height.

After Frank's passing, a faithful tenant who returned every summer took pity on my mother and sorted all the bolts and screws in the garage, putting them in jars with screw tops that hung neatly from the ceiling. Then, in the eighties, this space was converted into a sunroom for my mother. Our friend Thiemen the carpenter sawed

---

* Randy Saharuni became a photographer and took the jacket photo of the three of us.

a huge hole in the south wall of the garage and installed a bay window. When she wasn't outside soaking up the summer sun in her blue bathing suit, Gaby pretty much lived in that room. Around the same time, she got to redesign her kitchen. It was a great improvement on Frank and Flynn's original design, though it could stand an update today.

My mother always hated the Gardencourt Cottages sign, which, after the 1976 victory of the Parti Québécois and the passing of Quebec's new language bill, was now technically an illegal unilingual English sign. One Saturday night in the late eighties, a drunk driver backed into it and knocked it down. My mother was delighted with this turn of events, but less so when my husband, Dane, dragged the old sign onto the property, restored it, then erected it in the middle of the property as a shrine to Frank, where it stands today and again is in need of restoration.

THE BARONESS
(Jane)

Since my father spent a short time in Russia as a soldier with the Canadian Siberian Expeditionary Force in World War I, for the rest of his life he was something of a Russophile. He spoke a little Russian and liked to relive his experience by demonstrating the use of his souvenir World War I bayonet and reminiscing about some Russian customs that were different from ours. Did we know, for example, that Russians took their tea in drinking glasses, not cups? Or that they held cigarettes between their third and fourth fingers? He deplored the Communist regime and the Iron Curtain, and dreamed of going back to Russia for a visit if ever the Iron Curtain was lifted. As it was, the closest he ever got to Russia after his stint in the war was the Samovar Club in Montreal, a Russian-themed café on Peel Street, a few doors up from the Seagram Building where my mother worked. But still he yearned.

It may have been his fascination with Russia that brought him into contact with Baroness Baranovsky, a dispossessed member of the Russian aristocracy who had settled in Saint-Sauveur. I can't think how they would have met unless he sought her out. She was an elegant gentlewoman—I don't quite see her tottering over to The Pub for her evening tipple and running into him there. He must have chased her down.

My father, who was a big thinker in his own way, foresaw career opportunities for anyone who could speak Russian when the Iron Curtain was eventually lifted, something he predicted would happen about fifteen or twenty years thence, and prevailed on the Baroness to teach me Russian. I started my lessons in June 1951 when the school year ended, and went to her house twice a week until Labour Day, when school started again.

Madame Baranovsky lived in a small house at the other end of the village, up behind the church, and on most days I got myself there and back on my bike, my *Hugo's Russian Grammar* and copy-book in a school bag over my shoulder. My father liked to visit with her and would occasionally drive me there. When he picked me up, he and Mme Baranovsky would have tea—in a cup, of all things—and discuss my progress.

I remember her as being old though not elderly, perhaps sixty, with bluish-grey hair, draped in shawls, and wearing tasteful but pronounced makeup. Her voice was low and melodic, and she spoke both French and English beautifully. She looked a little pained when I showed off my French, and French diction lessons were added the following week, along with drawing and watercolour painting. Her house was modest but comfortable, cluttered with curios and *objets d'art*, the walls hung with paintings, many of them her own work.

As the summer progressed, the Baroness worked harder on my French than she did on my Russian. She took the *joual** out of my speech and taught me how to roll my *r*s properly. Over the summer, my rough country accent changed and became more refined and Parisian-leaning. She threw in deportment tips in the course of the lessons, and by the end of the summer I was well on my way to becoming a junior *grande bourgeoise*.

I was going into grade six when school started again in September, taught by Soeur Emile-Arthur, who was an intimidating character though quite a decent teacher. On my first day back, I was asked to read something from our *livre de lecture*. I read a paragraph or two in my hard-earned accent and well-modulated tones, and the nun stopped me in mid-sentence. *"Pour qui tu t'prends, Laury Jane McGarrigle? Parle comme du monde!"* ("Who do you think you are, Laury Jane McGarrigle? Speak normally!") My

---

* *Joual,* according to TERMIUM, is a Quebec French dialect characterized by a set of features (mostly phonetic and lexical) that are considered to be incorrect or objectionable, generally associated with street language and often seen as a sign of acculturation. To speak *joual* is considered hip among educated young people, especially in political circles.

classmates had a good laugh and I reverted in shame to my pre-summer French. The following summer, I refused further lessons from the Baroness.

I've wondered over the years what brought the Baroness to Saint-Sauveur. I can't find her in any historical records or accounts of her time there, so it's hard to know for sure. Since so many thousands of White Russians fled their country after the 1917 revolution to end up wherever they could, tracking down a member of the minor Russian aristocracy is too big a job, even for this grateful pupil. So I fall back on speculation.

There were other members of the Russian noble class established in Saint-Sauveur, and she may have been part of the entourage of the exiled Duke Dimitri of Leuchtenberg. To my knowledge, he was Saint-Sauveur's highest-ranking aristocrat, a Romanov no less, whose ancestors included Empress Josephine of France and Czar Nicholas I of Russia. Dimitri and his wife, Catherine, arrived in Saint-Sauveur in 1931, after a prolonged stay in the family-owned Castle Seeon in Bavaria. The castle had also housed for a time their pseudo-relative Anna Anderson, who was trying to establish her bona fides as the Grand Duchess Anastasia. Dimitri's father, Duke George, had extended hospitality to Anderson on this basis, but many in the family, including Dimitri, doubted her claim and she moved on to other patrons.

There is talk of family friction over Anderson and support of her claim. In any case, the money was running out, and Dimitri and Catherine struck out on their own for a new life in Canada. Upon their arrival in Saint-Sauveur, Duke Dimitri opened a ski school that counted among its first clients guests of his cousin, the Marquis d'Albizzi, who operated an inn in a former schoolhouse on rue Principale, across from the church. The Marquis had also bought a mountain, on the other side of the village and developed it as a ski hill. When the Marquis left Canada in 1939, Dimitri took over the inn and it became Pension Leuchtenberg.

It was the toniest of the Saint-Sauveur boarding houses, and over the years the Leuchtenbergs received Canadian statesmen and many other distinguished guests. The Duke died at seventy-four, reportedly from a fall that occurred while he was removing snow from the roof of the *pension*.

The link between Mme Baranovsky, if in fact she really was a baroness (see "Anderson, Anna"), and the Duke is only a guess on my part, but it makes sense; it seems likely those exiles in tiny Saint-Sauveur would have stuck together.

The Baroness was definitely a painter, possibly of some talent. Years ago I attended a wedding where I was seated alongside a member of the Molson clan, the beer barons whose family had extensive property in Saint-Sauveur until the early 1970s. We reminisced about the village and I asked him if he had ever known the Baroness (there's a Russian connection in his part of the family). He didn't remember her, but he did mention that there was a Baranovsky painting on the family's boat. I would love to see it; I should call him up and get an invitation.

NIMBY

ANNA: In the summer of 1953, Frank and our uncle Austin, Gaby's brother, ran for Saint-Sauveur town council on a team with their friend Frank Kelly as the mayoral candidate. All three were English transplants from the city. Their main objective in seeking office was to block the proposed expansion of a grey cinder-block clothing factory that had sprung up on rue Principale under the watch of the previous village administration. They had a list of incidental issues to address, such as whether or not the town should shell out twelve dollars to buy the lone policeman a new pair of boots, the only item of interest to an eight-year-old with a shoe fetish.

Back in the fifties, if you wanted to get your message heard, you hired a car with a loudspeaker on its roof and drove up and down the streets of the village barking into a microphone. The ultra-Catholic, right-wing Pèlerins de Saint Michel, or *bérets-blancs* (Pilgrims of Saint Michael, or white berets), used this system to spread their word until my father chased them down rue Principale with his horn blaring. Now my father and his cohorts were behind the wheel broadcasting their campaign platform. For a couple of weeks leading up to the August elections the village was a noisy place, and when Kate and I heard the sound getting closer, we would run out onto the front lawn in our bare feet to see if it was Daddy's people so we could wave at them.

On the face of it, our father and his team seemed to be campaigning against the creation of jobs, or at least factory jobs. They felt that the future of the village lay in tourism, not manufacturing. Their opponents, the old conservative French element, were furious. These transplants from the city were daring to plot the future of their village. Families from as far north as Mont-Laurier had already descended on the village to fill the positions of pattern-cutters, seamstresses and packers at this manufacturer of denim jeans, and more would be expected with a larger factory. My father had seen enough factory towns with their blocks of cheap tenements to know he didn't want to see this happening in Saint-Sauveur.

Aside from the obvious drawback of the cinder-block factory ruining the integrity of the picturesque rue Principale, with its graceful old houses and mature hardwood trees, there was also the issue that the factory drew its workforce from the local schools. The girls in particular dropped out as early as grade five or six, either because they lacked the necessary aptitude or the girl's family needed the extra money.

I remember walking home with Kate when we were in the lower grades and being taunted by some older girls who had left École Marie-Rose just a few months before. Now these former students were standing outside the factory on their cigarette break, teasing and luring us with penny candy and cigarettes they'd throw at us. "*Viens t'en, catin*," they'd call. ("Come closer, little dolly.") We must have looked pathetic to them in our navy, box-pleated tunics and beige, ribbed stockings.

Our parents warned us not to engage with these girls, fearing we might eventually fall for the allure of factory life ourselves, though we were a bit too young to think about dropping out of school just yet. But they needn't have worried. We were intimidated by the girls, with their heavily made-up faces and matte red lips, and would cross the street to avoid further encounters with them.

JANE: Some of the girls Anna describes had been classmates of mine at École Marie-Rose, and my parents held their fate over my head in the form of a veiled threat: "Look at poor So-and-So, she didn't apply herself and now she's working at The Factory. *Do you want to end up like that? At The Factory?*" The idea of being allowed to wear lipstick and have a few dollars didn't seem so terrible, but I knew better than to say so.

ANNA: The romantic in me now views the girls as mid-twentieth-century versions of Carmen and her friends working in the Seville tobacco factory, as immortalized by Georges Bizet in what may be the world's most popular opera, *Carmen*.

Look at them! Impudent glances,
Saucy airs,
all of them puffing away
at a cigarette.

If our father had had his way, he would have kept Saint-Sauveur as he had first found it back in the early 1930s, in a state of suspended animation, like a Clarence Gagnon painting, its colourful little cottages set in a rolling landscape of perpetual snow, the inhabitants travelling hither and yon in horse-drawn sleighs. Team Kelly wasn't against progress, but it was for the promotion of the ski industry and tourism in general. Happily, this is the direction the village took after they won the elections. But there were some downsides too. Our father did not live long enough to see the hills converted to garish, noisy waterslides in summer, these same ski hills that had been named after the Allied positions in World War I and where a wreath of poppies, commemorating the Great War, was laid on the big rock halfway up Hill 70 each Remembrance Day.

SAINT-SAUVEUR TODAY

(Jane)

Saint-Sauveur of the 1940s and '50s is a permanent state of mind I can drop into when I want to escape the Saint-Sauveur of today. Much has changed. It was always a tourist destination, but the former village now has a permanent population of 20,000 people and what feels like 10,000 restaurants to service the more than one million annual visitors. I wonder if my father in his wildest dreams would have predicted the scope and dynamism of the tourist industry when he originally championed it as the town's best destiny. The ski hills are still there, as is the big Catholic church in the centre of town, the lantern in its steeple a luminous magenta at nightfall. The Anglican church on rue Saint-Denis, a beautiful little log structure, is still standing, though its old parish hall is gone, the logs disassembled and carted away for some other use, and the land a present and future parking lot. The Dagenais family's hardware store on rue Principale is thriving in its original location, now as a Rona franchise, and has taken over the former Howick Clothing Factory, so abhorred by our parents, and expanded into the décor business for the benefit of all the new condominiums that continue to spring up.

With one or two exceptions, all the charming French-Canadian houses on rue Principale, and many on the side streets, are now bustling restaurants, or boutiques selling trendy clothes and what my mother used to call "gewgaws." On weekends the sidewalks are as packed with people as the streets are jammed with cars. Gone are the days when a Crackpot could stop his car in the middle of rue Principale to salute a fellow Crackpot. Horns would blare, road rage a real possibility.

There's a shop now where the blacksmith's workshop used to be, and where Daddy used to take us along as kids when he was having ironwork done. M. Ratelle shoed horses and repaired snowploughs and farm equipment. He was always coal black, covered in soot from head to toe, and his place stank of horse manure. Sparks flew off the forge, and it was fascinating to see him bend red-hot iron into various shapes with his hammer and tongs. My father took advantage of these visits to recite a bastardized version of the Longfellow poem:

> Under a spreading chestnut tree
> The village smithy stands;
> The smith, a mighty man is he,
> With large and sinewy hands;
> And the muscles of his brawny arms
> Snap back like rubber bands.

He delivered it with panache, his inflexion rising as he got to the last line, and held up his far from brawny arms. We loved it and never got tired of it.

Gone too are the days when you knew the village cops, in our day Tom Durocher, who for years patrolled on a bicycle before the town council voted in a budget for a police car.

There are no local police anymore; we are now served and protected by the Sûreté du Québec. They are an anonymous lot, and I miss the days of Tom's law enforcement. Our old friend Joan Green told me a good Saint-Sauveur cop story not long ago. It seems her parents, Bill and Betty Green, drove up to Saint-Sauveur one Sunday afternoon with Joan and her brother Billy to visit us. When they arrived at the house, our car wasn't there and no one was home. Her father Bill climbed up onto the second-floor balcony, let himself in through a window and unlocked the front door so his family could join him inside the house. They were just making themselves at home when we McGarrigles arrived, probably from an after-church visit to Lorne and June's. We were no sooner inside than Tom turned up at the door in uniform. Little Joan thought he was there to arrest her father for breaking in (which may well have been the case if a neighbour reported it), but my father invited him in for a drink and he joined the party.

The general mentality of the village in those days was laissez-faire in other ways that wouldn't be possible today, not all of them desirable. One of my classmates had a "funny" uncle who roamed around town. He was a short, corpulent man dressed in overalls and a goofy cap. He had a dull, unsmiling stare that he liked to fix on people, and we always crossed the street if we saw him coming. I was sitting at the village soda fountain one summer afternoon in my play shorts, when I was about eleven, enjoying a pineapple soda, when Alcide came and sat on the stool next to mine. There were no other customers and the waitress was in the kitchen. He sat and stared at me for a while, then put his fat, grubby hand on my thigh and stared at me some more. I slurped up my pineapple soda and rushed home on my bike. When I told my mother about it, she said, "Next time, tell that dirty old devil to keep his hands to himself." Next time! Today, he would probably be registered as a sex offender.

A sadder case was Luc, the father of a couple of boys who were Kate and Anna's age. The family lived a few streets away from ours, and Luc ran a small business from a home office, something like an insurance agency. We only knew him by sight, a nice-looking man of about forty. One fall day in the early 1950s, he began taking long walks around town, and always walked by our house at the same time of day. He continued through the winter, and on the coldest days we'd look out our living room window at dusk and there he'd be, trudging by. My mother said you could set your clock by him. Over a couple of years we noticed that his posture was changing a little at a time, his body leaning further and further forward, till he was almost bent in two. His general appearance took a steep dive; he became shaggy and unkempt, his face thin and weather-beaten, with a frozen sullenness.

He walked by one day and we noticed he was carrying a hatchet tucked under one arm, his hands jammed into his coat pockets. Now, when we came across him in the village, we crossed the street.

One day our parents' friend Esther Dinsdale came to see my father for advice about Luc. She was a widow who lived in a beautiful little stone château on a property that was bordered by a hedge. The yard didn't have a gate. Luc had been stationing himself in her hedge, sometimes for hours at a time, standing very still, hatchet at the ready. She had taken advantage of his absence to make a dash to our house and see what my father thought about the situation. Frank told her that Luc was probably just trying to protect her and not to worry about it. That seemed to soothe Esther, but not my mother, who wondered aloud if the two of them were not as crazy as poor Luc.

Still, no one intervened that I know of, and then one day Luc's walks stopped. The family, who were not from Saint-Sauveur, packed up and left not long after. As far as I know, he never hurt anyone, though he frightened a lot of people. That could never happen today; the authorities would be called, social services would step in and he would be processed through the system, as would the funny uncle—on balance a good thing, but at least then you knew where your peril lay.

GOOD TIMES

ANNA: In the spring of 1953, the family took a road trip to Ottawa. We had been to Ottawa once before, on a leisurely drive to visit my father's cousin Vesta Gillis and her family. Their place was close to the inner city, on a dark, tree-lined street with tall, narrow Victorian houses, so different from our bright Laurentian valley. But we wouldn't be visiting with family this time. Our daddy sold airplane jacks and this was a business trip.

The postwar expansion of Trans-Canada Airlines (TCA), Canada's civilian airline, might have accounted for the bump in demand for these big yellow jacks, and the purpose of the trip was either to deliver a tender to supply the jacks or to pick up a purchase order for them from the federal government.

JANE: The excursion had a festive feel to it. We must have gone there on a school day if Daddy was calling on his customer, and we never missed school unless we were sick and running a temperature. If you remember, we were the kids who walked to school on a day when it was too cold to take horses out. We think Gaby was probably tired of the long winter and wanted a trip herself, and since she never left us with anyone, we got to skip school and have a little holiday.

ANNA: While Daddy wheeled and dealed on Parliament Hill, our mother did her bit to boost the economy, taking us shopping at Ogilvy's, Montreal's elegant boutique department store on Rideau Street. It was the year of the new queen's coronation, and the hoopla and commercialization surrounding this event were in evidence everywhere. In keeping with the royal theme, Kate and I got matching grey cotton frocks with an embroidered red and gold crown on the bodice and, to complete the outfits, green-and-cream-check

Édouard Côté & Catherine Bannon, Gaby's grandparents, *circa* late 1870s. He was a Montreal tailor and she was a first generation Canadian (pre-Confederation), born at the Irish settlement of Sainte-Marthe, Quebec.

James McGarrigle and his mother, Rose Conway McGarrigle (our grandfather and great-grandmother), *circa* early 1880s.

Our grandmother, Laury Côté, with her sister Dora and brother Percy, *circa* early 1890s. Our uncle Percy's death at Passchendaele in 1917 continues to haunt us. Like so many other fallen soldiers, Percy's body is still in the mud though his name is engraved in the arch at Ypres, Belgium. Cold comfort.

Laury Côté with mandolin, *circa* 1894. We remember there being a pot-bellied mandolin like this one and a piano in the house at Sainte-Dorothée.

Thomas McGarrigle
(our great-grandfather),
little Jim McGarrigle
(Frank's oldest brother)
and James McGarrigle
(our grandfather),
circa 1900.

Our grandmother Laury and some of her brood, 1910. Standing, Eddy, and front row, Myrtle, Laury with baby Ruth and Gaby (our mother).

Private James McGarrigle (Uncle Jimmy) *circa* 1914–18. He served in France and was possibly at the Battle of Passchendaele, Belgium. He drowned after falling off a boat near New York City in 1939.

Gaby's younger sister, Ruth Latrémouille, *circa* 1918. Remembered for her beautiful red hair. She died at twenty-four.

Frank McGarrigle cutting up with some friends in Saint-Sauveur in the mid-1930s.

Gaby and Frank pleasure sailing *circa* 1935 on a friend's yacht.

Frank McGarrigle and Gaby Latrémouille on their wedding day,
November 16, 1935, at the Windsor Hotel, Montreal.

The Patriarch: Grandpapa Arthur Latrémouille on the lawn of the
Bussey Convalescent Home in Dixie (Lachine), 1943.

Gaby and Janie in Lachine, Quebec, 1945. Janie's first hotrod. Even
then Jane loved to drive.

Janie, Anna and Kate at the Blacks' in Ste-Adèle, 1948. We often called on people after Sunday Mass.

With our friends in Saint-Sauveur: Judy Hinds, Gogerty the dog, Kate, Sheilagh Byrnes, Nina Hinds and Anna, mid-1950s.

The Booth boys: Wayne, Ronnie, Dean and Sean, with barefoot
Anna. Watch for nails! 1951.

Anna, Gaby, Frank and Kate, north side of Frankenflynn, the house
that Frank and the carpenter Flynn made from spare parts, Saint-
Sauveur, *circa* 1954.

A picture we really like of our mother at home, *circa* 1956. Note, phase one of camp construction at right.

Anna and Kate, Montreal, 1961. A cold day for busking—note ski gloves.

Dave and Janie Dow in their MGA sportscar in St. Andrew's, New Brunwsick, *circa* 1962.

Daddy at home in Saint-Sauveur, 1962. The cards are a prop, Daddy didn't play cards; he thought it brought out the worst in people.

Anna near St. Paul Street, 1962, just up the street from the
Bonsecours Market where Grandpapa Arthur bought his pig's
heads. The area became known as "Old Montreal" in 1964.

Dane Lanken sweeps Anna off her feet in Saint-Sauveur in the mid-1960s. Chris Weldon's Austin Healey 3000 makes an appearance.

Projections during a light show in November 1966 in the ballroom of the McGill Student Union building. The light show was inspired by Kate's and Dane's trips to the West Coast earlier that year.

A rare photo of The Mountain City Four performing at Moose Hall, Montreal, in 1964. Left to right: Kate, Jack Nissenson, Anna and Peter Weldon.

Anna between rides during
hitchhiking trip with Dane
to the West Coast in 1967.
Looks like the prairies.

Kate and Chris
Weldon with
muddy faces after
a motorcycle ride,
in Montreal,
circa 1967.

Philippe Tatartcheff peering out of the Birmingham Apartments, *circa* 1968. In the 1960s a lot of our friends lived in this building at de Maisonneuve and avenue du Parc, now gone: Deborah Adler, Dane, John Weldon.

Anna peering out of the Birmingham.

wool coats with dark green velvet collars and matching straw hats that tied under the chin. We looked like proper little toffs in our fancy new duds, and ready for the St. Patrick's Day parade.

JANE: I was outfitted in a double-breasted coral jacket with brass buttons, and a navy and green tartan kilt with a jaunty matching tam-o'-shanter. There were no coronation adornments that I remember, but I didn't miss them. I loved my new spring outfit and thought I looked like a million dollars.

ANNA: On the way back home, we stopped in the Papineauville–Montebello area to visit with members of Doc Byers' family, Jesse and Bronwyn. Dr. Byers' first wife was Martha Jane Curren, the young widow of Louis-Joseph-Amédée Papineau. LJAP was the eldest son of Louis-Joseph Papineau, prominent Quebec leader of the 1837 Rebellion. The Seigneurie Club in Montebello is built on what was the old Papineau seigneurial property—hence the name—that overlooked the majestic Ottawa River. Our father worked on the construction of the lodge in the early thirties and must have known the Byers family since that time.

While we were in Papineauville–Montebello, our father walked into a Ford dealership and on impulse bought a new black '53 Monarch, a model of Ford available only in Canada. This sleek model was also designed around the upcoming coronation and had a red and gold crown-shaped escutcheon around the keyhole on the trunk, and another bigger one on the front just over the carmaker's insignia. It sounds garish now, like a pimpmobile, but it wasn't then. We drove this car right out of the showroom and headed for home along the scenic north shore of the Ottawa River.

STRANGERS IN STE. ANGÈLE
(Anna)

One of our father's friends was the writer Phyllis Lee Peterson. There was a certain cachet in knowing a published author, one whose stories had appeared in the *Saturday Evening Post* and the *Canadian Home Journal*. I'm not sure where they met, whether it was in a sanatorium (Frank made many friends this way) or through a mutual acquaintance.

There's a family story about Phyllis and her husband, Miller, visiting us once in Saint-Sauveur when Kate was about four. Seeing the balding Miller for the first time, little Kate is said to have blurted out, "What happened to your hair?" before kicking him squarely in the shins. The poor man replied that it was because of little girls like her that his hair had fallen out, and muttered audibly to his wife, "Horrible child." Kate loved to hear this story about her younger self. It was more fodder for the Kate legend. She caused men to go bald!

In the early sixties, CBC Television produced an episode of Phyllis's *Strangers in Ste. Angèle*, the first in a mystery series set in a fictional Quebec town. It would star Bruno Gerussi of *Beachcombers* fame, and Phyllis had Frank hired on as location manager. This was a happy time for him, scouring the Laurentian back roads in search of interesting settings. He may not have been able to locate his chequebook or his hammer in his own house, but he knew where every sawmill and cemetery was within an eighty-kilometre radius of the village.

The script called for an old farm as a locale. Frank found them the most charming of subsistence farms in the mountains just a few miles west of the village. The old square-log house with an attached shed, a small barn and a couple of open fields belonged to a spinster, a woman around forty years old at this time. All through the 1950s we had seen this rangy woman in a horse-drawn rig shopping in the village or going to Sunday Mass. The village anglos called her Annie Oakley.

Frank went to pay Annie a visit on her farm in an area known locally as *le grand ruisseau* (the big creek). The creek flowed out of Lac des Chats and tumbled down the mountains till it reached the flat plain of the Saint-Sauveur valley. The homestead had no electricity, which was not unusual for a place as out of the way as hers, but my father was a little surprised to see that she and her horse lived under the same roof. That is, the horse's box stall and her living quarters appeared to be in one room, the horse being a source of heat in this cold climate.

On her trips to town, her outfit was always the same: a blue denim mid-calf skirt with a bib, like a man's overalls but for a woman, a boxy denim jacket, thick brown woollen ribbed stockings and felt boots, the footwear farmers and schoolboys in the country wore, slipping rubbers (or "claques") over the felts when they went outside. Her face was deeply tanned from the sun and she wore her hair short like a man's. When driving a rig, her head was encased in a brown leather helmet with a peak and a strap under her chin. In her own way she was very stylish, a sort of backcountry Amelia Earhart. But this is where the resemblance ends. She chain-smoked roll-ups, had few teeth and always had a butt dangling from her lower lip. In the early sixties she still travelled to town by horse and buggy, the last holdout, hitching her rig to a post in front of Belisle's general store on rue Principale, where she got her supplies. In winter she drove a small utility sleigh, one she stood up in with the reins in her hands. She had a name, Thérèse Beausoleil, but like Annie O., she was a crack shot.

Mlle Beausoleil had a cameo in an episode of *Strangers in Ste. Angèle*, posing in an open window of her *chaumière* (cottage) while squinting down the barrel of her rifle. As I remember, the CBC used this shot of her with the gun to advertise the show.

In 1966, when my husband Dane's parents bought a house on Lac des Chats, his father hired Annie to cut down some trees on their property. The woman also wielded a chainsaw and by then she would have owned a pickup.

All through the filming, people came and went. Gardencourt was a hub for the crew and actors, and some may have even stayed in the cottages. At the end of the day's shoot Frank would have taken them to The Inn (formerly The Pub) or the Pow-Wow Room for libations.

I remember our family watching *Strangers in Ste. Angèle* when it aired on the CBC. It made television less of a passive activity, having met some of the people responsible for bringing this project to the small screen, including our father, who was immensely proud, as were we, to see his name in the rolling credits. *Location Manager: Frank McGarrigle.*

ST. MARY'S SCHOOL, COMBERMERE

(Jane)

École Marie-Rose ran only through grade nine, and I was done with it in 1955. I had skipped grade eight and thus finished a year early, perhaps catching my parents a little off guard. They had always planned for me to attend an English high school, most likely as a boarder since there wasn't a day school close by, but I wasn't enrolled anywhere.

Mummy thought she could get me into the Sacred Heart Convent in Montreal without too much trouble, because it was headed up by her old school chum Reverend Mother May Carter. Gaby and May had been best friends through their grammar school years at St. Patrick's, and Gaby had good stories about the fun-loving May who surprised everyone by becoming a nun. In Gaby's day, Father Gerald McShane was the pastor of St. Patrick's parish and ran it as his personal fiefdom. He exerted tremendous authority over the lives of his parishioners and used what influence he had to boost their prospects out in the greater world. It's fair to say he was both feared and revered by his flock. He must have taken particular pride in the advancement of the Carters in the Church. May Carter became Mother-General of the Sacred Heart Order, Father Alex Carter was consecrated a bishop, and Father Emmett Carter was also consecrated a bishop and later elevated to archbishop of Toronto, eventually becoming a cardinal.

Father McShane and the teachers at St. Patrick's thought Gaby very smart and wanted her to continue her education, but they knew too well that Grandpapa Latrémouille couldn't wait to send her out to work to help support his big family. They managed to keep her in school an extra year so she could earn normal-school accreditation and a teaching certificate. It was an informal scholarship—the school fees were waived. I see the fine hand and iron fist of Father McShane in this arrangement.

Mummy went to see May Carter to enrol me and learned to her dismay that there was a ten-year waiting list. The Sacred Heart Convent was a snooty school, though the fees weren't much higher than at other convents, and families were registering their daughters at birth. Gaby pleaded, but May wouldn't bend the rules to let her old friend jump the queue. According to Mother May, she had been obliged to refuse Cardinal Léger's niece, whose parents had also failed to register her in time. I doubt May Carter got to be the head of the Sacred Heart Order by saying no to cardinals, but my mother accepted it, and she and Daddy scrambled to find another boarding school for me.

We visited a few places and passed on them—too strict, too ordinary, too great a distance from home—and then one day my parents were introduced to the Ross family, who had recently moved to Saint-Sauveur from Ireland. Judith Ross had gone to school in Ireland, with an order of sisters called the Faithful Companions of Jesus. It was a congregation of pious, well-educated women and, except that it was a semi-cloistered order, the FCJs were closely modelled on the Society of Jesus; like the Jesuits, they emphasized a classical education. The order had opened up shop seven years before in Combermere, Ontario, a small village in beautiful, wild country on the fringes of Algonquin Park. Mrs. Ross called her school friend Mother Zoe O'Connell, who was then the Reverend Mother of St. Mary's Convent, and arranged for us to visit the school.

It was a long drive for the time, four hundred kilometres on two-lane roads, and our parents made a little family vacation of it. The Monarch was packed up for the trip and, being who we were, we made our usual late getaway and were only about halfway to our destination by suppertime. We put up on the road and arrived at the convent in late morning the following day.

"Combermere—Where the Magic Begins" is how I would have advertised it to my fourteen-year-old self once I got to know the place.

The entrance to the nuns' property was off Dafoe Road and bordered by stone walls. At the end of the long driveway was a modern white three-storey building, long and low-slung, with a stone and glass portico and wooden bell tower.

We were beautifully received by Mother Zoe, who was all Irish charm, and served tea and scones in her office while she told us a bit about the order and the school. We were all very taken with her. We left Mother Zoe's office for the short walk across the grounds to the day school, and were shown around there by Mother Miriam Ryan, its principal. She too was long on Irish charm, and the parents were smitten. I knew this was where I would be in the fall.

We spent the rest of the afternoon seeing a bit of the town, and looked in on Madonna House, a lay Catholic apostolate that established itself in Combermere around the same time as the Faithful Companions of Jesus (FCJs) did. Its leaders, Catherine and Eddie Doherty, actively promoted their mission and had an open-door policy for visitors.*

The apostolate's stated mission was to serve God and the poor, and the Dohertys and their followers made a point of going about barefoot and dressed in rags to identify better with the dispossessed. They cut a comical figure around Combermere, a community of mid-century rural Ontarians who could only wonder why people would go to so much trouble to look like ragamuffins. The nuns took a dim view of the whole thing and discouraged us from having anything to do with them, thus Mother Miriam's reply to my father when he mentioned a visit to Madonna House: "If you must."

I hadn't yet been indoctrinated when we dropped in on Madonna House that day, and when we met Eddie Doherty, I thought him a congenial and gracious man. He showed us around the place and introduced us to members of the apostolate as we came across them, describing their various duties. We met a couple of men whose job it was to clear the snow from paths in the winter. He

---

* It seems an odd coincidence that these two Catholic movements, wildly different in style if not content, ended up within a few miles of each other in the same small town in Ontario, but they were never connected and had very little to do with each other. Like much of Combermere, they were a study in contrasts.

referred to them as "our pathologists." We left Combermere with some pine saplings that the pathologists obligingly dug up for us and placed in the Monarch's trunk. My parents transplanted the saplings onto our Saint-Sauveur property, where they've since grown to a great height, fifty feet or more.

We loved everything about St. Mary's and Combermere, and my parents signed me up the next morning. School books and uniforms were ordered. On weekdays the girls wore a straight-cut dark green tunic over an apple-green blouse, and a dark green tie, a dark green blazer and green beanies. The Sunday uniform was a soft green box-pleated jumper worn over a pale yellow nylon blouse trimmed with lace, a pleasing feminine contrast to the boyish weekday uniform.

The FCJs' mission was to educate, and they had moved to Combermere to operate a secondary day school for the region. The principal industries in that part of the country were then farming, lumber and mining, and it was populated by Irish, Polish and German settlers. It was technically a parish school, but not all the boys and girls were Catholics. There were a few Protestants of one denomination or another, and one girl who was a Pentecostal. I remember her because she had to sit out the dances—Virginia reels, the schottische and the Highland fling—that everyone else had to learn. While the rest of Canada was jitterbugging, the FCJs were in the same comfortable last-century time warp as the McGarrigle family.

Once back home, we went shopping for the list of nightclothes, underthings and sundries on the nuns' list. My father and I made a special trip to Ogilvy's in Montreal to buy a hat box I would take on the train. It was plaid, about fourteen inches in diameter, and had a little hand strap. He told me that no well-dressed woman travelled without one. The nuns had arranged for me to meet Chris McGuire, a boarder who lived in Ottawa, and ride the train with her to Barry's Bay, where we would be met and driven the seventeen kilometres to Combermere. I had never been away from home on my own, but something about riding the train with a hat box made it seem like a grown-up experience, and I couldn't wait for this new adventure to start.

Chris and I arrived at the convent in high spirits, and I jumped right into the routine and got to know the nuns one at a time, according to what their duties were. Combermere is fishing and hunting country, and the convent was often presented with gifts of food straight from nature. Hunters, our parish priest Father Dwyer among them, would kill and field-dress a deer and drop it off to the cooking sisters, two Swiss women, who prepared it with great skill. We ate a lot of venison prepared any number of ways—steaks, roasts, stews, all delicious. The cooking sisters were versatile, and also made delicious cakes and pastries. They did their job a little too well. By Christmas, I had put on ten pounds and my uniforms had to be let out.

Mother Rita, who taught at the day school and organized our team sports, was a general favourite of all the kids, girls and boys alike. She had a special friendship with Moise Franswa, the old Indian who lived alone down on the riverbank below the convent. Moise was a World War I veteran whose family had owned a farm in the area at one time. He had been a fishing guide for a lot of his life and done odd jobs around the parish, but he was then close to eighty and less active. Mother Rita tended to him, and reminded us to keep him in our prayers as his health wasn't good. Moise was always a romantic and mysterious figure to me, living in his little cabin on the Madawaska River and getting about in his canoe.

Our subjects were English, Latin, history, geography, algebra, geometry and Scriptures. We also had regular classes in music and art, where Mother Mary's long rubber-tipped pointer was directed at our errant fingers on the piano keys and clumsy strokes at the easel. Mother Mary also taught deportment and supervised the dining hall. She walked around with her long pointer and rapped us smartly on the hands to remind us of our table manners. She was a dour person who looked a bit like Queen Victoria under her wimple, and she always seemed on the verge of saying, "We are not amused," as Queen Victoria is supposed to have done in response to something one of her grooms did. Mother Mary was rarely amused.

Latin was my favourite subject and was taught by Mother Miriam. I took to it very quickly and looked forward to the classes. I kept up my Latin chops during the other classes by trading notes in Latin with fellow keeners, my Latin grammar book always handy so I could look up the correct declensions. The notes were passed furtively from hand to hand, and when opened would read something like: *Larry non docetur in schola. Quare?* ("Larry not in school today. Why?") That would start a chain of correspondence in Latin about the whereabouts of Larry and other gossip.

We woke up to a little bell and an invocation, typically, "Jesus, Mary and Joseph," to which we replied, "Jesus, Mary and Joseph," the call-and-answer litany kept up through our washing and dressing, and the only speech allowed until we came down to breakfast. There was a short study period after breakfast, and we walked in pairs over to the day school, about ten minutes away. At the end of the school day, we walked back to the convent for supper and an evening study period before we were cut loose in the recreation hall. Half of our study hall was given over to desks and the other half was set up as a comfortable reading room. It had a well-stocked library of contemporary works and classics, though nothing as eclectic as the McGarrigle collection. The interesting thing about the FCJs as Catholic educators is that they encouraged us to question Catholic dogma and other received wisdom—up to a point. In the end, they always circled us back to the party line.

Either Father Dwyer or a junior priest said Mass in the convent's chapel every morning. Attendance was not compulsory but strongly encouraged. We left our shoes outside our sleeping cubicle if we wanted to be awakened for the seven o'clock Mass. I attended Mass a few times a week, not to suck up to the nuns but because I enjoyed it so much. We would think of it now as a meditative experience, as I became lost in the Gregorian chant and tranced out on the beautiful holy cards in my missal. It's part of the Combermere magic that I was sometimes transported to an altered state in chapel. I longed for those experiences and kept going back for more. My teenage mysticism didn't make me in any way a trouble-free charge to the good sisters. Far from it. I was often in hot water, usually for rebelling in some way and then digging in my heels about it.

I went home for the Christmas holidays and missed St. Mary's; I counted the days till school started again.

Chris and I learned on our return that Moise had gone downhill over the holidays. Mother Rita was going back and forth to his cabin more often now. Word came that he was dying, and special prayers were said and candles lit for him in the chapel. We had started school again on the ninth of January, 1956, and Moise died on the nineteenth. Much of that time is now a dreamscape of bleak, snowy fields and the freezing Madawaska River. I see a small group of us walking down the path to Moise's at dusk, and people gathered around a big bonfire outside his cabin. Inside the cabin are candles and oil lamps, and Moise lying on his deathbed. I can't remember if he was still with us or had already passed. I heard later that his body was placed in his canoe and floated down his beloved Madawaska. He's buried in the cemetery of the Holy Canadian Martyrs' church in Combermere, his grave not far from Father Dwyer's, who died after I left Combermere.

The sadness of Moise's death was offset a little by the arrival of a new boarder. Ann Bennett was Protestant, unusual for a boarder at St. Mary's. She may have been "serving time" at the convent— the mid-year entry suggests a hasty departure from another school— though St. Mary's was not in any way a disciplinary institution. Ann was a lot of fun and everyone liked her, including the nuns, even though she was a bit of a hellion. She challenged authority at every turn, especially when it didn't make sense to her, and I think everyone who was around for it would agree that it was a glorious moment for all of us when she made her statement about the "no pit stops" rule we had to live with on our walks.

Unless the weather was very bad, we went out every Saturday or Sunday for a long walk. Some of these excursions could last up to three hours. We paired up, a sister and student at the head, a student and sister at the tail, the sisters' faces veiled once they left the convent grounds. It was usually Mother Bridget or Mother Rita, and once in a while Mother Miriam or Sister Mary Agnes. We competed for the right to pair up with our favourite nun. Mother Rita was the most sought-after, although my favourite was Mother Miriam. There was one girl who had a terrific crush on Mother Rita, but her affection was not returned, and Mother Rita did her best to fight her off, often making a pre-emptive choice of her own. What's true in secular life with friends and lovers—we reject that which pursues us—was also true behind the convent walls.

On a particular Saturday afternoon, we gathered outside on the tiled courtyard at the convent's back entrance, chose our partners and set off. We were always reminded to use the lavatory beforehand because there would be no opportunity till we got back. We usually walked along remote backcountry roads with little or no traffic, and on one long walk Ann had an urge of nature and asked if she could go behind some bushes and pee. Absolutely not, said Mother Bridget. There were propriety issues and modesty issues, and St. Mary's girls didn't stop and do their business by the side of the road. Ann held on through the rest of the walk, until we were back within the grounds, and then made a mad dash for the courtyard. She dropped her drawers, squatted down, and peed all over the tiles. *Quel* audacity! We were thunderstruck at her nerve. There must have been consequences, but she was still in class on Monday, so they couldn't have been that dire. Word got around fast, and Ann Bennett was the hero of the moment.

I had incidents of my own, but they were small potatoes compared with Ann. Refusing to eat a piece of rhubarb pie and having to sit alone with it in the dining hall long after the others had gone to bed (I detested rhubarb). Taking a dozen Aspirins with Coca-Cola before a hamburger social at the day school (I had heard that it would get me drunk, but it didn't work; all I got was a ringing in my ears for several hours).

Those were merely warm-ups for my signature event, which came shortly after the Easter holiday. I had bought myself a 78 of Elvis Presley's "Heartbreak Hotel" and brought it back up to Combermere with me, packed with great care in my hat box. I was a huge Elvis fan and one of the first people I know to own the 78 of "That's All Right, Mama" backed by "Blue Moon of Kentucky," which I taught to some of the girls in the rec hall and later to Kate and Anna. I couldn't wait to play "Heartbreak Hotel" on the rec hall gramophone. Mother Bridget was on duty when I broke it out on the first night back, and she went ballistic about one minute into the song. She knew a spiritual threat when she heard it. She walked over to the record player, took my 78 off the spindle and smashed it over her knee. "There's your devil music," she said, handing me the pieces.

I was shocked at the destruction of my property and ran up to the dorm. I barricaded myself into my cubicle—as much as you can barricade yourself in a space where three of the walls are cotton curtains—and refused to come out until she replaced it. That effectively put me on a hunger strike, and except to use the bathroom I didn't come out that night, nor the next day. Mother Zoe had been moved since our first visit, and her replacement, the Reverend Mother Madeleine, paid me a visit in my cubicle to threaten me with expulsion if I didn't back down. I didn't care for Mother Madeleine or her negotiating skills, and her strong-arm tactics didn't work on me. Mother Miriam called my father that night. He must have left Saint-Sauveur at dawn the next day, because he showed up in Combermere early in the afternoon. By this time I was starving and praying for a way out of the box I'd put myself in. Daddy mediated the situation and worked out that he would replace the record, I would be suspended for ten days with plenty of work to take home, and I would never again bring any records to St. Mary's. On the way home, we stopped at the first place we saw that served food, and then drove back to Saint-Sauveur in a straight shot.

The rest of the school year was just one great day after another. With Mother Bridget's coaching, we put on *Oklahoma!* to thunderous applause from the local audience. We held a fundraiser for the missions, for which I became a fortune teller. Costumed in scarves and beads, with a string of pots and pans around my waist, I began to believe the tea leaves I had learned to read only hours before. I became quite a good basketball player; I was a guard because I was so short, but I was a very aggressive guard.

We wrote our final exams and I got top marks and looked forward to re-entry at St. Mary's that fall—but it was not to be. When my father came to get me at the end of the term, Mother Miriam told him the sisters felt I had a vocation. Not just any vocation, but as a Sister of the Precious Blood, a contemplative order. I had confided this to Mother Miriam, possibly swept up in the excitement of a senior girl who was going straight from graduation to being a postulant in the order. My father was floored. The teenager who had gone to the mat about her Elvis record two months before was now considering life in the cloister. He didn't say much one way or the other to Mother Miriam, but I knew it wasn't going to fly.

At that point, the universe intervened, as it has a way of doing. The church organist in Saint-Sauveur was getting married that summer and moving away. Would Laury Jane McGarrigle like the job? It meant living in Saint-Sauveur to be available to play for Sunday Masses, certain evening services, and the weddings and funerals that would come up. By all means, said my father, relieved that I would escape the nunnery without his direct intervention. I was sad at first to think I wouldn't be going back to St. Mary's, but got used to the idea over the summer. It was an honour to be the village organist, and a paid honour at that, so we turned the page on St. Mary's in Combermere and started looking around for another high school.

ORGAN GRINDER

(Jane)

When it came to his daughters, our father had big dreams and high expectations. He never let us pass up opportunities to advance ourselves; in fact, he sought them out for us. When the job of organist at our parish church was offered to me, it must have seemed like Divine Providence lending a hand.

I remember having a few misgivings at the time. The offer came with a big job description I didn't feel that well prepared for. Among other things, my sight-reading wasn't as good as it should have been, considering I'd been studying music for eight years, nine if you count Mme Landoska in Lachine.

It was also a demanding schedule. I would be playing for 10 a.m. High Masses on Sundays to accompany a male choir, and occasional 8:30 a.m. Low Masses on special Sundays; these were known as *la messe des anges* because the hymns and sacred music were sung by the children's choir under the direction of the Music Sister. There were any number of feast days throughout the year that required a sung/played Mass, and occasional vespers and other evening services. And, of course, weddings and funerals as they arose.

All that said, there was never any question of me turning down the job, too much was riding on it: personal distinction, parental pride, even a small honorarium. My parents accepted the offer from the parish on my behalf, along with the annual salary of five hundred dollars, a lump sum paid by cheque that went straight into the Daddy Bank.

The Daddy Bank was our own personal financial institution. Any money that came into Kate's, Anna's or my hands, such as occasional windfalls from visiting friends and relatives, went into the Daddy Bank, with the understanding that withdrawals could be made if Daddy approved of the expense. Elaborate records were kept, using forms from my father's inactive bank accounts. Whenever I put money into the Daddy Bank, a deposit slip was filled out and the entry noted in an old passbook. To make a withdrawal, I filled out a blank cheque made out to myself, wrote in the amount and signed it. Daddy gave me the money and noted it in the passbook, all very businesslike. There was always a discussion about how the proposed expenditure squared with the sense of values my parents wanted me to have, but Daddy generally honoured his end of the deal.

My new instrument was a three-manual Casavant pipe organ with a pedal board played by the feet. I was familiar with stops and settings from playing our harmonium at home, and had learned what I could from Hélène, the girl I succeeded as organist, before she left town, but I was by no means a full-fledged organist in the manner of E. Power Biggs or our uncle Jimmy's hero Marcel Dupré; I never properly mastered the foot pedals, which should be played with both feet, and I got away with using the left foot on the pedal board and the right foot on the volume pedal, or "swell." This is considered bad form by accomplished organists, but it's how I was taught and I never took it any further, despite my father's urging and willingness to pay for lessons.

It says something about the wealth of the Catholic Church in that era that a small town such as Saint-Sauveur, not a rich parish, could afford such a magnificent instrument in its parish church. Casavant Frères is a renowned Quebec pipe organ manufacturer in Saint-Hyacinthe that still makes and restores these splendid beasts, and ships them to customers all over the world. Perhaps the Church offered the Casavant brothers a few indulgences in trade?

The organ was in the choir loft, which was reached by a set of narrow winding stairs, and from which the altar and first ten or fifteen rows of pews were visible. This helped cue the organist to the officiating priest's next move. The pipes, four to sixteen feet in length, and arranged by graduated size on the back wall, made a dramatic backdrop to the choir standing behind me. Once the organ was fired up, and I pulled out all the stops, so to speak, I was in command of an impressive sound.

Hélène was always beautifully turned out on Sundays, and I have a vivid picture of her on her last day, in a lime-green Dior-style shirtwaist dress, with a matching straw picture hat and matching high-heeled shoes, a fashion standard her replacement would never live up to. Once seated at the organ, she kicked off the high heels and played the pedals in her stocking feet. I wondered if splinters from the wooden pedals ever made runs in her nylons.

The church seats 450 people, not counting the choir loft or the lofts on either side of the altar, and in those days, before the secularization of Quebec, they packed them in on Sunday mornings. Each Sunday Mass was a performance that I wanted to be ready for, and I practised a lot, with Marcel the choirmaster and by myself. I had keys to the church and to the organ, and sometimes went over after supper when the church was likely to be deserted. It was quite spooky when the church was dark and I had to feel for the switch that would flip on the light at the head of the staircase. *The Phantom of the Opera* comes to mind, though it was the Phantom who was scared out of her skin when someone occasionally wandered into the church I had left unlocked, and up to the choir loft to see what was going on.

I learned a few Masses and many pieces of occasional music. My sight-reading improved, and it didn't take me long to feel at home with the Casavant's dashboard.

The Eucharist is a quiet part of the Mass when no particular music is prescribed, so I began improvising music to get the communicants in the right frame of mind. It was very sweet-sounding music, with a lot of suspended chords in it that gave it a churchy authenticity.

People in the congregation felt free to comment to a kid in a way they probably wouldn't have done to an adult, and I received some praise (It was beautiful!) and the occasional complaint (It was too loud!). Sometimes there would be a question about what I had played during Communion. I was too shy to admit I had made it up on the spot, so I attached some obscure or imaginary composer's name to it. Inevitably, the parishioner would nod wisely and say, "*Ah oui, je reconnais…*" ("Oh yes, I recognize it.") It was a real gig and, except for that little deception, I took it very seriously.

When I played my first funeral, I was excited because Marcel chose Pietro Yon's funeral Mass, one of my favourites. The solemn High Mass was celebrated by five priests dressed in their black and gold vestments, three at the main altar and one at each side altar. Say what you will about Catholics, they knew how to give a sense of occasion to religious ceremonies before Vatican II ushered in guitar Masses and replaced Latin with the vernacular.

Years later I read a partial thread of letters between Uncle Jimmy and Pietro Yon *circa* 1930. They met following an organ recital by Yon at Carnegie Hall in New York and went out for drinks. Evidently Uncle Jimmy complimented Yon on his playing but criticized the programme for being light on Bach. Yon must have written a defensive letter which we don't have, but the rest of Uncle Jimmy's side of the thread is a downward spiral ending with Uncle Jimmy busting Yon for playing too many of his own compositions in concert and not enough "first-class composers." Ouch.

After playing for a lot of services and seeing how casual Marcel the choirmaster could be—poking fun at the priest's bad intonation, rushing his way through a funeral—I was becoming irreverent myself, especially after I started playing for the skiers' Mass at noon on winter Sundays. It was a very different sensibility from *la messe des anges* and probably should have been called the drinkers' Mass, such was the bedraggled state of many congregants. Herb O'Connell, who owned Mont Gabriel, a luxury ski resort about five kilometres from Saint-Sauveur, filled his sleigh with guests from the lodge and transported them to the midday Low Mass. Himself was at the reins, in his big fur coat and hat, the guests seated in the sleigh under their blankets. Upon arrival at the church, Herb left the sleigh and the team with a boy from the village, and marched with his guests up the centre aisle of the church to reserved pews. His bar singer,

Jerry Travers, often under the weather from the night before and looking a bit press-ganged, scrambled up the stairs to join me for the music his boss wanted. Jerry carried sheet music under his arm the first few times we did this—some hymns, Cesar Franck's "Panis Angelicus" for the Offertory, other greatest hits such as "The Lord's Prayer" (composer Albert Hay Malotte) and both the Gounod and Schubert versions of "Ave Maria." We started breaking some new ground once we got used to each other, and played hymns we were familiar with from our days in Catholic choirs. We discovered we both loved "In a Garden," a saccharine but affecting hymn from the Sankey–Moody hymnal (Protestant, but the roof didn't fall in), and worked it into our repertoire. There was no additional compensation from the parish, but Himself gave me an occasional tip and a yearly ski pass to Mont Gabriel.

In the summer of 1958, our uncle Gus and aunt Muriel visited us from New York for a couple of weeks with their two boys, Frankie and Jimmy. "Great Balls of Fire" was a big hit that summer for Jerry Lee Lewis, who as far as I know was the first piano-based artist to make it big in rock 'n' roll, all the others being guitar players. This was exciting to a young piano player, and I had taken to playing and singing "Great Balls of Fire" at home, complete with Jerry Lee's glissandos. Jimmy and the other kids enjoyed it and kept at me to play it, trying to goad me into banging the keyboard with my feet, as Jerry Lee was famous for doing onstage, as though I would dare attempt this on the Steinway.

A funeral came up during their visit, and Jimmy came along to keep me company while I played for it. The choirmaster had sung the Mass solo and left as soon as he could get away. I was playing the recessional, an unknown Kyrie composed by a friend of mine, and I asked Jimmy to let me know when everyone had left. He was leaning over the rail and gave me the sign that the church was empty. I decided to see how "Great Balls of Fire" would sound on the organ and launched into it, pulling out more and more stops as I went along. I was going full throttle, glissandos and all, pedal-to-the-metal on the swell for volume, and saw Jimmy at the rail shaking with laughter. The church was *not* empty, there were still a few mourners straggling out. Jimmy was a devil and I should have known better than to trust him.

I eventually gave up the organ job and didn't play any kind of sustained keyboard again for quite a while.

MY YEAR OF LIVING DANGEROUSLY

(Jane)

While I was settling into my new job as organist during the summer, my parents were pondering my education and what to do about it now that they had pulled me out of St. Mary's. They wanted me in an English school, close enough that I could live at home and be on hand for the Sunday Masses and other services that were part of the parish schedule. There was one obvious option, Sainte-Agathe High School, but it wasn't a given that I'd be accepted. It was governed by the Protestant school board and, being Catholics, we paid taxes to the Catholic school board. There was also the question of disparity in scholastic levels. We'd been told that Protestant educational standards were more demanding and that the same grade level didn't necessarily mean equivalency. My parents chalked this up to anti-Catholic sniping, but there was something to it, as I later found out.

To prepare the ground a little before attempting to enrol me, my father decided we should pay a call on Bruce Smail, a teacher at Sainte-Agathe whom he knew slightly through Brownie Byers, our friend in Papineauville. The idea was that if we could charm Mr. Smail into presenting my application, I had a better chance of getting in.

We arrived at Mr. Smail's with my report cards and settled in for a bit while he and my father had a few drinks and talked about things—mutual friends, the good old days in the Laurentians, the threat of Communism, and other topics of general interest. It was a well-used strategy of my father's: break the ice first, then home in on the mission, in this case enlisting Smail to help with my schooling. When they got around to it, Smail looked over my report cards and agreed to run with my application. I don't see how he could have refused.

A few days later, we were driving once again to Sainte-Agathe, this time to meet Principal Jacobsen and register me. Another uniform was ordered—Dress Gordon tartan pleated skirt and a dark green cardigan over a white blouse. The boys wore grey flannels with a dark green V-neck sweater over a white shirt.

Sainte-Agathe High was a consolidated school, at the centre of a roughly thirty-kilometre population radius, and was attended by kids who came from all over that part of the Laurentians: Saint-Sauveur, Piedmont, Sainte-Adèle, Val-Morin, Val-David, Sainte-Agathe, Saint-Jovite and Mont-Tremblant. There were no school buses, and students got to class any way they could. Some of the boys had cars of their own, or were able to use family cars. When possible, kids carpooled. I rode most days by taxi, the driver stopping along the way for other students who were signed up for the car service. I was the farthest away and the first pickup of a core group of five—occasionally swelling to seven—who piled into a boxy Oldsmobile every morning and afternoon. It was the Rocket 88 model, and rocket we did on the old Highway 11, burning up the road trying to make up for time lost to weather or some student's tardiness.

I was in for a huge shock when I fell into Sainte-Agathe. It was a far cry from the cosseted environment I was used to. The students worked semi-autonomously—no sister breathing down your neck to make sure you understood the lesson, no lingering for the benefit of students who didn't get it. I had very little background in math and science, the subjects Mr. Jacobsen taught, and Jake, as we called him, ran a tight ship; classes moved ahead through their work very quickly. I knew after the first few weeks that I was in over my head, but I didn't know what to do about it.

I couldn't go to Mr. Smail, my homeroom teacher and erstwhile family friend. The sympathetic educator I'd met with just a few weeks before had somehow turned into a misanthropic monster once school started. He had a reputation for using his caustic wit to humiliate students, and he'd already taken a few runs at me for no reason that I could see. I was actually good at the subjects he taught—English and literature—but he was an equal opportunity bully: no one was spared. I lost interest in his classes.

After years in convents, I was as unused to the permissive atmosphere of my new school as I was to its demanding curriculum. If Sainte-Agathe High had been a girl, we would have said she was "fast"—a word used in the 1950s to mean sophisticated, worldly-wise, a little edgy. School romances abounded out in the open. One of my classmates, who couldn't have been more than sixteen or seventeen, was dating a beautiful twenty-four-year-old blond teacher, and spending his weekends at her place. No one seemed particularly bothered by it. There was an active party scene—sock hops in the gym, and house parties almost every weekend, thrown by kids whose parents might or might not have been at home. There was almost always liquor at these parties—beer, or hip flasks of rye or rum to spike the 7-Up or Coke, and sometimes sloe gin or Manischewitz, the thick, sweet kosher wine.

I had a hard time breaking in at first. Music, my usual currency, had little value in the Sainte-Agathe set. When I brought my father's guitar to school once in a while, only a couple of people showed any interest. One of them was Harry Marks, who was a year behind me. He was keen to learn to play it and I showed him a few chords. Years later, when I was married and living in California, Anna ran into him at a club in Montreal where his band Wizard was playing. They reminisced about Sainte-Agathe and he told Anna that I taught him his first chord. He also said, according to Anna, "I used to love watching Janie play, the way her breast fit nicely in the curve of the guitar." Well. I guess my currency had more value than I thought.

At the top of the social strata was a sort of A-list of pretty girls who had their sights set on a corresponding list of attractive, well-heeled boys. At the bottom were a few untouchables of either gender, and in between were the rest of us, trying to hold our own in the gene pool.

My high school crowd was open enough to include the non-A-listers in most of their parties. Complicated arrangements always had to be made for rides back and forth, or sleepovers with friends who lived closer to the party-giver, but one way or another we made it to someone's house on Saturday night with stacks of records to play and dance to.

If they weren't coupled up, the girls took their chances that they would be asked to dance, and there were always a few Sadie Hawkins numbers sprinkled throughout the evening when girls could invite boys to dance.

There was a small radio station just north of Saint-Jérôme with a dedicated hit parade music show. Rockin' Eddy was the disc jockey, and he would spin the platters we requested during our parties. He had a strong fan base in our part of the world, and a couple of us got the idea of calling him to see about having a party at the station. Rockin' Eddy couldn't have been happier to arrange it, and a dozen of us piled into cars one Saturday night and drove down to CKJL with records to play and a list of requests for songs we didn't have. It was a raucous evening of boisterous teenagers and cool fifties music going out live to all Rockin' Eddy's listeners in the broadcast area. It seems like something I would have read about in American teen magazines, and here we were doing it in our very own Laurentians.

The party of all parties that year was given by Peter Ryan, who lived in Mont-Tremblant. In point of fact, Peter Ryan's family *was* Mont-Tremblant. The internationally known ski resort, now the largest in eastern Canada, was developed single-handedly in the 1940s by Joe Ryan, Peter's father. Peter was being groomed as an Olympic contender in alpine skiing and living in Mont-Tremblant with his widowed mother, though truth to tell, she wasn't around much. He relied for parental support on his ski coach, Ernie McCullough.

Peter's event was a dress-up party, and I wore a black taffeta skirt over crinolines, and a white nylon peekaboo blouse, nylon stockings, and the black high-heeled shoes my uncle Gus had bought me in New York the previous summer. My mother didn't care for the outfit, she found it very ordinary, but I made a withdrawal from the Daddy Bank for the occasion, which would explain how I was allowed to choose my own clothes. In retrospect, she was right: those peekaboo blouses were hideous, especially on a bosomy girl like me.

Group transport was organized as always, and Peter sent out station wagons from Mont-Tremblant Lodge to pick up and return kids who couldn't get rides. When we got to the house, there was a full bar set up and a bartender from the Lodge taking drink orders. He was whipping up Grasshoppers and Pink Ladies, and I ordered a Zombie, a concoction of several kinds of rum sweetened by fruit juices. The Zombie was touted as the drink that could really get you there fast, and it did—much faster than my Aspirin-and-Coke concoction of the previous year. There was no sign of Mrs. Ryan anywhere.

Kids were jitterbugging to "Sh-Boom," and bear-hugging to "I Saw You Crying in the Chapel." One by one, couples peeled off to bedrooms and closets all over the Ryan home. It was a long way from the hamburger socials at St. Mary's, where the girls and boys danced together, stiff-armed, in the robotic box step we'd been taught by Mother Rita.

We called it a night around 2 a.m. and I was delivered home an hour later by a professional driver in a Mont-Tremblant Lodge station wagon, and woke up in the morning with my first hangover. I was sixteen.

Looking back at the whole party scene that year, it seems miraculous that we travelled those wintry Laurentian roads, sometimes with impaired teenaged boys at the wheel, without anyone ever getting hurt.

Exams were coming up. I had more or less abandoned ship around the Christmas holidays, but reality was starting to close in on me. In a desperate panic, I began hitting the books, but it was too little too late. I did moderately well in subjects that were easy for me, less well in a couple of Jake's subjects, and rather poorly overall. My parents decided to end the public school experiment and started looking at other schools for the coming fall term.

FRIAR'S BALSAM

(Anna)

My father may have felt that as long as we were healthy and happy, staying in Saint-Sauveur shouldn't be an impediment to us fulfilling our ambitions, if we had any. Some people had actually made it out of the village and onto the world's stage, though not many. Usually, if a local girl suddenly dropped out of the picture, the rumour was that she had been snatched by *la pègre*, as Montreal's underworld was known. One of the success stories was Miss Latreille, the daughter of the humble CN Rail station master and his wife. Maybe it had something to do with her growing up alongside the railway tracks, but somehow she had gotten herself all the way to New York City, where she became the assistant to Dag Hammarskjöld, the secretary-general of the UN.[*]

Frank, too, harboured dreams for his daughters. He must have told me a dozen times how he'd happily cut off his right arm to send me to Trinity College in Dublin. Perhaps it was my lack of enthusiasm for this rather grand plan, but nothing was ever done to move it along. And I was just as happy. In June 1958, I was a shy thirteen-year-old doing okay in school and with a sudden interest in boys. I didn't want to go away, not now or ever. And besides, I didn't want my father to lose an arm. He was already a bit of a physical wreck.

Maybe I took my father a little too literally, but growing up with a chronically ill parent was no laughing matter, and he wasn't one to shield his young daughters from the truth. "I'm living on borrowed time, girls," he'd avow ominously. Frank was an asthmatic prone to bouts of bronchial pneumonia. When he came down with it, which was a couple of times a year, our normally easygoing father became very agitated and we were ordered not to upset him lest we worsen

---

[*] Miss Latreille went down in the plane with her boss in 1961 on his way to mediate in the Congo.

his condition. Then, like some evil portent, the aroma of friar's balsam would fill the house, the tip-off that daddy was sick again. This fragrant, tarry essence is what he put into the old glass vaporizer, a fixture by his bed, in hopes the hot steam would relax his constricted airways. For days, the poor man would be hunched over this gurgling, rickety contraption with a towel over his head until his lungs cleared.

The precarious state of his health filled me with so much anguish that through childhood I suffered from nightmares of him dying. I would wake in tears, and go down the three steps to his small room on the landing to see if he was still breathing. He always was. Satisfied he was alive, I'd crawl into bed beside him, but I could never tell him what my bad dream was about. I was a softie where my father was concerned, a daddy's girl, and in gratitude, he passed his finicky lungs on to me.

Our mother was less sympathetic. "Why oh why did I marry a sick man?" she would rail with a desperate smile, though never to his face. And as we got a little older and our father grew frailer, the mantra became a warning: "Never marry a sick man!"

Frank saw his situation in a more poetic light.

My Life

Is there then more happiness than this?
Those simple hours, all too fleeting, the bliss
Of being among the ones who love me most
And loving me would ask no more than that I
Rest awhile.

E'en as we toss the jest, watching the loved ones play
A great dark shadow, forming too swiftly in the East—
Taking a horseman's form, apocalyptic—
Bearing across my path, causing me to pale,
Veers, and brushing past, whispers
"Next time without fail."

Gathering courage I bid them fond adieu
Gabrielle, Janie, Anna Ruth and Kit
And hurry to the marketplace for grubbing battle,
Bartering my wits and sweat for daily bread
That I might hear their cries of joy 'ere Sun goes down
And giving thanks, embrace them all and rest.

—*Frank McGarrigle, 1950*

Kate also took my father literally. There was a British woman living on the next street over from us about whom our father had remarked to my mother, while Kate was in earshot, "I think Mrs. So-and-So has a chip on her shoulder." The next time the two of us were over playing with her little boy, Kate was on the lookout for the chip. It was summer and Mrs. So–and–So was in a sleeveless sundress, and Kate spotted a large depression on her upper arm. Our father's suspicions were confirmed. Kate blurted out triumphantly, "Daddy's right. You *do* have a chip on your shoulder." The "chip" was the crude scar from a vaccination. The woman was none too happy with what my father had said, and I don't remember us being invited back. Another story about Kate that bolstered her reputation as an outspoken if outrageous character—even at an early age—which she believed herself to be.

JUVIES

(Jane)

On Sunday, May 11, 1958, I had a terrible row with my mother and ran away from home with my friend Pandy (so nicknamed by her parents because of the pandemonium she caused wherever she went). By unhappy coincidence, it happened to be Mother's Day. We were missing for almost a week, and every night that I was gone Daddy lit a candle and left it burning in the window of our front room until the family went to bed. He sat by the candle for hours at a time, reading or playing the piano, waiting for me to come home. On the sixth day, his prayers were answered and his missing daughter returned to him, though not as he might have wished.

Anybody, except for the people involved, could have seen this coming. My parents had realized too late what a mistake it had been to drop their sheltered daughter into a fast public high school. They then over-corrected by reverting to the boarding school option, this time a convent in Montreal that would allow me to come home on weekends and carry on my duties as church organist. It would be my fourth school in four years, and I put up strong resistance. If I had to be a boarder, why couldn't I go back to St. Mary's? They were very clear, the organist job was the determining factor in choosing a school, and Our Lady of Angels in Ville Saint-Laurent was the closest English convent to Saint-Sauveur. I believe they honestly thought they could reverse the effects of the freedom I'd experienced during my year at Sainte-Agathe, and put the genie, or in my case the Janie, back into the bottle.

And so it went. I started school in the fall, delivered there on Monday mornings by my father or one of my uncles, and picked up again on Friday evenings for the weekend at home.

The school had a big student population, which was divided by language, the French girls on one side, the English on the other. There were at least twice as many French girls as English girls, and though we took our meals together, we didn't mix much. The dining hall was crowded and noisy and served mediocre food, and I was introduced to the crude practice of washing our own dishes at table. An empty tub was passed from girl to girl, into which we scraped our leavings. Another tub followed, filled with soapy water in which we washed our dishes and cutlery then wiped them dry to use for the next meal. By the time the tub reached the last couple of girls at table, the water was cold and greasy, with bits of other people's meals floating around in it.

A handful of rich South American girls had been sent to my school so they could learn both English and French. One of them, Elena Lemus, was the daughter or niece of El Salvador's then president, Colonel José Maria Lemus, now known to have been a brutally repressive dictator in that troubled country. The girls were nice enough but received special treatment, which didn't endear them to the rest of us. They were exempt from washing their own dishes or any other routine chores. It was galling to have to launder our own underwear and hose while the Latinas threw theirs away and drew from a fresh stash. They were taken shopping every so often to replenish the supply, and that was galling too—we never left the convent grounds. Let's just say the place lacked the quaint elegance and egalitarian feel of St. Mary's, and I couldn't wait for the year to finish.

I got on all right in class, doing a combined junior and senior year, and earning good monthly grades. I was on track to graduate and write college entrance exams.

On the weekends, my parents had me on a very short leash. I recall going to a movie one Saturday night with a boy who lived across the street. He could have driven us in the family Buick, but I was no longer allowed in cars with boys, so we walked to the Nordic Theatre. I was embarrassed to see our black Monarch creeping along about a hundred feet behind us. It was waiting at the theatre when the movie was over, too, and my father drove us home. The irony is that the previous summer, when I had gone to a movie and was stood up by the girl who was supposed to meet me, one of my father's friends came and sat next to me. He put his arm around me and cupped my breast in his hand, stayed for a few minutes and left. I sat there like a zombie, not knowing what to do. I never told my parents; I was certain they would say I had somehow attracted it. My parents were getting it all so wrong, and I went from chafing to seething to boiling with resentment. Something was going to blow.

Pandy was a big, beautiful girl, *Junoesque*, my father called her. She was often described as "precocious," a gentle way of saying she was burning through her teens at a fearsome clip. Pandy was charming and provocative, wilful and fearless. She had attended several of Montreal's finest private schools and been expelled from nearly all of them, and was proud of her "no jail can hold me" bragging rights. I had just turned seventeen and Pandy was fourteen, but she was far ahead of me in the ways of the world.

The Mother's Day quarrel was caused by a clandestine romance Pandy was having with an older guy we'll call Roman. She had been seeing Roman against her parents' wishes and using me as a decoy to do it. When my mother discovered what we were up to, she was furious at Pandy for making me her teenaged beard, and called me an idiot for going along with it. She picked up the phone to tell Pandy's parents what was in the works, and I threw a fit.

We stormed out the front door to the street and broke into a run, cut through some fields and headed towards the ski hills. Pandy was determined to find Roman and we set out for his house, avoiding roads where we might be seen. Having to bushwhack up and down mountains and through farmers' fields gave an added sense of drama to our adventure. When we arrived at his house, around six o'clock, Roman wasn't there so we set out again, not quite sure of our next move.

At the time, I was in year three of my job as organist at the Saint-Sauveur parish church. In Catholic liturgy, May is the month of Mary, and I was due at the church at 7 p.m. to play for a special evening service honouring the Mother of God on Mother's Day. Still in a rage at my own interfering mother, I made the fateful decision not to return to Saint-Sauveur. Seven o'clock came and went, and I pictured the empty organist bench up in the choir loft, the restless congregation, my parents' embarrassment and anger at their no-show daughter. I began to regret my actions and the path they had put me on but it was harder than ever to go home, which suited Pandy very well; she was happy to stay in the general vicinity of Roman's place until we came up with a better idea; meantime we needed a place where we could stay the night.

We pointed ourselves deeper into the woods, toward the Rivière du Nord, a beautiful little river that runs more or less parallel to the Montreal highway. We walked until we were tired, and came upon a ramshackle summer cottage on the riverbank that we were able to break into without much trouble. Having secured a place for the night, we rummaged in the kitchen cupboards for food and helped ourselves to some canned goods and soggy biscuits before we bedded down.

Monday came and went. I didn't turn up at Our Lady of Angels and was now officially missing.

We couldn't stay in the cottage forever and decided to hit the road. It was my idea to hitchhike to Combermere and my old boarding school, St. Mary's, a distance of about four hundred kilometres north and west of Saint-Sauveur, where I imagined we might find some sympathetic friends. Plus, for some time I'd had an idea about going back to St. Mary's and doing my senior matriculation year. I'd been happy and academically fulfilled there, and I thought if I could somehow get back to it and pick up where I'd left off two years before, it would expunge the years in between and give me a fresh start.

Hitchhiking was an accepted mode of travel for girls in those days, provided they were in pairs, and we weren't particularly concerned for our safety. Actually, we were most worried that we would have been reported missing, and that some alert driver would take us to the nearest police station to be turned over to our parents. Still, Pandy had taken a big kitchen knife from the cottage and put it in her purse.

I had mapped out our trip. We would head for Ottawa, a route I knew well from the many drives I had taken there with my father, and then head west to Barry's Bay. From Barry's Bay, it would be an easy hitch for the last seventeen kilometres to Combermere.

Much of that night is a blur, but I do remember one very nice man who bought us coffee and something to eat. Another character who gave us a ride put his arm around Pandy, seated next to him in the front seat of his truck. He quickly withdrew it when she opened her purse and whipped out the kitchen knife. He pulled right over to the side of the road and dumped us. We were stuck there for some time. There were long waits between short rides, and we may have been on the road all night. At any rate, we arrived in Combermere sometime in the morning and went to the home of Shirley Pastway, a classmate at my old school who lived in the village with her family. We didn't call ahead, just turned up at her door. I was surprised that Shirley was reluctant to let us into her house, but I hadn't considered our appearance: dirty, rumpled clothes and grimy, scratched-up hands and faces.

We walked over to the convent, where we were admitted and led to the Reverend Mother's office. Both Reverend Mother Madeleine, the Grand Poobah of the convent, and Mother Miriam, the principal, were expecting us. Shirley or her folks must have called ahead to let them know we were on our way. I loved Mother Miriam but was not a fan of the Reverend Mother. She was a bit of a sourpuss whose appearance went against her: she had a beaky nose and prominent, yellow front teeth, and was nicknamed "Bucky" (even my mother referred to her as Bucky).

Both Bucky and Mother Miriam were taken aback at the sight of us, and Mother Miriam was cold and reserved, not a side of her that I knew, and it chilled me to the bone. I was crushed when I asked her about returning to St. Mary's that fall and she said no, it was quite impossible. When Mother Madeleine made as though to call my parents, Pandy and I fled the convent and hid in the woods overnight. Next morning, we were on the road again. We stuck out our thumbs, and as luck would have it, the first ride we caught was headed for Toronto.

Meanwhile, our fathers asked the Sûreté du Québec to put out an all-points bulletin for their missing daughters, and were doing some detective work of their own. They paid a call to Roman's house and accused the family of hiding us. Roman's parents were Russian émigrés who had survived a famine, a revolution and World War I before finally finding peace in Canada. The last thing they would have done was harbour two underage girls. I'm told the father was outraged at the suggestion, and shouted back at our fathers in his heavy Russian accent, "What?! Do you think we're going to eat them?"

Next day, the fathers visited Roman's place of work. The police pulled Roman off the job and leaned on him for a couple of hours, *Dragnet*-style, trying to extract a confession as to our whereabouts. They eventually accepted that he had no idea where we were and allowed him to return to work.

While the cops were sweating Roman, we were on our way to Toronto, making good time down Highway 62, and were at the city centre by early afternoon. We had now been away for five days. We feared our parents would be angry enough to send us to reform school, as they'd threatened many times, so going home was out of the question. We sat in a coffee shop drinking water and making further plans. We would first get jobs, then an apartment, and establish ourselves in Toronto. We would begin a new life.

To get a job, we would need clean clothes. What little money we had started out with was long gone, and we would have to shoplift our new wardrobe. Except for nicking a lipstick or two, I was an amateur, but Pandy claimed to be a past master at it. We scoped out that the nearest department store was Simpson's at Yonge and Queen, and the good folks at Simpson's were going to stake us. Many a successful career has been built on shakier beginnings.

We had a productive time at Simpson's, pilfering skirts and blouses that we thought would make a good impression on future employers. We wore some of the purloined clothes, and stuffed others under our coats. We had just made it out the front door when we were grabbed from behind by a couple of store detectives. I felt physically sick.

Pandy and I were taken to separate rooms for interrogation, and the grilling began. I broke down very soon and admitted to being a runaway. I gave the store detective what he needed to contact my folks and blubbered like a four-year-old when, during a telephone conversation with a superior, the detective was mulling over whether or not I would be charged. If he was trying to throw a good scare into me, it worked. It seemed as though I had taken a shortcut to the reform school I so dreaded.

Meanwhile, in another room, Pandy was stonewalling her interrogator and admitting nothing. She had some ID in her purse but stuck to the prisoner's old standby, "name, rank and serial number," when questioned about it. Later, when we all reassembled, she sneered at me for breaking, as I had known she would.

After talking to our parents, the Simpson's security people arranged a flight home for us. We were handcuffed to a Toronto cop and loaded into the back of a police car for the ride to Malton Airport (now Pearson International). We were flown home, cop and all, and were met by our fathers at the Dorval Airport (now Pierre Elliott Trudeau International). As we were alighting from the plane, Pandy's father spotted a colleague who was meeting the same flight; he quickly headed him away from the awkward family reunion, leaving my father to greet the two desperadoes, still manacled to a Toronto policeman. We were released into the custody of the fathers and taken home in separate cars. That was the last I would be seeing of Pandy for a long time.

There was no mention of reform school, just enormous relief that I was home safe and sound. It was my father's idea to let me have a homecoming party the following weekend in one of the cottages on our property. He moved a record player and some nibbles and party favours into the cottage, and at the last minute threw in a case of beer, his way of saying that my folks were going to let up on me a little. For the moment, I was home where I belonged.

When I was returned from my trip to Toronto, the good sisters at Our Lady of Angels wouldn't take me back. A month later, I sat for my junior matriculation exams with other outliers, mostly adults, in a cold industrial space temporarily outfitted for the occasion. I got a passing grade in eight subjects, enough to complete high school but two short of the college-track requirement. That was fine with me, as I was ready to get a job and have some independence.

RETURN TO MONTREAL

PART THREE

Montreal, Fredericton, San Francisco,
Saratoga Springs, London,
New York City

The McGs Go to the City . . . 155

Bring Me the Head of . . . 161

Continuing Education . . . 164

Gaby Gets a Job . . . 169

Sundays in the City . . . 172

Skigirl . . . 177

The Dating Game . . . 182

First Guitars . . . 189

Trio Canadien . . . 190

The Mating Game . . . 199

Visiting New Brunswick . . . 206

Tickertape . . . 209

The Mountain City Four . . . 214

Derek Lamb . . . 225

Dane . . . 227

Hearts Are Trump . . . 229

Montreal Clubs After 1965 . . . 239

Coast to Coast . . . 241

In the Un-merry Month of May . . . 251

Bob Dylan . . . 256

Good Art . . . 258

Flower Shop . . . 260

My First Apartment . . . 264

"Sisters McGarrigle" by Derek Lamb . . . 270

Peace and Love . . . 272

Hitchhiking to the West Coast . . . 278

Altamont . . . 286

Caffè Lena . . . 292

Roma . . . 300

Kate and Loudon's Wedding . . . 302

Fiddle . . . 305

Kate and Loudon . . . 307

Moving Pains . . . 309

"Work Song" . . . 311

"Kitty Come Home" . . . 319

Epilogue . . . 321

THE McGS GO TO THE CITY

ANNA: After Jane's unscheduled visit to Toronto in the spring of '58, and the likelihood of a repeat performance down the road by either Kate or myself, our mother wisely stepped in and chose another path for us. We would move to the city. The alternative, staying on in Saint-Sauveur with all of us in different schools and in different localities, was unthinkable. Our eleven-year Laurentian idyll was coming to an end, much to my father's chagrin. Building the house in Saint-Sauveur and then the cottages had been his "big work," and his cottage rental business at Gardencourt was generating income.

So while Kate and I whiled away the summer, Gaby would have been busy making plans for our departure. Because she didn't drive, she depended on either my father or her brother Austin to get her to Montreal so she could scout out schools and apartments. She wanted very badly to return to Westmount, where she had lived with her family before marrying Frank. Then as now, Westmount is, arguably, the most desirable neighbourhood on the island, a separate enclave hugging the downtown at Atwater Avenue. Gaby may have seen herself once again strolling down Sainte-Catherine Street to the corner of Peel, which was the centre of her universe, and meeting up with old friends who were still at Distillers Corporation, where our mother used to work. Her sister Myrt was just a short trolley ride over the mountain in Snowdon. Gaby's old school friend Nora Leonard, who lived near Westmount Park, had told her about a place for rent just up the street from her. The pieces were falling into place. Kate and I certainly thought we were headed for Westmount.

But unbeknownst to any of us, my father was also scouting locations and had already gone ahead and signed a lease on an apartment in the Town of Mount Royal (TMR), without my mother seeing it. And that was the end of that. The lease was signed.

The Town, as it's called, is built on the flat land just below the north side of Mount Royal, and its proximity to the newly opened Laurentian Autoroute must have been what sold my father on this location. This new toll road cut the commuting time to Saint-Sauveur in half, to forty-five minutes. His cottage rental business was centred there and he needed to protect his interests. Besides, he was probably annoyed with my mother for abandoning the "Laurentian experiment." Kate and I were not really privy to any plans our parents were hatching, but we did pick up on our mother's disappointment in the abrupt resolution to the upcoming move. The Town also happened to be where Janie was living, at least temporarily, with Gaby's brother Lorne and his family, when she started work that summer at the head office of Bell Telephone on Beaver Hall Hill.

The yearly lease on our new apartment ran from October 1, a seemingly arbitrary date as it did not dovetail with anything really, certainly not the beginning of the school year, which in those days was the Tuesday following Labour Day, in early September. Like many things in Quebec, it may have been a vestige of the province's old civil code, perhaps allowing for the harvest to be brought in.

Whatever the reasons, no provisional arrangement had been made for my mother, Kate and me for September. School started in two days, so we had to act fast. Frank knew the apartment in TMR was unoccupied, and the landlord had already given him a key. He would take a chance and show up Labour Day weekend and work it out from there with the landlord, whom he took to be a reasonable man. My father, a landlord himself, was a flexible one. His seasonal leases for the cottages in Saint-Sauveur began on November 15 for the winter season or June 15 for summer. If someone wanted to come in two weeks early, he always accommodated them, at no extra cost.

We arrived in the Town under cover of night on the Sunday, a couple of mattresses tied to the roof of the '53 Monarch, and probably Daddy's old Gibson arch-top guitar. That thing went everywhere with us. But by Labour Day morning, Frank's clumsy plan to finesse a free month's rent had backfired when the irate landlord turned up and ordered us out. We were caught in a snafu, with the lease already signed and nowhere to live. Frank offered to pay the difference, but the landlord refused to back down, making my father look like a fool in my mother's eyes. This incident soured the relationship 'twixt my father and the landlord, and they never trusted each other after that.

JANE: I was in TMR a few weeks ahead of the family, farmed out to Uncle Lorne and Auntie June Latrémouille for the last three weeks of September 1958, so that I could start my job at Bell Telephone right after Labour Day.

Lorne and June lived on Canora Road, near the Port Royal station, the last stop before the commuters' train entered the Mount Royal tunnel on its way downtown to the Gare Centrale. My aunt and uncle were good to me during my stay, especially June, the aunt-by-marriage, who was softer at home than her persona at family gatherings would have suggested, and a tolerant, loving aunt *in loco parentis*. I had discovered Buddy Holly and was a bit obsessive about his music. The first thing I unpacked when I moved into Lorne and June's was my 78 of "That'll Be the Day" to play on Uncle Lorne's state-of-the-art hi-fi system. I played it over and over again all afternoon, and when my uncle got home from work and settled into his big chair with the *Montreal Star*, Buddy Holly was going full blast in his living room. After about three spins, Lorne shouted at me to stop. June, a nurse by training, adopted her best bedside manner—"Oh Lorne, she's just a teenager, that's how they are"—and brought him his gin and tonic. I really was just a teenager, and had been on a rocky ride for a couple of years. I think June understood that, and had some sympathy for the chaotic situation the family was in.

ANNA: In the meantime, Gaby, Kate and I went to stay with Gaby's father, Arthur Latrémouille, in his house near Sainte-Dorothée, about as inconvenient and out of the way as a place could get, while our parents devised a way for the two us to travel to our new schools in the Town. The small farmhouse on a half acre was perched on the banks of the Rivière des Prairies, commonly called the Back River, and had been the summer residence of the Côtés, Gaby's maternal grandparents. When the old folks died off, our grandmother, Laury, inherited the house and spent the summers there with Arthur and their brood of twelve children. There's a very out-of-focus picture of the family on the front porch, snapped by a passing photographer astounded to see that many people on a porch at one time. No features are discernible on their blurred faces, but my mother and her siblings are easy to identify from their distinctive body stances.

That September, our mother shared the one downstairs bedroom in the farmhouse with her father. It was a sombre room on the east side of the house, furnished with two brown metal single beds, each with its own HBC blanket, a red four-point for Gaby and a green five-point for Grandpapa. Today, when I see the Bay's trendy merch flyers, I'm always reminded of our old grandfather, not exactly the person today's marketing people are pitching their fine products to.

Gaby was always civil to her father, but she did not respect him. She was still full of resentment toward him for keeping their beautiful mother Laury in a perpetually pregnant state. For that and for making Gaby turn over all her earnings to him, "for your little brothers and sisters," as he put it. Or as she put it, "for his bloody bastards." One day her boss, who had noticed her wearing the same outfit for several days running, said to her, "Gaby, you must have a tidy nest egg salted away?" implying a certain miserliness on her part. She confessed that she handed over all her earnings to her father. Her boss was furious and told her that from that day forth she would remit to her father only enough to cover her room and board, no more. On her next payday, when Gaby arrived home, Arthur was standing at the door with his hand out. She handed him five dollars. He said, "Where's the rest?" She said, "My boss, Mr. Stinson, says I'm only to give you this much for my board." Arthur mumbled, "*Qu'il se mêle donc de ses maudites affaires*" ("Why doesn't he mind his own goddamn business").

But in my mother's eyes, Arthur's worst moment was as his twenty-four-year-old daughter Ruth lay dying of a heart ailment upstairs in the house on Metcalfe Avenue in Westmount. He complained to Gaby, "When is she going back to work? We need the money." Gaby said, "Don't you understand, Dad?! She's never going back to work. She's dying." Ruth did die and Gaby recalled that at her funeral, a terribly sad affair, Arthur managed the greatest display of grief, sobbing uncontrollably as he followed her coffin down the aisle. "He was a big hypocrite!" Gaby didn't mince words.

Arthur was an old-fashioned French-Canadian conservative, what used to be called a *bleu*. I don't recall a crucifix or a picture of the Virgin in his house, icons normally found on the walls in a French-Canadian Catholic home. Our grandfather didn't go to church. Politics was his religion. The walls of his farmhouse kitchen were decorated with political calendars bearing the likenesses of the Honourable John Diefenbaker, a.k.a. Dief the Chief, then the prime minister of Canada, and l'honorable Maurice Duplessis, the leader of Quebec's Union Nationale, who were in power in Quebec. This was just prior to the Quiet Revolution. These two staunch characters stared each other down over a low-set enamel sink where Kate and I would rinse out our stockings and undies at night.

The upstairs of the old house consisted of two large rooms. Years ago, my mother and her four sisters would have slept in one of these rooms while her seven brothers took the other. Now Gaby was up there cleaning and arranging a pallet on the floor under an eave for her two youngest daughters. After being subjected to the vagaries of the adult world, it was a comfort to sleep that close to the ground. At least we couldn't fall any farther.

Sometimes we were too cozy in our nest, oversleeping and missing our morning ride with the neighbour who was hired by our father to drop us at the commuter train station a few miles away, across the Cartierville Bridge. The couple of times this did happen, our frantic mother, afraid we would be late for school (my mother had a great respect for school, unlike her father, who used to brag about only making it to grade three), ordered us out to the road to hitch a ride with the local farmers. We were only twelve and thirteen, but there were two of us. Before long we would be climbing into the cab of an old truck, redolent with manure and pipe smoke. If these smells lingered on us, we were unaware of it as we boarded the train at Val-Royal station for the twenty-minute ride to the Town. It might as well have been twenty light years, as we left behind the nineteenth century of Sainte-Dorothée and climbed the steep stairway to the alien New World. We who had roamed free and never felt lost in the mountain forests and thick swamps around Saint-Sauveur now had to find our way through the planned maze that was the Town, with its confusing street layout designed around a circular park.

BRING ME THE HEAD OF . . .

When Grandpapa Arthur turned eighty, he began living for a month at a time with each of his remaining ten children. He was grateful for the clean bed and regular meals, less so for the occasional forced bath. He certainly looked a lot nicer than when he was on his own.

But sometimes he had a yen for something called headcheese that was his comfort food. This gruesome delicacy is made by boiling down a pig's head and it was never on the menu—he would have to make it himself. A former tramway driver for the Montreal Street Railway, Arthur used public transportation to get around town. After securing a head at the Bonsecours Market in Old Montreal, where you could get this kind of thing, he rode the bus with the porker's head in an old suitcase, back to where he was staying that month.

On one occasion it was to the home of a daughter-in-law, a fastidious no-nonsense woman. When Arthur turned up on her doorstep with the bloody suitcase, she said, "You're not bringing that thing into my house" and directed him back toward the bus stop. As a courtesy, she phoned the other Latrémouille women to warn them, "He's coming with the head."

His next stop was our house because his own daughter Gaby could be counted on to indulge him and allow him to prepare his treat in the kitchen of 1415. The head would first have to be shaved, cleaned then plunged into cold water, teeth and all, with onions and celery, and simmered till the flesh came off the bones. The meat and some fat were packed into a large dish and stock poured over, and after chilling for several hours, they formed the gelatinous mass that so pleased our grandpapa. The final product netted out to a couple of pounds that Arthur was left to enjoy on his own. He tried urging it on us but only Gaby ever partook of his special treat.

ANNA: When Grandpapa stayed with us he didn't want to be a bother to our mother, pitching in to help her whenever he saw an opportunity. His vision was poor—opaque cataracts (like antique milk glass) covered his eyes—and his hands had a tremor, so he was limited to doing small things like clearing the used napkins off the supper table and throwing them down the incinerator chute in the kitchen. But more than once the old man scooped up either Gaby's reading glasses or her watch by mistake, which necessitated a trip to the boiler room by our poor mother to pick through the building's trash in search of the lost items.

I remember another time when Arthur was more trouble than help. It was summer and we were all in Saint-Sauveur. Gaby was thinning out the junk in the basement and Arthur insisted on helping. They formed an assembly line of two, each one filling a cardboard box with stuff from the poorly lit basement, then coming upstairs, through the "little door" to the living room, and emptying out what was mostly old papers and bits of broken furniture into the fireplace. When the fireplace was good and full—our mother had a habit of stuffing the papers right up into the chimney—she threw in a lit match, then jumped back. Gaby was a certified pyromaniac and Daddy always suspected her of trying to burn the place down. This time, something exploded in the flames. Great fiery projectiles like horizontal fireworks shot out from the hearth, right through the screen door of the living room (until someone had the good sense to open it) and out into the street. Our father, who was already angry with the two of them messing around in his subterranean preserve, ordered us all out of the house while he investigated the cause of the explosion. Not surprisingly, it was Arthur's improper disposal of an incendiary bomb, a souvenir of our father's from the Great War. The Taliban had nothing on Grandpapa. That put a stop, at least temporarily, to our mother's efforts to clean the basement (or burn down the house).

Back in the city, my classes at the Mother House, on Atwater at Sherbrooke W., ended at 1 pm and when Grandpapa was staying with us it was my job to go home and give him lunch. Even with his bad eyes he could still read body language, particularly if it were a woman's body. He told me once, over our lunch of Campbell's cream of tomato soup and white toast, that he found it attractive when a woman walked slightly pigeon-toed and on the insides of her feet,* something I avoided doing in his presence. The old man could have written for *Cosmopolitan* or had his own charm school.

Another time at the city apartment Kate was preparing to attend a prom. She'd had a pink and white silk formal made by one of Arthur's tenants, the same woman with whom he sometimes boarded. She was a talented seamstress despite having only one good arm. (She also made my grad dress.) On the afternoon of the dance, my sister was in a flap looking for the silk pumps that she'd had dyed to go with the long dress. "WHO THE HELL'S TAKEN MY NEW SHOES?" she screamed accusingly at me and Gaby, blaming us for the disappearance of her shoes. Grandpapa, who was in the living room listening to Kate's rant, quietly materialized in the hallway outside her room cradling the black street shoes that he'd just taken off, and presenting her with the still-warm lace-ups, he said with just a tinge of sarcasm, "*Tiens, ma noire, prends les miens*" ("Here, my dark-haired one, take mine"). A gentle dig aimed at a frivolous granddaughter coming from one who had walked barefoot from Ottawa to Montreal at four years of age.

At least this time Arthur diffused a potentially explosive situation, instead of causing it, and we all had a good laugh. My sister's pink pumps turned up under a pile of clothes on the floor of the room she and I shared, and Kate, looking like a teenage Jackie Kennedy, was off to her dance.

---

* He got up from the table to demonstrate "the walk" for me.

CONTINUING EDUCATION
(Jane)

After Labour Day, I started working for the Bell Telephone Company, which at the time was a sort of generic finishing school for young ladies who "went to business," as my mother liked to put it. The entry level pay for file clerks, the lowest of the low, was $35 a week, with a bonus of $2.50 a week for fluency in both languages. By day, I worked in Bell's medical department, where I learned proper telephone manners and office etiquette; by night, I attended O'Sullivan's Business College to study shorthand and typing.

The medical department kept files on all Bell's people and had three or four doctors who followed patients with conditions that were related in some way to their jobs. There was a big focus on "time of the month" distress, because of the number of female employees at the company, and the amount of productivity lost to dysmenorrhea. The medical department was forever coming up with solutions to ease the pain of menstrual cramps. I suffered from this myself and was a guinea pig for a number of remedies they were trying out, including some exercises that proved very helpful.

I became friends with a few of the girls who were secretaries to the doctors, in particular Gail Hartt, a beautiful, auburn-haired girl with almond-shaped eyes and a lovely figure. She had a wacky sense of humour and the ability, so endearing in beautiful people, to make fun of herself and not take her looks seriously. Bell put out a company periodical and once its editor discovered Gail, she was often called on to do photo layouts, especially vacation spreads so the editor could put her in a two-piece bathing suit.

Gail had friends at Bell who became friends of mine, and we began going out and around together, as girls do, but Gail and I became particular friends because she was so musical. She was a good singer and played the guitar, and was as big a fan of the Everly

Brothers as I was. We bought ourselves Stella guitars and learned all their songs, particularly from the album *Songs Our Daddy Taught Us*, which we sang in the same harmonies as the Evs, and started bringing our guitars to parties.

In the meantime, there were some young men I palled around with, not sweethearts, just fellows I skied with or hung around with, and my new girl gang merged with them. One of them, Bryan Jones, would pretend to cringe when he saw the guitars come out, and teased us without mercy. We'd start to sing, "I'm not in this town to stay," our favourite from the *Songs* album, and he'd yell back, "I'll say you're not." It wasn't very long before Gail and Bryan were dating, and they later married.

Our family was now officially in residence in a flat on Sherwood Crescent in the Town of Mount Royal. I say "family," but my father spent most of his time in Saint-Sauveur. The conflict about the flat we ended up living in later escalated when my mother got herself a job. He complained that it put him in a higher tax bracket, something my mother dismissed with a laugh, but there's no question he was upset about it. He may have felt he was losing control of the womenfolk, who weren't as dependent on him anymore. We weren't living in "his" house, amid his treasures, and we had a source of income other than the Daddy Bank. I think he was overwhelmed by the power of femaleness, our strong feminine wills, and our bathroom full of dripping nylons and undergarments.

It was actually quite a good-looking flat and in a tony part of town—my parents were of that address-conscious generation—but my mother accepted living there only grudgingly. She did hunt down a grand piano that we stored for the owner until we bought it a few years later, and gave the place a few touches, but it never felt like home.

Until then we'd been living in our own house and had the run of the place, and now, in our rented flat, we were cooped up and on top of each other. Kate and Anna shared a bedroom, Gaby's room was next to theirs, on the other side of the bathroom, and she shared it with either Daddy or Grandpapa, depending on which of them was around. I was assigned to the alcove off the living room, a small open space that faced the grand piano. I kept my clothes in Gaby's closet, and many's the blouse I had washed and ironed for work the night before, only to find that Kate or Anna had gotten to it first. There were loud words, and lectures from my grandfather about sharing with my little sisters. It was all part of the morning scramble to get in and out of the bathroom, and out the door to our respective schools and workplaces.

In the evenings, Kate and Anna and I fought about the telephone, a convenience we'd rarely needed in Saint-Sauveur. At the suggestion of someone at work, I had my own line installed in the alcove. I loved having my own phone, until one night when I had so many calls, and was on the phone for so long, that my mother, in complete exasperation, yanked the cord out of the wall in the middle of a call. She got on to Bell the next day and cancelled the line. Among other things, she thought it a shocking waste of money to have two telephone lines in one apartment. I saw it differently. I had been paying for the extra line, along with room and board, and it seemed very unfair. Where was Auntie June to throw oil on those troubled waters and tell Mummy, "Oh Gaby, she's just a teenager, that's how they are"?

Although I was now a business girl, and Kate and Anna were in high school, we still spent some of our evenings playing music together, and became friends with another family of musicians, the Maniatis boys, Peter, Tommy and Jimmy, who sometimes came over and joined in the music. My mother encouraged these get-togethers; she thought it was good wholesome fun, even if it got quite loud.

One evening, when some combination of the Maniatis brothers and the McGarrigle sisters and a few other musical types were singing and playing instruments in our flat, the doorbell rang; it had been ringing for a while, unheard because of the racket. My mother answered it to find a couple of Town of Mount Royal cops with a complaint about noise. My mother was very stern with them. "How many complaints?" she wanted to know. "Two," they said. Gaby said,

"Come back when you have ten," and slammed the door on them. They did come back, more insistent this time, and we had to stop.

My parents had decided to rent the house to skiers for the winter, and Daddy had equipped a little room for himself in what was originally intended to be a garage. It had a powerful electric heater, a two-burner stove and oven, a little sink, a couple of beds set head to head, a table (formerly a tool space) affixed to a wall, a working toilet, and a showerhead that was never connected to a water source. Gaby now got involved in fixing up the garage. She made blue and white gingham curtains for the window, and a skirt out of the same gingham to mask the pipes under the sink.

When I went up north on weekends with my friends, I usually stayed in a modest *pension* that had a couple of rooms outfitted as small dorms; the girls bunked together in one room, the boys in the other. Often we stayed in for the night, singing and telling stories and drinking our favourite tipple. My father, who was a realist about some things, advised me to drink sloe gin and soda, heavy on the soda.

I didn't generally go to our house—it was too disturbing to see strangers coming and going from it, and to think of my father holed up in the old garage—but I did stop in one Saturday when I was walking by and saw my father's car in the driveway. I was surprised to find my mother there, sautéing mushrooms and getting ready to cook a steak. She asked me to stay to supper. The place was cozy and warm, I could smell potatoes baking in the oven, and my father read aloud from the weekend paper as my mother prepared dinner. I'd never liked mushrooms, but Gaby pressed them on me that evening, and I've loved sautéed mushrooms ever since. The steak was delicious, my parents were getting along, and everything in that moment seemed perfectly right. I was sorry to have to leave, but my gang was waiting for me at Mrs. Curie's *pension*.

Later that same winter, I had a few dates with a boy named Jean-Guy who was in the same loop as my boy gang. He was a rich kid whose father was someone important in (or important to) the

Duplessis government, and his allowance was more than my family's annual household budget.

He was exceptionally generous and picked up the tab for everyone at the table whenever we went out for the evening. Among his other attractions, he owned a white Pontiac Bonneville convertible that he sometimes let me drive. Between Ronnie Booth's indoctrination and a love of cars passed on by my father, I was, and still am, a bit of a car nut. People used to say I had gasoline in my veins. I took myself home in the Bonneville one night after an evening at the Chiriotto Lodge in Sainte-Adèle, when Jean-Guy was either in his cups or couldn't be bothered to drive me himself. I was staying with Daddy in the garage, in the narrow second bed that served by day as a couch. Daddy had made up the bed for me and I crept into it at 3 a.m. with all my clothes on, and left my purse on the tool space/table.

When I woke up the next morning, both my father and the Bonneville were missing. Eventually it turned up in the driveway with Frank at the wheel. He'd been burning to drive it and had rifled my purse for the keys. He handed me the keys when he came in and said: "I just took it for a spin—what a beauty." I said: "Yeah, it is. I'd better get it back to Jean-Guy." Daddy said: "You be careful, the roads are slippery." No lecture about how late I got in, or about driving around on backcountry roads in the middle of the night with a few sloe gins under my belt.

GABY GETS A JOB

(Anna)

With Jane out working and Kate and me settled in our new city schools, Gaby talked about getting herself a job. She liked being out of the house. It was her sister-in-law June who told her about a job posting she had seen in the Town of Mount Royal *Weekly Post*. The ad called for a part-time secretary reporting to the director of security at the Marconi Corporation.

With June's prodding, she decided to apply. What did she have to lose? At this time, Gaby was fifty-four and had not worked in an office for over twenty years. She was concerned, however, that she looked too old, at least on paper. When she filled out the application, she lied about her age, using the birthday of her deceased sister Ruth for her own and making herself five years younger. Now she was forty-nine. So much for security. In her defence, Gaby never thought she stood a chance. But just in case, she began brushing up on her very rusty shorthand. This involved one of us girls reading a text out loud, usually from the Montreal *Gazette*, and her jotting it down as quickly as she could in the Pitman shorthand she had taught herself thirty years before. For good measure, she had her salt-and-pepper hair dyed a pinky blond, a colour then popular with middle-aged matrons.

A few days later, when the call came asking her to report for an interview, she couldn't believe her ears. Our equally astonished father drove her to the interview and, after dropping her off, rolled down his window and yelled after her, "Hey Gaby! You forgot your crutch." This cattiness was uncharacteristic of our father. He must have seen himself slowly losing influence over his wife and daughters, and if this remark was meant to shake her confidence, it had the opposite effect. After thumbing her nose at my father, she pushed on in her slow, determined swagger through the main entrance of Marconi and came out with the job. Gaby had the last laugh.

The Marconi headquarters were at the southern limits of the Town of Mount Royal, on the east side of the CN Rail commuter tracks. The TMR is dissected diagonally by two main arteries, Graham and Laird Boulevards, with several shorter spoke roads radiating out from its centre, where the Mont-Royal train station and a large circular park are situated, while the cross streets weave concentrically through these. All the town's streets have Scottish names such as Carlyle, Dunsmuir, Dunvegan and Glengarry, leading one to wonder if its origins are Masonic. Any fans of *Holy Blood, Holy Grail* or *The Da Vinci Code* might want to take a closer look at this place.

Her walk to and from work took Gaby past the shops at the town centre, including the big Dominion food store where she would stop every afternoon to buy groceries for the evening meal. That is, after she had fortified herself with a couple of G and Ts at June's, which was conveniently on the way. Then, loaded up with her customary two large paper bags, she'd make her way across the bridge over the CN tracks to the west side of town and through the big circular park with its lawn bowling courts and endless beds of pretty tea rose varieties. From there, she'd take a well-worn footpath that cut along the south wall of the grey stone United church and past the shrub-lined yard of our white stucco building, where the ladies of leisure in the neighbouring apartments would sometimes sit in the late afternoon sun, enjoying a cup of tea and a cigarette. This was to be Gaby's not too glamorous routine for the next few years, and aside from her bridge club and the Dollar Symphony concerts at the old Forum at Atwater, she had few diversions. At this point I should mention that with every passing day we girls were getting less popular in the building, with the piano going constantly and the loud parties when our parents had gone north to Saint-Sauveur for the weekend.

One late September afternoon, when I was already home from school with my boyfriend Michael, Gaby came trudging up the stairs and through the door with her heavy bags, visibly upset—not crying so much as fuming. She complained that the younger matrons in the garden had snubbed her, or at the very least had not acknowledged her. I remember feeling sheepish for having made my mother a pariah in the building, but Michael was incensed, and before either of us could stop him, he ran to the open window of the living room that looked out on the back garden and bellowed at the top of his lungs, "PEASANTS!," stunning the women out of their complacent stupor and then slamming the window shut. We laughed so hard we cried, Gaby's spirits now restored. After years of being browbeaten by her father and older brothers and to some extent by my father, my mother appreciated a guy who stood up for her. And I think his reaction to the slight she suffered showed an uncommon sensitivity for a teenaged boy, coming as he did to the emotional rescue of a beleaguered middle-aged woman, and one not even his mother. She never forgot this, and often held him up as an example when we brought other boys home.

SUNDAYS IN THE CITY
(Anna)

After the move to the city, on those weekends when we didn't go to Saint-Sauveur, our father liked to take us to different downtown churches for Sunday Mass. We were unanimous in finding our local suburban church in TMR to be on the bland side; besides, Montreal had so many interesting downtown churches to choose from. Mark Twain's quote about not being able to throw a brick in this city without breaking a church window is pretty accurate.

Frank was partial to the Catholic church on De La Gauchetière West in Chinatown, a modest little church where the Gospel was read in Chinese and where the McGarrigles were often the only non-Chinese congregants. My father was very accepting of and interested in other cultures, yet when we followed Chinese Mass with a Chinese lunch at the Jade Garden down the street, he never failed to address the waiter as Jim, which embarrassed the hell out of us girls.

St. Patrick's was Gaby's favourite, the old Irish greystone parish church at Saint-Alexandre and Dorchester West (now René-Lévesque or, as my son Sylvan calls it, René-Dorchester) that she had gone to with her family. Stern old Father McShane was still at the helm, his body now so bent over that his chasuble dragged on the floor, but he was no less fearsome to Gaby.

We girls loved the sparklier Marie-Reine-du-Monde (Mary, Queen of the World) Cathedral up on Dorchester West near Dominion Square, with its imposing black and gold rococo baldachin with twisted columns, said to be a half-scale replica of the canopy over the altar in St. Peter's Basilica in the Vatican.

Montreal, which we were just getting to know, was a half- and quarter-scale kind of town, an appetizer of a city. My high school graduation dance was held in a private function room in the Queen Elizabeth Hotel, with no booze and plenty of chaperones. A bunch of us, bored by the sobriety of that scene, snuck up to the Panorama Room, the elegant bar atop the hotel, for something stronger than 7-Up. This popular nightspot had an unbroken view of the city's skyline, including the cathedral of Mary, Queen of the World, which was directly across the street. That evening, after a couple of rum zombies, I thought the fifteen-foot-high statues of the saints along the roofline of the church we were looking down on were people waiting for the 150 bus. LMFAO.

This was just prior to the Second Vatican Council (1962–65), or Vatican II, after which Mass in the vernacular was instituted. New altars were built so that the priest who previously had his back to the congregation now faced it, making the ceremony more inclusive. Seeing the priest head-on took away from the Church's mystical experience, and this new accessibility was thought by some to be a dumbing down of the liturgy. Still to come was an abomination known as the hootenanny Mass, where hippie priests in homespun surplices strummed guitars and sang inane tunes with simple lyrics ("Michael row the boat ashore, Hallelujah!") that were easy for the congregants to sing along with.

Before these changes, the Catholic Church, through its thousands of franchises worldwide, had served up a Mass in Latin, *Credo in unum Deum*, to the accompaniment of stirring organ music and with a plain white wafer for Communion, whether you were in Djibouti or Winnipeg. Only the condiments changed: the Gospel lessons and parish news read from the pulpit were in the mother tongue of the flock.

Over the ensuing decades, the Church faltered for reasons that are all too obvious now, and people in Quebec and elsewhere parted from the institution in droves, leaving most parish churches in Montreal empty and broke. They continue to be sold off to developers for condos and gyms.

Following Mass, my father liked to visit close friends. Were these visits organized beforehand or did we simply drop in on people? Knowing my father, it was probably the latter. Often it was to Jane's godparents, Beth and Stephen McGivern in the lakeshore village of Valois. Beth Tobin, a Maritimer from Pictou, Nova Scotia, had been a good friend of our father's older brother Jim. She and her husband had one child, an adopted son, Frank Toby, a couple of years older than Jane and named after our father. There's an old Christmas card from the McGiverns in the house in Saint-Sauveur, a faded, staged photo from the 1930s showing Beth and Stephen seated, staring wistfully at a decorated tree, as if waiting for someone. The absence of children in this photograph always struck me as sad, so I imagine Toby's arrival must have put them over the moon.

The highly theatrical Beth, an accomplished musician and painter, was careful to nurture in her son her own God-given talents, and from the time Toby was a babe, she sang to him as he lay in his crib. All her efforts paid off when one day the little boy sang back to her, whereupon she was said to declare joyously, "Oh, Stephen! He can carry a tune!" Kate tried this technique with baby Rufus and had the same results.

I'm not sure what method Beth used to impart her drawing and painting talents to Toby, but as a child he was allowed to draw all over the pages and spines of his books. His old books were passed down to us and we girls greatly admired his doodles of women's heads in profile, not unlike those "Draw Me" ads on the back of 1950s comic books, but less cheesy, more Egyptian in style, with elaborate hairdos and big long earrings. Toby's drawings were an inspiration to me, a born doodler, as I was growing up.

Beth's old aunt Kate, an infirm but sharp-tongued octogenarian, lived with the family. Once, when our family was visiting, Toby dressed up the old lady in a long velvet gown with some of Beth's gaudier necklaces, rouged her cheeks and stuck a black lace mantilla on her head. Because she couldn't walk, he threw her over his shoulder like a sack of potatoes and carried her down from his third-floor lair to the main floor, depositing her in an antique wheelchair with a cane seat and a high back. After whisking her around the house at high speed to her screams of protest, he parked her in the middle of the living room for all to admire. The old girl was reminiscent of those dried-apple dolls, but we told her she looked lovely.

On that long-ago winter afternoon, in the amber light of the McGiverns' antique-filled living room, Beth and our father took turns at the piano, singing the genteel parlour songs of their youth. Then Gaby would have requested Toby's big number, as she always did, the romantic ballad from *Brigadoon*. Toby was only too happy to oblige. Moving to the upright, back straight, hands upon the keys, head poised like a swan, he turned to face her and in his warm, slightly nasal and wonderfully affected voice, he went into the pre-amble of the song before settling into the schmaltzy hook of this bygone hit, "Come to Me, Bend to Me." All the ladies swooned.*

After high school, Toby studied fine arts and later worked in the advertising department of Ogilvy's, where he drew the department store's distinctive newspaper ads. Mother and son formed an insep-arable pair in music and art, perhaps to the exclusion of the father, who did not share their talents.

After old Aunt Kate passed on, Beth and Toby took an extended trip to Europe, leaving Stephen behind. While they were away, the poor man died alone in the house in Valois. As I remember, our father was called to identify the body and put in charge of inform-ing Stephen's next of kin, unreachable on another continent.

Other Sundays we might drop in on the Blacks at their city apartment across from Westmount City Hall. Jack Black was a tall Newfoundlander with a booming voice, who usually greeted our father this way: "Frank McGarrigle! As I live and breathe! How the devil are you, you goddamn Catholic SOB?" LOL. He and his wife, Bert, had one daughter, Barry, privately educated, a few years older than Jane, and what my mother would have called a bluestocking. Jack and Bert were very proud of their daughter, who lived and

---

* To my ear, Andrew Lloyd Webber was heavily influenced by Lerner and Loewe and in particular this song, using the first two melodic lines of the chorus in "Music of the Night" in his *Phantom of the Opera*.

worked abroad at some interesting job, in either New York City or Europe. The Black women had androgynous first names that I think Kate and I associated with worldliness and sophistication.

We really only knew Barry from tales of her various exploits in whatever world it was she moved in, and by the books she had outgrown that were passed on to us along with her hand-me-down clothes, many of them hand-knit by her mother. There's one sweater of hers that all three of us wore before Kate's kids took it over. I expect we'll see Martha's kids, Arcangelo or Francis, in it down the line.

SKIGIRL

(Anna)

When Kate was fourteen, she signed up for a downhill race at the Alpino Lodge, a family ski resort a few miles west of Morin-Heights. Our father drove her to the Alpino early that Sunday, dropping her off at the base of the small hill where the race was taking place. He recognized a couple in the parking lot, whose kids were also in the race, and asked them if they would mind taking Kate back to Saint-Sauveur when the race was finished, as he had to return to take our mother to church. He went back to where Kate was putting on her skis and told her, "When it's over, check in with the So-and-So's, they'll take you back to Saint-Sauveur."

I imagine he wished her luck before returning to Saint-Sauveur to collect our mother for the twelve o'clock Mass, and as he didn't have to return to the Alpino for Kate, the two of them went to Uncle Lorne's for après-Mass cocktails and the buffet lunch Auntie June usually put on. Kate, our mother and I were living in Montreal during the week, with Daddy spending most of his time in Saint-Sauveur, so he especially looked forward to these informal get-togethers with family, to laugh and tell stories and listen to music.

My uncle and aunt didn't have a piano, but they did have a fancy stereo system in their modern country house on the Simon River Road, with floor-to-ceiling windows that looked out over the village and the ski hills. Lorne loved the big singers of the day such as Mario Lanza and Bing Crosby, and these artists would have done time on the turntable that afternoon. Lorne himself was a gifted tenor, bursting into song when the moment seized him, with or without the piano accompaniment my father or Janie would have provided had they been at our house. His big number was "Brother, Can You Spare a Dime?," a Tin Pan Alley tune written during the Depression about a once-brave army lad fallen on hard times and now forced to beg in the streets. Lorne would walk to the centre of the room and, fists clenched and arms swinging, begin marching on the spot, setting up the song. Lorne, the cool-headed businessman in classic après-ski wear, was so convincing in his delivery he embodied the narrator, a teenage conscript at the onset of WWI, full of irrational enthusiasm for the war, who becomes a sobbing downtrodden veteran, forced to beg on a busy city street.

Lorne had played the saxophone as a kid but lost most of the fingers on one hand during an explosion at a construction site while he was on a summer job. Despite this drawback, or maybe because of it, he worked hard and became a successful businessman.

The downhill race ended. For reasons that are still not clear, Kate failed to connect with her ride. Her version was that the family were not in the parking lot when she went to look for them. The only option as she saw it was to ski home. She hitched on her skis and headed back toward Saint-Sauveur along the crest of the snowbanks bordering the road she and Daddy had taken to get there. Night began to fall. She forged on, her snowy path illuminated by whatever bright star was visible in early evening in the late winter sky.

Back in Saint-Sauveur, my father and mother had left Lorne's and returned to the house to find Kate still not home. When my father called the couple, they told him that they hadn't seen her after the race and assumed he had come back for her. Our mother was furious with them and with our father for his poorly executed plan. I imagine they were both feeling guilty after spending such a lovely afternoon at Lorne's. Daddy got in the car and headed back toward Morin-Heights in search of his youngest daughter, while Mummy stayed behind in case Kate turned up.

The road to Morin-Heights was well travelled, but Kate was beyond that small village, on some back road to the west of it. It was pitch-black when he finally came upon her, as he told it, "a lone figure in the car's headlights gliding along the top of the high snowbank." When she saw his car, she collapsed in tears. Our father tried to comfort her, but she was beyond comforting.

Kate never forgot the feeling of abandonment and it was a long time before she forgave my father this lapse in his parental duties.

It was a late summer weekend a few years later. Kate had gone to Saint-Sauveur and, instead of staying with our father, who was alone, stayed with her friend Nina down the street. She hadn't bothered to check in with him, perhaps still harbouring a grudge since "the abandonment." Well, the grudge was for this and because she felt he had worked her too hard over the years, making her stack the firewood for the house and the four cottages. I reminded Kate that I had always been right beside her doing this annual autumn chore. While we're griping, Kate and I regularly cleaned the camps for the changeover of seasonal tenants, and did this from a very young age.

That Sunday afternoon, she left Nina's and was travelling back to Montreal on the Voyageur bus. The southbound bus took Route 11B, picking up fares in the villages as it went along. After Saint-Jérôme, it joined the Laurentian highway for the rest of the journey to Montreal.

Earlier that summer, our father had opened a very modest little travel bureau that he called Agency 29. He had rented a small, free-standing cabana with an open front, formerly an ice cream vendor, and stocked it with colourful brochures from various Laurentian hotels, motels and tourist attractions. His hopes were high for Agency 29, going so far as to have letterhead printed up and a phone line installed. The address was 29 Route 11B, in Shawbridge, Quebec. For those travellers who bothered to stop and avail themselves of his services, he would call ahead and make reservations for them, earning himself a small commission from the hotel.

In 1963, the new northern extension of the Laurentian Autoroute from Saint-Jérôme to beyond Sainte-Adèle was opened, cutting the traffic on this section of old Route 11B to a trickle. We girls teased him about his Agency 29 being a flop, but I don't think he cared what we thought. He was likely quite lonely, something Kate and I, being self-centred teens, hadn't stopped to consider. Our father knew the Laurentians like one who had been born there; he was familiar with all the characters and the local lore, and he loved meeting people. Those people who did stop would have heard the story of *le loup garou*, a local werewolf that roamed the dark mountains. And Agency 29 was a good place to snare customers for his other enterprise, Gardencourt Cottages, which also had its own letterhead. Our father headed up a conglomerate, but we couldn't see that then.

The bus Kate was travelling south on had rolled into Shawbridge and was stopped at the traffic light. From her window seat, looking east, she saw our father across the highway, sitting alone on the balcony of Agency 29, reading his paper in the late afternoon sun. Seeing him there, older, vulnerable and alone, she now deeply regretted not going to see him, and with tears welling up in her beautiful hazel eyes she rushed to the front of the bus just as the light went green and demanded to get off. The bus driver thought she'd lost her mind. She ran across the intersection, against the light, calling out, "Daddy, Daddy!" He looked up from his paper, surprised and very happy to see her. She collapsed in his arms in tears. Much later she told me that at that moment she made some kind of peace with our father.

In 2008, Kate launched the Kate McGarrigle Foundation for research into and treatment of clear-cell sarcoma, an underfunded "orphan" cancer she was fighting. For a couple of years my indomitable sister organized Christmas concerts to benefit her charity. As well as picking the songs and deciding who would sing what in the shows, she was involved in designing the merchandise for the swag bags given to donors. In the summer of 2009, Kate was driving around the Hamptons with her friend Mae Mougin, a New York ceramicist based in Southampton, trying to come up with an idea for an illustration to adorn a soap dish, tea towel and clay tree ornament. Mae handed Kate a scrap of paper and a felt pen. Without hesitating, Kate drew a little girl in a long skirt on a pair of skis, and named her Skigirl.

The drawing of Skigirl is reproduced on Kate's white stone monument in the Saint-Sauveur parish cemetery, which just happens to be situated between Lorne's house, where my parents were enjoying themselves that Sunday afternoon, oblivious to Kate's predicament, and the village.

THE DATING GAME

(Jane)

Our move to 1415 Sherwood Crescent had gotten off to a rough start. Quite apart from the row with the landlord about occupancy, and my mother's resentment toward Daddy for his high-handedness, Kate and Anna and I weren't keen on living in the Town. We thought it very square. It had good-looking houses, substantial apartment buildings and plenty of green space, but you could say about the Town of Mount Royal what Gertrude Stein said about Oakland: "There is no there there." For years there had been a sign at the Graham Boulevard entrance to the Town that read, in big letters, "MODEL CITY." It suggested planned lives, a failure of imagination.

On the positive side, the Town yielded some interesting new connections. I met the boy across the street, Bobby Kirk, who lived with his parents and sister in a pretty stone house that I'd admired when we first moved there (admired as in, "Why can't we live someplace like *that*?"). The first thing to get my attention was his car—a black TR3—but he had other things to recommend him. He was warm and upbeat, and had a breezy, humorous personality. My mother loved Bobby, found him very entertaining and looked forward to seeing him when he called for me.

Bobby was a crack skier and was attending Middlebury College to take advantage of Vermont's fine skiing, in between fraternity parties and getting an education. After we'd been going together for a few months and writing letters back and forth, he invited me to visit him at Middlebury over their Winter Carnival weekend. It was my first visit to a boy at a college campus and I was very excited. There was a ski meet and a dance, some frat events and plenty of partying. Five decades later, the details are a little hazy, but I do remember a clandestine visit to the boys' quarters, where there were already other giggling girls. We had a great time at Carnival and continued to correspond till he came home again.

Bobby and his friends were fond of riffing on certain words and expressions, and the word of the moment was "winner." They were forever using it to describe people or situations, positively ("What a winner that guy is!") or sarcastically ("There goes a real winner!"). When Bobby came to call for me during one of my grandfather's periodic stays, I was a bit embarrassed about my toothless old Grandpapa, who shuffled around our apartment in his scuffed slippers and worn clothes that were usually at less than optimal freshness. I was trying to steer Bobby away from him and toward the front door, but Bobby stayed where he was and said, "Hey! Your grandfather's a winner," and listened patiently to Grandpapa's wheezy tale.

I made the dumb mistake of breaking up with him to take up with someone else who was disappointingly ordinary, and a bit of a jerk into the bargain. Live and learn. My mother never forgot Bobby and his kindness to my grandfather, and for years after we lost touch, she asked about him: "Do you ever hear from Bobby Kirk? What a winner he was."

Through Bobby, I met Bob Dykes, and we double dated a few times with his girlfriend. Later in the year, during Christmas break, Bob brought his friend Dave Dow over to 1415 one evening. Bob might have had some idea about fixing us up but I had plans for the evening, so we went our own ways.

By 1959, The Pub in Saint-Sauveur had changed hands and undergone a bit of a facelift before being rechristened The Inn, but it was still the skiers' hangout on weekends, as it had been in my parents' day. My father dropped in occasionally mid-week for "a short one," but it wasn't his crowd anymore and he rarely played the piano. Doc Reid was now the house piano player and had a regular paid gig on weekends. I was at The Inn with the usual suspects on a wintry Saturday night, sitting at a big table covered with quart bottles of

Molson's and Labatt's beer. Doc Reid was playing a waltz on the piano. A young man fought his way through the haze of cigarette smoke at our table and asked me to dance. It was Bob Dykes's friend Dave, who was home on another break from university and up north for some skiing. We had our dance and saw each other a few more times during his holiday. I remember one of our evenings when we sat in a snowbank in Saint-Sauveur, snogging and sipping away at a bottle of Brights Manor St. Davids, a truly awful wine that my uncle Austin referred to as "Brights Disease." We wrote to each other after he went back to Fredericton, and he invited me there for the UNB Winter Carnival.

I don't really have to reverse-engineer the Dave of today to get back to that long-ago first impression, because he hasn't changed that much, give or take five decades and a little filling out: a strong face with intense blue eyes that bore into you, not quite six feet tall, on the skinny side, wry sense of humour; then as now, a person to be reckoned with. I liked that he had a bit of a subversive edge and thought outside the box.

Dave lived in the Town of Mount Royal with his parents, Don and Irene Dow, and his sister Debbie, who was ten years younger. His older sister, Joan, was married and lived with her husband, John, at the other end of the Town.

I didn't know much more than that about him when I flew to Fredericton for the 1960 Winter Carnival, and I knew very little about UNB. It was not at all like Middlebury. UNB wasn't considered a strong academic school at the time (not that I checked its accreditation before visiting) and there were no fraternities, but there were plenty of high-spirited boys from Canadian establishment families getting into different kinds of mischief, and Dave knew all of them.

Dave met my flight, and we went straight to his apartment on Queen Street, where he and a couple of other fellows were engaged in rigging up some dynamite caps with the intention of blowing up a dam. Their last experiment had blown up Dave's kitchen sink, and they had fled the apartment after calling the landlord to report that there was a problem. By way of explanation, they stood a plunger in what was left of the cast-iron sink. One pictures the landlord scratching his head at the sight of the twelve-inch–hole. Dave's friends referred to him as the Deacon, I think because he could maintain composure no matter what circumstances he happened to be in. We set out for the dam soon after my arrival. It was a very small dam, and they sure enough blew it up. Satisfied with their work, the Deacon and his merry band of vandals went home and cracked a few beers, in those days more easily said than done.

At that time, 1960, New Brunswick, while not technically a "dry" province, was one of the most inconvenient places in Canada to get a drink, thanks to the Women's Christian Temperance Union and an unyielding Baptist population. There was a provincial liquor store that I remember as being open at odd hours, but there were no bars in New Brunswick, and no wine or beer was served in restaurants, not even in the elegant dining room of the Lord Beaverbrook Hotel. But where there's a will, there's a way. Licensed service clubs (the Elks Club, the Air Force Club) extended memberships to the general public, and many preppy college students from "away" became honorary members of the Benevolent and Protective Order of Elks, and exercised their club privileges on Saturday night. We dropped into the Elks Club during my stay for a little taste of Fredericton's nightlife, a boisterous group of happy Elks tearing up the dance floor to a hometown band.

The following night, we went to a show on campus featuring a supergroup of the day whose name I can't be sure of. Dave remembers them as "the Four Somethings." At the time there were many popular male vocal quartets: the Four Lads ("Standing on the Corner"), the Four Preps ("Sh-Boom"), the Four Aces ("Three Coins in the Fountain"), the Four Freshmen ("Graduation Day").

Whoever they were, it was not the kind of music either Dave or I listened to. Once introduced to jazz, I paid less attention to mainstream pop music. At that time, my favourite LP was the soundtrack from the film *I Want To Live*, a terrific score by Gerry Mulligan, with Art Farmer and Shelley Manne. Dave's musical taste was pretty eclectic—jazz, folk, R&B—and he introduced me to the music of Ray Charles, who would become, then and forever, my favourite piano player, and one of the artists I most admire and keep going back to. Over the Carnival weekend we listened to music on Dave's system, a portable record player with the speaker removed and placed in a metal wastebasket to improve the sound. Dave was a third-year electrical engineering student, so who was I to question his audio know-how? Dave also put me on to Jack Kerouac, George Orwell and Aldous Huxley. I returned to Montreal with a new cultural perspective and the sense of a growing attachment. Heady stuff.

Up until my visit to Fredericton, we hadn't seen much of each other's parents. Dave had been over to 1415 a few times, and I had been to a couple of family dinners at his parents' home. We continued to correspond and, besides sanctioned visits to Montreal on school breaks, he caught rides occasionally to come up and see me, and stayed with friends who were living on their own. His parents weren't aware of these visits, and it made my mother uncomfortable to receive him at 1415 knowing he wouldn't be checking in with his folks. She evidenced her displeasure by being a little short with him when he turned up on the first of these unauthorized visits. "I see you haven't put on any weight," she said by way of a greeting when she met him at the door. "I see you haven't taken any off," he shot back. Gaby had a good laugh; she had met her match.

I saw a lot of Dave during the summer of 1960 and got to know his parents. I was all admiration for Don and Irene Dow, people of uncommon decency who were good at managing their lives. Don was a self-made man and something of a legend. He had started at the bottom at the Nesbitt Thomson brokerage house in the 1930s and worked his way up to a sales desk. During World War II, the company sent him to Rouyn-Noranda, Quebec mining country, where he sold bonds to the miners. After he suffered a heart attack in the 1950s, the company kicked him upstairs. By this time Don was at the top of his game and he became the Bronfmans' bond man at Nesbitt Thomson. Not at all a glad-handing salesman, he was a gentle, unaffected person and a devoted family man. A lifelong autodidact, he spent his Saturday mornings at the Montreal Museum of Fine Arts, studying the paintings and educating himself. On Saturday afternoons he pored over photographs of paintings, his radio tuned to the CBC's regular Saturday afternoon broadcast of opera performances from the Met in New York. He acquired a collection of important Canadian paintings, one at a time over the years, and the Dows' home was a mini-gallery of works by Jean Paul Lemieux, David Milne, Jacques de Tonnancour, A.Y. Jackson and other celebrated painters.

Except for very prominent families, such as the Molsons and the Eatons, the history of Anglo Quebec has been somewhat ploughed under by the ascendancy of French in regions that were previously English-speaking. I was fascinated to look back at Irene's story. She was Irene Scott of Scotstown, a community in the Mégantic area of Quebec's Eastern Townships, founded by Scottish colonists in 1872. Her father was a prominent citizen; he was in the lumber business and operated a general store. He also owned the local electric power company at Bury, and one of twelve-year-old Irene's early duties was to drive around the countryside in the family car to collect from his customers. He was fluently bilingual, and the Quebec *Gazette* shows Nathaniel-George Scott being elected to the Quebec legislature in 1916, where he sat for seven years. He died suddenly of a heart attack at fifty, an event that coincided with the stock market crash that wiped out the family fortune. His widow and four grown children later resettled in Montreal.

From our earliest meeting, I was in awe of Irene Dow. She was a ninety-pound powerhouse with an indomitable will that made itself felt in the most genteel and feminine way. She had organizational skills a CEO could only envy and she used them to bring comfort and ease to her family, her friends and the community. I've tried most of my life to model my homemaking on Irene's (she was

188 • Anna & Jane McGarrigle

to homemaking what Meryl Streep is to acting) but, alas, have had only mixed success. I started out by appreciating Irene, then grew very fond of her as time went on.

I was invited to the Dows' for a family evening a few days before Christmas. Dave's sister Joan and her husband John were there, as was his little sister Debbie, home for the holidays from her school in Neuchâtel, Switzerland.

No one observed Christmas more flamboyantly than Don Dow. The exterior of the house was covered with decorations—lights and ornaments in all the windows and around the porch, and on the roof, a life-size cut-out of Santa in his sleigh being pulled by reindeer. We were on our second round of Don's Christmas-themed drinks when the doorbell rang. Someone recognized the car outside as belonging to Dr. Organ, pastor of the United Church that the Dows (nominally) belonged to.

Dr. Organ was known to be strongly opposed to alcohol, so we quickly hid our drinks behind the furniture. His ten-minute visit felt like an eternity, not because we were thirsty but because we all smelled like a distillery. Irene offered him tea, which thankfully he turned down. No sooner was he out the door than we reached behind our seats for our drinks in one synchronized motion and relaxed again. I felt a little sorry for Dr. Organ, who was probably experiencing the same reception on his other calls, but he was swimming against the tide.

After the holidays, Dave went back to school and we continued writing letters over the winter.

FIRST GUITARS
(Anna)

In 1960, when Joan Baez released her debut recording on Vanguard, she became a role model for many teenaged girls, including Kate and me. She was young and beautiful, with long hair, and performed barefoot even in the most formal of settings. We wanted to be her. Most folk artists of the day played guitars with a round sound hole, with either nylon or light-gauge steel strings; they had a natural wood finish and the really nice ones were made by C.F. Martin. These were the kind of guitars Kate and I wanted.

But our mother and grandfather Arthur, both of whom knew nothing about guitars, wanted to surprise us. The pair of them went down to Craig Street near Saint-Laurent, where the pawnbrokers were. These places also sold cheap new guitars.

On Christmas morning, 1961, two tell-tale trapezoid-shaped boxes lay under the tree, the kind of cardboard box inexpensive guitars come in. Gaby and Arthur looked on proudly, barely containing their excitement as Kate and I tore the wrapping paper off the boxes. Perhaps knowing what was coming, our father stepped out of the room.

The guitars were brand new, dark-varnished with a sunburst section in the centre and f-holes where the sound comes out. The strings lay a half inch above the fretboard. It was impossible to hold them down and make a chord. We didn't hide our disdain for these crude instruments and grumbled, "These aren't the kind of guitars we want! They're Western," and walked away. If they had only asked us instead of wanting to surprise us.

Our grandfather, the professional orphan, could not believe what ingrates Gaby had raised. We exchanged them for cheap, blond, nylon-stringed guitars.

TRIO CANADIEN
(Anna)

Kate and I attended TMR Catholic High/École secondaire catholique VMR. The late-1950s school, a rectangular box with a sage-green curtain-wall facade, was actually two schools, one English, one French, with a boys' side and a girls' side, which made it seem like four schools. The French students occupied the first floor, the English were on the second, and the gym and activities rooms were common areas for both schools. The Sisters of the Holy Cross ran the girls' side and did an excellent job of scheduling these common areas to ensure that the girls and the boys were never in the same place at the same time. In the unlikely event that a girl and a boy might have crossed paths, the girl's uniform would have been a complete turnoff: a grey accordion-pleated skirt cut well below the knee, made of an acrylic fabric that didn't appear to bend, a white blouse also in some new space-age material that caused the wearer to sweat profusely, and worn with a royal-blue necktie should any girl get ideas about undoing the top button to expose some young neck. A generously cut navy blazer completed this total eclipse of the female form, and in case there were any foot fetishists among the boys, the girls' feet were safe inside sensible brown oxfords. (Foot-fortresses.) Lipstick was verboten, but the French girls got around that by wearing foundation and lots of eyeliner. Generally, the English girls were more saintly, but a few bent the rules. The boys wore essentially the same type of uniform except their grey pants were not accordion-pleated.

Sometimes it seemed as if the nuns were more interested in maintaining the physical state of the gleaming new school than in teaching us. There was a well-equipped chemistry lab with enough Bunsen burners, beakers and test tubes to go around fifteen ways, ours was a small class, but we weren't allowed to touch any of it. Instead, we had to gather around the nun like in a kindergarten class and watch as she performed the experiment with pale, shaky hands while reading aloud the instructions from the chemistry manual. I suspect that some of the sisters knew little about the subjects they had to teach. Kate told me she was often asked by her teacher to conduct the math class. Our home-class sister, who was also the principal of the English girls' side, was so inept that the parents of all the other girls petitioned the school board to have her removed. My father was the only parent who wouldn't sign the petition. He thought it was cruel. She finished out the year but retired soon after.

In the fall of 1961, Michèle Forest was in grade ten on the French side. It was her first year at the school, which had opened two years before. Michèle was the kind of girl one took immediate notice of. She was animated and very funny and confessed to having been the class clown all through high school. Naturally curious, she searched out the action in this cheerless place. While wandering the corridors one day in late 1961, she heard music. She followed the sound, the way one scans a rainbow looking for the pot of gold, and discovered Kate in a small room playing the school upright and singing in what Michèle described as a pure, high voice, surrounded by a clutch of admiring students. My sister was in grade ten on the English side. The two soon got together outside school to work up songs.

I had graduated that June and was already at the Mother House Secretarial School, so I met Michèle through Kate. Michèle knew a lot of songs in both French and English, and in different idioms. I don't remember her playing an instrument, though coming as she did from a bourgeois background, the Forest girls would have had piano lessons with the nuns. She had a knowledge of French popular music that Kate and I did not share, from the worldly French chansonniers of the day, Gilbert Bécaud and Guy Béart, to Quebec's Mary Travers a.k.a. La Bolduc, famous for her "turlutage" (Irish lilting), whom Michèle could mimic perfectly. Growing up in Saint-Sauveur, we heard French country-radio hits such as Oscar Thiffault's "Le rapide blanc" (a.k.a. "Awigniahan"), a suggestive song about a man who calls on a woman with the intention of seducing her while her husband is away working in a logging camp, what's commonly known as "une chanson à double sens."

But most of the French songs Kate and I knew were school-yard rounds or lovely hymns such as "Mère du bon conseil" and "Rose d'Israël," stuff you sang in church. Jane had taught us some of the quaint country songs she had heard in Combermere, including "The Blackboard of My Heart," but in 1961 we were looking for songs like the ones Joan Baez had done on her 1960 debut recording. Joan Baez was a phenomenon, the understated Lady Gaga of the time.

Before long we three formed a trio, with Michèle on lead and Kate and me on guitars and harmonies. The first songs we learned were the American spiritual "Swing Low, Sweet Chariot," "Green Fields," an early eco-anthem made famous by the Brothers Four, and the Afro-American complaint "Every Night When the Sun Goes Down." Michèle remembers us taking the number 65 city bus over Côte-des-Neiges, guitars in tow (we didn't own cases), and going to the bar in the Berkeley Hotel on Sherbrooke West, a hangout with preppy McGill students who'd just come from a college football game. Our performance was impromptu. After finding a good spot to stand where we would be seen, Michèle burst into song while Kate and I followed on the guitars. There was no stage, no mics, and no one seemed to care that we were underage. I like to think our singing was appreciated by the bar's young clientele already acquainted with the likes of the Kingston Trio and other popular folk music of the commercial variety. La Poubelle ("The Trash Can"), a *boîte à chansons* on Guy Street owned by Quebec troubadour Tex Lecor, was another folk club we sang in, again informally.

It may have been Michèle who suggested we try out for Loyola College's Winter Carnival Concert. This Jesuit boys' school was famous for its theatre programme, and their student productions were first-rate. My boyfriend at the time, Michael, was a Loyola boy and an aspiring playwright. We had recently seen *Volpone*, the Ben Jonson play, starring the seventeen-year-old Richard Monette in the title role. This French-Canadian-Italian teenager with the posh classical stage accent was so convincing as the old Venetian roué that I remember thinking, "This person is going places." And he did, working for many years as the artistic director of the Stratford Festival.

The only live play I had seen up until that point was an amateurish production at our high school, one that Kate was in. Hers was a small role, but she had two rather important lines to deliver, the first being at the start of the play and the second near the end. In her nervousness, she blurted out the second line first, wrongly cueing her co-stars and abruptly ending the play.

The student in charge of hiring the talent for the Loyola concert was Seymour, himself an aspiring folksinger who later became a playwright. It was arranged that he would come to Michèle's house on Kenilworth Avenue in TMR to hear our trio. All three of us would never forget the dramatic entrance he made wearing a black overcoat, the bright red lining of which was revealed when he threw the coat over the modern sectional sofa in the Forest living room. We gasped. I remember feeling intimidated, our collective nervousness audible in our more than usually tremulous voices. Not surprisingly, this young suburban Svengali found our repertoire ho-hum, which I suppose it was, and he suggested edgier and preferably more obscure material. To illustrate his point, he grabbed a guitar and tore into "Kilgary Mountain (Whiskey in the Jar)," an Irish folk tune with the rousing chorus

> *Musha rig um du rum da,*
> *Whack fol the daddy-o,*
> *Whack fol the daddy-o,*
> *There's whiskey in the jar*

alternately strumming the guitar and slapping his thigh with his right hand when the word "whack" came around. We got the message and he booked us for the show.

Meanwhile, we consulted folk song collections at either the TMR library or Classics Bookstore and worked up "Two Brothers on Their

Way," about young immigrant Irishmen to the United States fighting on opposing sides of the Civil War, paid substitutes for well-to-do American lads whose families didn't want to lose their own sons in the war. "One wore blue and the other wore grey." We learned the spinning song "En filant ma quenouille," a French-Canadian *chanson à répondre* that Kate and I would record twenty years later for *French Record*. Another was the Canadian fisherman's ballad "Mary Ann," collected in Tadoussac, Quebec, by Marius Barbeau.

A lobster in a lobster pot,
a blue fish wriggling on the hook,
They're suffering long but it's nothing
like the ache I feel for you my dear Mary Ann.

My mother loved this last song, and when we were rehearsing at our place, she used to say, "Sing the one about the lobster pot." So taken were we with Seymour's performance, we called ourselves the Kilgary Balladeers, at least for that one evening. The show was reviewed and the *Montreal Star* followed it up with a piece on the three of us.

Shimon Ash and his wife, Neema, who had the Finjan Coffee House above the Arena Bakery on Victoria Avenue in Snowdon, took an interest an us. Because we sang in both English and French, Shimon named us Le Trio Canadien.

He was an enlightened South African who straddled Quebec's two solitudes. Somewhere along the line, Michèle acquired an auto-harp and we continued to add new songs to our repertoire—"Poor Wayfarin' Stranger," Guy Béart's "L'eau vive"—and before long we had enough songs to open for Finjan regulars. These were Québécois chansonnier Claude Gauthier, whose seaside ballad "Mouette de goéland" was a favourite of our mother's; Wade Hemsworth, a drafts-man at CN and composer of "The Log Driver's Waltz" and "The Black Fly Song"; Shirley Singer, Wade's girlfriend at the time, and her singing partner Shirley Brown, who sang in both French and Hebrew;

and Derek Lamb, a British animator at the National Film Board and interpreter of British music hall songs, whom we had already met at La Poubelle. The bulk of Le Trio Canadien's appearances were on the stage of this small Israeli coffee house that served falafel and Turkish coffee made on the old gas stovetop in the Finjan's kitchen. The route from our homes in TMR to the Finjan was well worn. The 16 bus that ran along Graham Boulevard took us west to Lucerne then south along this artery to Kindersley, where we transferred to the 124. From there we went past the Baron de Hirsch Cemetery and up Victoria Avenue to Côte-Sainte-Catherine Road, where we got off. The 124 continued along Victoria up into Westmount then down the hill to Sainte-Catherine West, where it turned around.

One winter a couple of years back, I took this bus for old times' sake and sat up front just as our grandfather Arthur had done. It seemed that the only other people riding the 124 with me that day were small brown Filipinas on their way to clean houses in Westmount. The women appeared even smaller in the oversized down jackets they all seemed to be wearing, castoffs, I surmised, of Westmount teens who had grown out of them. They reminded me of Melida, a cleaning lady from the Dominican Republic who used to work for Dane and me when we lived in Westmount. She usually arrived at our flat bearing bags of used clothing given to her by her other Westmount clients, which she would in turn send on to relatives. Melida was at our house one day when I was putting together an outfit for a TV show Kate and I were doing later that day and I needed something to dress up the jeans I was going to wear. Melida came to the rescue with an item from her collection, a rust-coloured satin jacket that did splendidly.

During the trio's short-lived career, we taped at least one CBC show that featured young talent. It was late summer of 1962 and Michèle and I were working downtown. Michèle was the reception-ist at Young & Rubicam, an ad agency in the new CIBC tower at Peel and Dorchester West (now René-Levesque West). The studio where the TV show was being taped was in an old church in the suburb of Ville Saint-Laurent, just north of TMR. She and I rode the CN commuter train to the Town, where we met up with Kate and picked up the instruments. We were already late and Michèle recalls us hailing an open-backed truck that was transporting apples to take us the rest of the way. Two of us rode up front in the cab with the driver and the other got in the back with the apples and the guitars. What a lovely record jacket this would have made, if we'd ever gotten around to recording one. The trio did make one demo tape at Studio Marko, which was then on Dorchester West in what had been the old Ford Hotel. Michèle's father was very supportive and he paid for the session. Regrettably, the tape is lost.

This may sound like a generalization, but I remember all the Forests, five girls and two boys, as tall and nice-looking, the older girls in their tan trench coats and kerchiefs like their idol Audrey Hepburn, who at that time was the brightest star in the entertainment firmament. The family shopped at Holt Renfrew, a small high-end store in an art deco building on Sherbrooke West at De la Montagne Street. This store was out of reach for the McGarrigle girls. A co-worker of our mother's at Marconi had told her about a bargain dress shop on Côte-des-Neiges Road, not far from TMR. It was run out of a pokey apartment by a morbidly obese gentleman, and this is where Kate and I shopped. The place was always full of teenaged girls and their mothers in search of a deal, rifling through racks of dresses and suits, all made in Montreal's once-vibrant garment district, many with the familiar Algo Originals label. From time to time our mother did spring for a designer outfit for us from either Ogilvy's or Eaton's Ensemble Room, but it had to be seriously marked down.

I think it was Michèle who suggested the trio dress alike. We'd look more professional and it would level the fashion playing field. We likely went to Marshalls Fabric Store on Sainte-Catherine West to buy the white duck for the straight skirts and the blue-and-pink-striped mattress ticking for the jackets. The Simplicity pattern we chose was for beginners, with no linings, collars or buttonholes, just a couple of darts at the waist with a side zipper for the skirt, and a dart at the breast on each front panel of the jacket, which had three snap fasteners to keep it closed. We wore the new outfits for a photo shoot Michèle's father had organized.

I was to meet up with Kate and Michèle at the coffee house after work. I didn't like the way the boxy jacket looked on me (I was short-waisted and already looked like a box), so I bought a lavender cardigan to wear instead, rationalizing that it was in the same tones as the jackets. When I walked into the room minus the official jacket, Kate and Michèle demanded to know where it was. I'd had a hunch they would enforce the dress code and had left it behind at work. Neither of them spoke to me that evening, either during the show or later, on the bus ride home, and maybe for longer.

The trio disbanded after a little more than a year and a half. Michèle remembers that Kate and I started missing rehearsals to do something else. At the time, Michèle was the only one serious about a singing career, and she told me recently that it was she who walked away. I was happy to hear it wasn't because of the stupid jacket episode. In any case, we three remained good friends and I am forever indebted to her for introducing me to the music of Claude Léveillée.

One summer's evening long ago, I drove with Michèle and her brother Gaston to the Domaine de L'Estérel in Sainte-Marguerite to see this Quebec singer-songwriter and self-taught piano player, who wrote some of Quebec's most evocative and enduring songs, "Le vieux piano" and especially "Frédéric."

He performed with pianist André Gagnon that night, playing back to back grand pianos with comedian/musician Yvon Deschamps on a stripped-down drum kit, and a contrabass player whose name I don't recall. The venue was in the art deco style, all white with rounded corners, and reminds me now of the set of Carl Dreyer's *The Passion of Joan of Arc*.

A few years before we caught Léveillée at L'Estérel, Edith Piaf had been in Montreal performing when some friends took her to hear Léveillée, who was playing in a small downtown boîte. By all accounts she was so charmed by him that she invited him then and there to come live with her in Paris and write songs for her. Martha was to cover one of these in 2009 on her tribute to Piaf, *Sans souliers, ni fusils à Paris*. The song was "Non, la vie n'est pas triste," written by Léveillée at 67 bis boulevard Lannes, where he spent all his time at the piano churning out musical themes and sleeping in a cupboard Mme Piaf had so kindly cleared out for him. The two years he spent in Paris are documented in *67 bis boulevard Lannes*, an NFB film by Jean-Claude Labrecque. Piaf carried a bell around with her in the apartment, and when she heard Léveillée play something she liked, she'd ring it. Piaf referred to him affectionately as "mon petit Canadien," but in reality he was her musical slave. It's funny to think that talented songwriters were so sought-after that you had to practically lock them up.

THE MATING GAME
(Jane)

Our spring wedding was a quiet one, generally the case when a Catholic married out of the faith, and was celebrated in the Lady chapel of St. Patrick's Basilica in Montreal. Dave had to take religious instruction beforehand, and make a promise that our future children would be brought up as Catholics.

Skippy Edwards was my maid of honour and Russell Bailey stood up for Dave. The flinty priest who married us didn't crack a smile during the ceremony, and we were happy to get out of there and over to our little party at the Queen Elizabeth Hotel down the street. Daddy arranged for the organist to play "Annie Laurie" as we left the church, a gesture to Dave's Scotch Presbyterian grandmother, perhaps to make up a bit for her great-grandchildren having just been commandeered by the Catholic Church. Nana Scott enjoyed the piece and thanked him.

The plan was to spend the summer in Montreal and be back in Fredericton in time for Dave's fall term at UNB. We rented an apartment on University Street in a row of old homes that had been made over into student housing and fraternity houses. It was near the McGill campus, and just down the street from the Royal Victoria Hospital. I remember the place as one big room with a kitchenette and bath and a few pieces of essential furniture, down the hall from some foreign students whose cooking filled the building with the most peculiar smells.

The apartment's main selling point, besides the groovy location, was a tall window that opened out onto a roof with a slope just gentle enough that chairs would stay in place and not slide to the pavement two storeys below. We put some potted geraniums out there and it became our terrace, a place to sit outside on hot summer nights. I'd never lived downtown, and enjoyed the traffic, the music drifting out of the frat houses, the sirens of the Royal Vic's ambulances coming and going during the night. Our terrace had no railing, and it's just blind dumb luck that we didn't end up at the Royal Vic ourselves.

Uncle Lorne had gotten Dave a summer job in the tool crib of an oil refinery in the east end of the city, handing out tools to the workers. I was already working for Morgan Realty, later to become the Hudson's Bay Development Company, another of Lorne's job placements. He had gotten me on there as a receptionist, and planned to push me up the ladder into the office of the head man, General Alfred Ernest Walford, as the General's executive secretary. The General (he was always referred to as the General) was a veteran of both world wars and had a long corporate history with the Henry Morgan Company. He was a natty little man with salt-and-pepper hair brushed back close to his head and a neat moustache. He favoured double-breasted pinstriped suits that he wore well because of his trim build and ramrod military bearing. Trim or not, the General was watching his weight and had put himself on a Metrecal diet. Metrecal was an early nutritional supplement in powder form that, when mixed with water, became a foul-tasting vanilla shake. Once in a while the General's secretary asked me to prepare his liquid lunch and take it down the hall to him. Uncle Lorne was always happy to hear of me having direct contact with the General, and confident about my long-term prospects at the company. When he found out that I would be moving to Fredericton in the fall, he was very disappointed. I had the feeling he thought I was throwing my life away.

Dave and I met up at the apartment after work every day and either went out on the town or had friends over to hang out with us on our improvised deck. My friend Anne Tripe had taken up with Johnny Sansome, a former classmate of Dave's at UNB who had dropped out to become a writer, and we saw a lot of them. John was an intriguing character—British by birth, brought up in Venezuela before going to UNB, and now in Montreal, living downtown in a slightly rundown apartment at the corner of Burnside and Drummond, with not much besides a typewriter and hopes of becoming the next Hemingway, his idol. He had beautiful manners and the understated sense of humour the British are known for, but never quite enough money. For that matter, none of us had enough money. On weekends we prowled around lanes behind apartment buildings, checking the balconies for empty beer bottles to turn into cash for beer of our own. An irate resident caught us in the act one afternoon and demanded to know if we were taking away his neighbours' bottles. John very politely, and in his plummiest accent, said, "Yes, yes, we're doing this for them," and scrambled off the balcony with the case of empties under his arm.

There was something deliciously clandestine about the guy. Without actually saying it in so many words, he gave the impression of being on the run, and was intending to leave any day for Tampico. His departure seemed urgent and necessary. We sat out on our terrace, eating pizza and drinking cold beer on those warm summer nights, listening to John spin his getaway plans. In my imagination, he would soon be sailing away on a tramp steamer headed for the Gulf of Mexico, but as it turns out, he and Anne got married and settled down in Halifax. So much for that fantasy.

We listened that summer to Los Tres Compadres, a Mexican folk music group that inspired Dave and me to get nylon-string guitars and learn "Malaguena Salerosa," which we played for anyone who would listen. Our version was pretty raucous, with friends joining in on the chorus while Dave and I crashed our way through the mariachi strums that were so much fun to play. We later saw, to our surprise and delight, that Los Tres Compadres would be performing in a boîte downtown. We went to their show, and they did not disappoint; we were thrilled to see and hear them live.

Before we knew it, summer was over and we were off to Fredericton. Dave had found us an apartment on York Street, above a beauty parlour owned and operated by Mrs. Cora Walker, our landlady. Cora wanted to know right off how I was able to get my hair so pouffy. She was still doing her clients up in pincurls and wanted to update their look. I brought my hair rollers down to the shop and coiffed one of her customers, and taught Cora how to backcomb. She got herself some rollers and from then on her clients left the shop with pouffy hair, thanks to the Montreal technology.

Through Bob Dykes, Dave arranged for me to meet Mike Gordon, a graduate student in political science who was executive assistant to the Honourable William R. Duffie, Minister of Youth and Welfare. It was a recently revamped department in the new Liberal government of Louis Robichaud, the first Acadian premier. It combined youth services with welfare services, the idea being that if there were proper counselling and vocational and recreational direction for young people early on, there would be less need for welfare down the line—an interesting proposition. It happened that Mike was looking for a secretary and I got the job. Mike was working on his master's thesis about the administration of a previous New Brunswick premier, Andrew G. Blair, and was steeped in New Brunswick's political history. He was the perfect political flack, dedicated and vigilant about Bill Duffie's image, sensitive to every nuance of his utterances.

New Brunswickers are good, open-hearted people and I made friends quickly in the department, usually in the canteen while getting coffee or lunch. The canteen was operated by the Canadian National Institute for the Blind, and as a rule, the counter person was sightless. You didn't always get the sandwich you asked for, and the coffee might get spilled in its transfer to the customer, but no one ever complained. People were on their honour to identify the bill that was changing hands for payment (a dollar? a fiver?) and I never heard of anyone cheating.

I loved the people I got to know in New Brunswick. They were, as my father liked to say, the salt of the earth. They called their home "God's Country" and were fond of referring to themselves as "poor but proud." They were outrageously proud of the province's attractions: the Reversing Falls, the Magnetic Hill, the longest covered bridge in the world.

Among the many interesting and colourful characters I met down there was Barry Grant, an old friend of Bill's. He had been one of Bill's speech writers during the campaign, and was now part of the Youth Services administration. Barry was some years older than Dave and me, and a former high school teacher.

We got to talking in the canteen one day, and when he discovered what a fervent reader I was, he began bringing in books for me to discover: James Thurber (*My Life and Hard Times*, *The Years with Ross*), more George Orwell (*The Road to Wigan Pier*, *Burmese Days*), others I can't remember. He was working on a dictionary of Canadian slang and colloquialisms at the time, and was always on the lookout for expressions to include in his work. The books kept coming, and often, when neither of us was very busy, we took long lunches at the canteen. I became a sort of disciple of Barry's. He was a great fan of *The New Yorker*, and put me on to the bons mots of Robert Benchley and Dorothy Parker and other wits of the famed Algonquin Round Table. Barry himself was highly literate, mordantly funny and a great storyteller. In that way he reminded me of my father, a fellow Maritimer. Barry also shared with my father an enjoyment of drink that may have led to the demise of his civil service career.

I came to work one day to find the Fredericton *Daily Gleaner* on my desk, open to an item about the arrest of a John B. Grant at one of the service clubs; the charge was attempted theft of a floor polisher. It was Barry, of course, who had tried explaining to the cops that he wasn't stealing the floor polisher, he was dancing with it (which made a lot more sense, if you knew Barry), but the cops didn't buy it and he spent the night in jail. In any case, Barry was not of that world, not a civil servant in his heart of hearts. I didn't see much of him after he left the department, and we eventually lost touch.

We moved out of Mrs. Walker's to a rented house on University Avenue, just down the hill from the UNB campus. We hadn't paid attention to the railway track between the house and the campus when we signed up for the place, and were awakened on our first morning and every following morning by a train that went by around 6 a.m. and blew its whistle just as it passed our bedroom window. We eventually got used to it and otherwise enjoyed the house. We had a lot of company, some of it planned but often just people dropping by on their way to or from school.

Even though I had a job and Dave was sent an allowance from home, money was tight and we lived on sausages and potatoes, a cheap New Brunswick crop. I dyed our mashed potatoes green on St. Patrick's Day and continued dying them different colours to break the monotony. In another economy move, we tried making our own beer. We made a mistake in the formula and produced a highly volatile liquid that spontaneously exploded caps off the bottles, making a sharp crack every time. Sometimes this would occur in the middle of the night and give us a fright until we remembered that it was the beer. We couldn't really drink it and idly wondered one day what would happen if we were to throw a bottle or two at the afternoon train when it went by the house. A very satisfying explosion happened, and we got rid of the entire batch over about a week, with friends dropping by to have a turn.

Dave received his engineering degree in May 1962 and we decided to stay in Fredericton for a while longer. The New Brunswick Electric Power Commission hired him and, before he even started work, we ordered a new sky-blue MGA convertible. After we took delivery of our beautiful ride, Dave had to teach me how to drive a stick. No synchromesh in first gear, and after grinding the transmission for a few days, I got the hang of it.

We moved out of the house on University to another rented house, this one in Marysville, about a twenty-minute drive north across the Nashwaaksis Bridge (now the Westmorland Street Bridge). We had looked at a couple of places, but this one had a piano. Up until then, my only opportunity to play the piano was at the Elks Club when I sat in with the band, and I was happy to have my own instrument again.

The house was a modern bungalow with three bedrooms, a bathroom, a living room and a good-sized eat-in kitchen. The owner had left his furniture in it and a large potted plant, and it was a comfortable, easy move for us. We got to know the neighbours on either side of our house, and a few other people on the street. They were a little older than us, and a good lot who would do almost anything to help the young carpetbaggers. We never locked our door, and would come home sometimes to find a casserole or baked dessert waiting for us on the kitchen table, other times a jar of preserves. We occasionally spent our Saturday nights with them and gathered around the piano towards the end of the evening for a beery, maudlin version of "In the Garden."

My mother and father had talked about coming to visit us, now that we had a couple of spare rooms and could put them up, but we hadn't set a date. One day, not long after we moved into the house, an odd thing happened while Dave and I were driving home from work. Through the passenger window, I was startled to see my sister Kate sitting on a fence. I made Dave stop so I could look back, but she was gone. About half an hour after we got home, to our great surprise, my father's car pulled into our driveway and out stepped Frank, Gaby and Kate. I said something like, "So that *was* you sitting on the fence. Why ever were you stopped there?" They hadn't stopped anywhere and had no idea what I was talking about.

I recounted my psychic experience, if that's what it was, and Daddy said, quite seriously, "Coming events cast their shadows before." In her later years, Kate claimed to be a witch—a good witch, but still a witch. Maybe she was, or maybe she had a sixteen-year-old double who lived nearby. All I know is that I saw Kate eight hundred kilometres from home, and half an hour later she was in my kitchen.

We had a good visit for a few days and they continued on to Saint John, Daddy's hometown.

Life changed when Dave finished school. Many of the people we palled around with had finished at the same time and gone back to their home cities. We made new friends through work and graduated to more refined entertainments like dinner parties, and I learned how to cook so I could host some of my own.

Later in the year, Anna came to see us.

VISITING NEW BRUNSWICK

ANNA: In the spring of 1962, I got my chance to visit Jane and David in Marysville, New Brunswick. This would be my first time in a flying machine, a TCA flight to Fredericton aboard a Viscount turboprop. I wore my best outfit, a beige wool bouclé Chanel knock-off with brown leather trim on the pockets, and a kerchief on my beehive hairdo à la Empress Farah Diba of Iran, the third wife of the Shah of Iran and a major fashion icon of the early sixties. How times have changed.

The night I arrived, we were sitting around their bungalow when someone mentioned in passing that Fred McKenna, the blind guitar player on CBC's *Singalong Jubilee*, also lived in Marysville. Kate and I both admired Fred McKenna's unusual guitar style, seated in a chair with the instrument across his lap (the way one spanks a child), fretting it by placing the fingers of his left hand perpendicular to the fretboard and fingerpicking wildly with his right hand. (Jeff Healey played the guitar the same way.) With his rich, searing baritone, McKenna struck us as the real deal, a seasoned country musician and not some latter-day folkie.

I think it was Jane who said, "Why don't you call him up?" After finding his number in the local directory, I dialled it and waited nervously. A woman picked up. "Is Mr. McKenna there, please?" I inquired meekly. "One moment," she answered in a pleasant nasally tone, and cupping her hand over the mouthpiece, she hollered, "FRED? It's for you."

In the background, I could make out the muffled mutterings of an angry man who was probably enjoying a Friday night beer (as we were). I could hear him shuffling toward the phone, knocking stuff over in his path and swearing. I began to regret ever having dialled the number. I considered hanging up, but I couldn't after all the trouble he was going to to take my call.

"HELLO," he bellowed in his familiar searing baritone.

"Oh, I'm so sorry to disturb you, Mr. McKenna," I offered earnestly. "I'm a fan of yours from Montreal and happen to be in Marysville visiting my sister. I just wanted you to know how much I enjoy your songs on *Singalong Jubilee*."

Silence, then, "Well, thank you for calling," and that was that. I vowed I would never again call a celebrity out of the blue; what a completely stupid idea that was. Over the years, Kate and I got our share of calls from fans in faraway places. Calls from complete strangers always raise the hair on your back.

One afternoon Dave and I went out for a drive with me behind the wheel of their new blue MGA. This was my first time driving a shift, and he was coaching me. We were out in the countryside at the top of something called Mill Hill. There was a steep descent, as the name implies. I didn't know about downshifting, and as we careened down the hill, I possibly had my foot on the clutch thinking it was the brake, and panicked. Usually, when I panic, I put my hands over my eyes. I'm pretty sure it was Dave who stopped the car with the handbrake, causing it to spin out and come to a halt. He pointed out that we had narrowly missed a pile of stones and then, cool as a cucumber, said, "Would you like me to drive now?" I was struck by how easy it would be to kill yourself, yet at the same time how difficult it was to die.

JANE: There would be another car mishap before the weekend was out.

Our bachelor friend George Gunter came over to the house on Saturday to meet Anna, and we decided to go out for dinner. We travelled in our separate sports cars. After dinner, we travelled back in convoy, Dave and me in the lead, Anna and George following in his TR3. No one can remember for sure whether Anna or George was driving, but the TR3 went off the road as it was turning into our driveway behind the MGA. What to do? We left it in the ditch for the night, thinking we'd call a tow truck in the morning.

George stayed over, and when we got up the next day, the car was out of the ditch and properly parked in the driveway. Our neighbours had pulled it out for us. Dave called on his usual subversive humour about this kindness. "Prying do-gooders," he said. "How did they know we didn't want it in the ditch?" Of course, we thanked them for coming to our rescue.

We went home to Montreal for Christmas that year and the following year. It was a long trip, ten to twelve hours as I recall, on icy two-lane roads, in a drafty car built for the British climate. Dave did most of the driving and I tried not to think about us spinning out. He distracted me with scientific explanations about why an object travelling in a straight line would maintain its trajectory, ice or not. I would fall asleep around Rivière-du-Loup—about halfway—and wake up safe and sound in the Dows' driveway in Montreal. A week later, we turned around and went back—a bit of a harrowing journey all around, but worth it to be home for the holidays.

Dave didn't see himself as a career man with the New Brunswick Electric Power Commission but wasn't sure what he wanted to do next, except see some new country. He decided to go to graduate school, and applied to Stanford in Palo Alto, California, and to the University of California at Berkeley. He was accepted at Berkeley, and we started planning for our trip across the continent and our new life in California.

TICKERTAPE

(Anna)

In the summer of 1962, I got my first job. This was after a year-long programme at the Mother House Secretarial School, where I learned to type and was taught an obscure French/English shorthand invented in Montreal called Perrault–Duployé, as well as business accounting. One school year seems like a long time now to learn just three subjects when today's health care workers in Rwanda are given only six weeks of training, or so it was reported recently on TV.

My employer was an old-style stock brokerage firm at McGill Street and Notre-Dame West, on the western limits of what was then Montreal's financial district. If the district were a Monopoly board, our office would have been the Baltic Avenue property, a bit down-at-the-heels and in a rented ground-floor space of a terracotta-clad edifice a few blocks from the Montreal Stock Exchange on Saint-Francois-Xavier Street, now the Centaur Theatre.

Officially, I was the secretary to the comptroller, but being the newest and youngest employee, I filled a lot of gaps. At lunchtime I relieved the switchboard operator, a stout woman who dressed straight out of the forties and came to work in a voluminous black coat and a hat with a little veil over her eyes. Her large, uncorseted body hung in soft folds from the rickety swivel chair on casters she rolled around on in the small space she shared with an old-timey switchboard. The woman was deft at handling the dozens of heavy-cloth-covered cables with quarter-inch phone jacks at either end, which she used to connect clients to their respective salesmen, all the while barking buy and sell orders into a direct line to the firm's trader on the floor of the stock exchange. Adjacent to the switchboard room was a small lounge with a noisy tickertape machine that fed a jerky paper tapeworm into the veiny hand of a gaunt old British gentleman in a grey smock who recorded the stock trades on a large blackboard with a piece of white chalk. I wonder what my old friend would make of today's three tech giants, AAPL (Apple Inc.), MSFT (Microsoft Corporation) and GOOG (Google), and the action they generate? He'd have to lay in some extra boxes of chalk for sure.

A few of those old, heavy, varnished wooden armchairs, generic office issue that you can't pay people now to take off your hands, lined the wall across from the blackboard for those clients wishing to keep track of the day's action. Many of them sat there for the five hours the markets were open, their bony behinds on the hard chairs, leaving only for trips to the lavatory. Unlike the high-speed mega-trades in today's volatile markets, the blue-chip stocks our clients held might move upward or downward only one-quarter of a point in the course of a week, unless there was a crisis, as on the day John F. Kennedy was shot. I was at lunch when the shot or shots were fired, and found out about the president's assassination upon my return to the office. I have no recollection of how the markets reacted and had to google what impact JFK's assassination had. Stocks were in a free fall for over an hour before the NYSE called a halt to trading. I don't remember what we did in Canada, but we must have followed suit. We usually do.

Before the start of the business day and again at market's close, the forty-something family man who ran the cage would go down the street to the vault with a large briefcase carrying stock and bond certificates that needed to be processed that day. One of my jobs was doing the ownership transfers when these stocks and bonds changed hands. Most clients kept the certificates of their holdings in the company's vault, but if you didn't and you sold a stock, you had three business days to surrender the certificate. Alternatively, if you bought a stock, you had three business days to pay for it, unless you had margin. Our brokerage house was reputed to be the most conservative in the district, and its two conservative partners dressed in well-cut, sombre grey suits. I remember telling Kate how the old men I worked for had hair the colour of money, by which I meant silver coins. She liked the analogy. And everybody smoked—cigarettes, cigars or pipes. It could get tense, but these weren't the high-flying, risk-taking brokers of today in their cartoonish black-with-white-pinstripe suits and pastel shirts with white collars. Only the dapper floor trader dressed in that manner, and we only saw him at the end of the business day when he returned to the office to report on the day's trading. He was the knight who did battle on the floor from ten until three for the firm.

My father would occasionally meet me downtown and we'd go to lunch somewhere nice, somewhere other than Murray's, that venerable old Canadian restaurant where my co-workers and I usually ate. He liked the French restaurant in the Aldred Building at Place d'Armes, the windows of which looked out onto Notre-Dame church across the street. This art deco structure with setbacks is said to resemble the Empire State Building, but it's about eighty floors short of that famous landmark. Another favourite eatery was Le Petit Havre, a tiny Breton bistro over an old garage in Saint-Vincent Street, and just a couple of doors away from the old city morgue, as my mother was fond of reminding me.

My father liked these outings. Strolling arm in arm with me down St. James Street made him feel he was in the thick of things, which of course he wasn't. He was a sixty-three-year-old in an outmoded suit, and rapidly coming up on the end of the line, though we didn't know that then. He'd lean over to me and say with a smile, "People must be wondering what a young thing like you is doing with an old goat like me."

A year after I arrived, the company was sold to a young, bilingual entrepreneur whose plan was to move operations uptown to the cruciform of Place Ville Marie. The two partners were getting on and seemed anxious to retire. Around this time, I had a copy of *Cité Libre*, a left-leaning magazine famously edited by Pierre Elliott Trudeau, displayed prominently on my desk. The new owner spotted it and lit into me about it being a subversive rag. He ordered me to put it out of view. If I was an anti-capitalist, what was I doing working for a stockbroker? he asked. A fair question.

When he moved the company uptown, taking half of the staff, I was not invited to join them. The fat lady on the switchboard didn't go either, nor did most of the unilingual staff, including the old scribe in his grey smock with his piece of chalk. In the new office he would be replaced by an electronic tickertape. It was then that the two old partners who had sold their highly reputed brokerage with its long list of well-heeled conservative clients did an about-face and registered a new company, thereby staying in business. I like to think they did this because they didn't want to put people out of work, and because their old clients might have objected to the change. They didn't mind the old, hard chairs.

Place Ville Marie, Place Victoria and the CIBC building, three monoliths that would change the skyline of Montreal, were going up, and within a couple of years the Montreal Stock Exchange along with many of the brokerage houses moved into these shiny new city landmarks, leaving the old financial district moribund. Around this time, the first mailbox bombs began exploding in the anglo bastion of Westmount. The Quiet Revolution was growing noisy and violent. It was to be many years before this part of town recovered, finally becoming the western extension of historic Old Montreal.

I loved working for the broker, handling the beautifully illustrated, multicoloured stock certificates printed on banknote paper. In this electronic age, I doubt they are printing any more of these intricately designed certificates; along with paper money, they will soon go the way of the dodo.

In my time there, I even talked my mother into buying a couple of blue-chip stocks, CP and Bell. During her lifetime, these accrued in value and split a number of times, begetting more and more little stocks like fruitful families.

After two years at the brokerage house, I decided to go back to school and enrolled as a full-time student at the École des beaux-arts for the 1964 fall term. In the interim I took a job uptown with a small firm that sold TV and radio time to advertisers on commercial stations across Canada. I was working in advertising even if it wasn't

Kate on the ferry Rivière-du-Loup St-Siméon, 1968, the same ferry she mentions in her song *Matapedia*.

Philippe and Kate on the ferry, 1968. Philippe was Kate and Anna's co-writer for many years.

Gaby and Kate at
Val Royal Station,
Saint-Laurent,
Quebec, 1968.

Caroline Holland raising an arm on the steps of the Capitol Building
in Washington, DC, in the late 1960s. Caroline and Kate were in
engineering together. Anna and Caroline would co-write "You Tell Me
That I'm Falling Down," recorded by Linda Ronstadt in 1975.

Kate and Roma Baran, a.k.a. Catherine Carr and Roma Blackwell, the spiritual wives of legendary piano and guitar blues duo Leroy Carr and Scrapper Blackwell, Saratoga Springs, New York, 1970.

Vinnie, Anna, Dave Dow and Janie at home in San Carlos,
California, 1973.

Gaby with Jane's son, Vinnie, in Saint-Sauveur, *circa* early 1970s.

Anna with Audrey Bean in Montreal, off to a game of pick-up hockey. Anna and Audrey wrote "Cool River," recorded by Maria Muldaur, and "Louis the Cat" on K&A's *Odditties*.

Uffe and Gudda Lanken at Chas. J. Hill, the Lanken family flower shop in Westmount, in the early 1970s, around the time an FLQ bomb blew out the back of the store.

Kate and Loudon in 1973. A serenade in the grass, shortly after Rufus's birth.

Dane and Anna at the farm in Alexandria, Ontario, early 1970s. Anna is wearing Barry Black's hand-me-down sweater, which has since been passed down to Kate's kids.

Rufus Wainwright with his G-Pa, Loudon Wainwright, *circa* 1978.

Gaby with baby Martha at Anna and Dane's apartment, 4378 de Maisonneuve W., Westmount, 1976.

Uncle Austin with lil' Anna (Jane's daughter) in 1974.

Gaby and Sylvan with the Gardencourt sign our mother hated so
much. After it was knocked down by a drunk driver Dane re-erected
it on the property in our father's honour.

Rufus, Sylvan, Lily and Martha in Venise-en-Quebec, a bit early for swimming, March 1980.

Sylvan and Lily Lanken skating on the pond at the farm in
Alexandria in the 1980s.

Kate, Gaby and Anna backstage at Mariposa Folk Festival, Toronto Island, 1975.

Kate and Anna, Mariposa Folk Festival, Toronto Island, 1975. This photo was on the front cover of our debut album on Warners.

Jane recovering at Carmel Beach, California, Memorial Day Weekend, May 1974.

Deborah Adler, a.k.a. Dancer with Bruised Knees, with Kate, Anna and Andrew Cowan at the ticket counter, Mirabel Airport, Quebec, on the way to London in the summer of 1976.

Kate's drawing of Skigirl, inspired by the time she had to ski home alone during the night. Her drawing is reproduced on her white stone monument in the Saint-Sauveur parish cemetery.

Gardencourt, the property at Saint-Sauveur. Kathleen Weldon made this drawing as a wedding gift for Martha Wainwright and Brad Albetta, wed on September 2, 2007.

for an actual creative agency such as Cockfield, Brown or McKim or MacLaren, who were clients. The two young partners definitely saw themselves as movers and shakers. Their choice of location at Crescent Street near Sainte-Catherine West and close to the action reflected this perception. The office was only two blocks from Le Bistro on groovy Mountain Street, a favourite haunt of Montreal's more artsy types, where Kate and I would meet our friends on Friday evenings.

Years later, when the two of us toured Canadian cities doing the requisite interviews and live in-station performances to promote our music, I recognized the call letters for many of the country's commercial stations with the most clout. Unfortunately, our music didn't get played much on these stations, until 1981/82 when we released *Love Over and Over* with the brilliant Mark Knopfler on guitar for the title track. It was the only one of our songs to make it onto the Canadian hit parade.

THE MOUNTAIN CITY FOUR
(Anna)

The trio met Jack Nissenson at the Loyola concert. This fine baritone with a repertoire of songs from the British Isles would intro-
duce Kate to his friend Peter Weldon, a McGill graduate student
in Biochemistry,* a tenor who played banjo and guitar. Kate would
be the third member in a group the two were forming. Both Jack
and Peter had done studio work for Montreal impresario Sam
Gesser, who was also the Folkways Records rep in Canada.

Acclaimed Quebec fiddler Jean Carignan was another musician
in the loop.

Both Jean Carignan and Peter had worked with Canadian folksinger Alan Mills, accompanying him on the Potato Festival circuit
in the Maritimes. Later, when Sam Gesser was putting together Les
feux-follets, a folk-dance troupe based in Montreal, Carignan
became the featured fiddling act and toured the world playing his
show stoppers, "Le reel du pendu" ("Hanged Man's Reel") and
"Le rêve du diable" ("Devil's Dream"). For a while Jack joined the
outfit as a soloist. Through him we met dancer Deborah Adler, a
small blonde girl with very long braids who was one of the troupe's
stars and who became a close friend.

Jack and Peter started coming to Saint-Sauveur on weekends with
a car full of instruments. Often Michèle and I were there too, our trio
was still extant, but wouldn't be for much longer. Kate and I learned
to fingerpick guitar from Peter and all three of the Trio Canadien had
crushes on him. We weren't alone. When Peter did "Willie Moore" in
a drop C tuning he'd learned from Peggy Seeger, we girls all pretty
much turned to mush. This Appalachian song is a tearjerker to start

---

* If memory serves me well, he was studying the effects of carbon tetrachloride on the
liver. CCl_4 was used in the dry cleaning process. I stopped having my clothes cleaned.

with. Willie's girl, "fair Ellen," drowns herself when her parents forbid them to marry, leaving the heartbroken boy to wander the world.

Willie Moore scarcely spoke to his friends they say,
And at length from them he did part.
When last heard, he was in Montreal (really?), *
Where he died of a broken heart.

The mental picture I retain of Peter sitting on the steps of camp 67 playing this song was the inspiration for my "Goin' Back to Harlan" (a.k.a. "Appalachian Dream") on our 1996 recording *Matapedia*. It's about inhabiting the world of folksong.

... and if you were Willie Moore,
Then I was Barbara Allen
Or fair Ellen, all sad at the cabin door,
Weepin' and a-pinin' for love.
Frail, frail my heart apart
And sing me little Shady Grove,
Ring the Bells of Rhymney
'til they ring inside my head forever,
Bounce the bow, rock the gallows
For the Hanged Man's Reel
And wake the Devil from his dream.
I'm goin' back to Harlan. **

Peter, Jack and Kate's first gig was at the Hotel Vermont in Sainte-Agathe, a family-run establishment in the Laurentian borscht belt.

---

* Legend has it that Peggy Seeger and Ewan MacColl stayed at the Weldon family home when the two were appearing in Montreal sometime around 1960. We conjectured that Peggy Seeger changed Willie Moore's last stop to "Montreal" after she'd met the twenty-something Peter. Folk process? Maybe.

** Harlan County, Kentucky, a birthplace of sorts for Anglo-American folk music.

I went to see the show and before long I too was singing with the group which now called itself the Mountain City Four (MC4).

Both Peter and Jack knew a lot of songs, many of them learned from Library of Congress and Folkways recordings they got from the Record Centre, a record-lending library on McKay at Burnside (now de Maisonneuve West) owned by Edgar Jones and his wife, Charlotte, a Québécois actress. Edgar was legally deaf, a result of the quinine cure for the malaria he'd contracted while living in India. Despite the handicap he hadn't lost his love of music and there was always something unusual on the turntable to grab the attention of the browsing client. Edgar was on the gruff side and didn't engage with the public. He left that to his amiable assistant Edward Ruznak, a lute-maker and a good friend of Peter's.

Jack was the most-seasoned of the MC4. He had been to the UK, met the McPeake family whose music he greatly admired and while in London had performed a short set at the Singers Club, the near-mythic folk venue run by Ewan MacColl and Peggy Seeger. Jack stressed that one had to be invited to sing there.

The four of us rehearsed at either Jack's parents' home in Côte-Saint-Luc or at the Weldons' on de l'Épée in Outremont. Besides the songs learned from Library of Congress and Folkways recordings, we heard the music of living African-American legends like Jesse Fuller, the one-man band, who regularly played the downtown coffee houses, stops on the east coast folk circuit. The Mountain City Four covered "Twelve Gates to the City" as sung by the Reverend Gary Davis, another visiting artist. This blind twelve-string-guitar virtuoso had an idiosyncratic style that incorporated bluesy bass note runs with a lot of syncopation, a style Kate taught herself to play; she also sang lead on this spiritual that suggests there might be a ring-road around Heaven.*

---

* I imagine it's like the Boulevard Périphérique around Paris built where the old Thiers wall had stood, its exits and entrances coinciding with the *portes* or gates of this once-walled city.

There's three gates in the East,
Three gates in the West.
Three gates in the North
And three gates in the South.
That makes twelve gates to the city,
Hallelujah!

Peter took the lead on "Hesitation Blues."

I ain't good lookin' and I don't dress fine,
But I'm a ramblin' boy with a ramblin' mind.
Tell me, how long do I have to wait? (Not long!)

Jack took us down into the coal mines of Appalachia with Merle Travis's "Dark as a Dungeon." Sadly, Jack left us just as I was rewriting this chapter, and the memories of him singing about the miner's wish for his body to metamorphose to coal upon his death are all the more poignant.

Kate's and my "big" number was the a cappella "Motherless Children," an Afro-American complaint with the refrain "Motherless children have a hard time when their mother is dead." Our most elaborate arrangement was of Arthur "Big Boy" Crudup's "Mean Ol' Frisco," a most unforgiving train.

A former girlfriend of Peter's, now living in NYC, sent him a copy of the first Bob Dylan record. From the initial playing we were committed fans of the boy from Hibbing, Minnesota, eventually working up his "One Too Many Mornings."

The MC4 also covered original compositions by Wade Hemsworth, by day a draftsman for the CN, and at night a songwriter and performer, who penned some of Canada's most famous folk songs. Jack was the best interpreter of Wade's songs apart from Wade himself, and helped to popularize "The Blackfly," written by Wade when he worked on a survey crew—

I'll die with the blackfly pickin' my bones,
In North Ontari-o, i-o, in North Ontario.

and "The Story of the *I'm Alone*," the real-life saga of a Canadian rum-running ship sunk by the Americans in international waters during Prohibition.

Stern in the air, the I'm Alone *went down,*
A heavy sea around her,
It's a wonder only one man was drowned.
The bos'un was the one who was pulled aboard the cutter
When his life was gone.

Most of Wade's songs were written to be sung by men, but there were two "girl" songs, as Wade called them, that Kate and I sang lead on: "The Log Driver's Waltz" and "Foolish You," both of which we later recorded.

In about 1963, Jack introduced us to songwriter Galt MacDermot, a former Montrealer who had done his music training in South Africa. He lived (and still does) on Staten Island, making periodic trips back to Montreal to see his aunt, the Canadian painter Anne Savage. During one of these visits, Jack made a date to tape Galt at the Nissenson home where Jack had a microphone and an immense Ferrograph mono tape machine set up. Seated at the Nissensons' upright in the family's finished basement, Galt gave us a sampling of his and his friend and lyricist William Dumaresq's quirky compositions—often the central figure in the song was a guy who's in trouble with the law.* The MC4 took up "No Biscuit Blues," a lament by a child who's lacking in the basic necessities, and whose father turns to crime to rectify the situation, landing himself in jail.

A few years on, all the stars in the heavens would align for his collaboration with librettists James Rado and Gerome Ragni to

---

* I read somewhere that William Dumaresq's father was a policeman.

write *Hair*, the smash-hit Broadway musical celebrating the Age of Aquarius. Both Rado and Ragni acted in the original New York production while MacDermot led the live band. I saw *Hair* in NYC during a Beaux-arts school trip in 1968. Nobody in my class had heard of it, so I went alone and sat in the gods. I was on my feet with everybody else in that theatre swaying in a giant love fest to "Let the Sunshine In" as the show concluded, and remember thinking it was just a few years back that Galt was playing the Nissensons' upright for a little known folk-group in Montreal in the hopes we would take up one of his songs. In the late 1970s Kate and I recorded "No Biscuit Blues" for *Dancer with Bruised Knees,* our second album with Warners.

In 2008, when Kate was already sick, she went to a holistic clinic in NYC where people bathed their feet in a solution of hydrogen peroxide and water. She struck up a conversation with the tall, thin, white-haired man in the chair next to her. It was James Rado. (He wasn't sick.) They talked about Galt and *Hair* and the wonderful sixties. She would have told him that the cast recordings of both the NY and London productions of *Hair* were all-time favourites in our homes.

When Peter moved out of the family home to a downtown apartment on Lincoln Avenue just west of Guy Street, the MC4 practices took place there. Rehearsing was always the most interesting part of being in that group, with the four of us trying to cover as many notes as are in a chord, throwing in a dissonant one from time to time to avoid sounding commercial. (God forbid!)

In 1966, Kate was asked to write music to lyrics by filmmaker Derek May to go under a segment featuring the schooner *Bluenose* in *Helicopter Canada,* an NFB film made to commemorate Canada's Centennial in 1967. She stayed up all night working on the tune instead of studying for an exam she had the next day, which she flunked. But she never regretted writing the song. She and I recorded the *Bluenose* song early that summer in the big sound studio at the NFB complex in Ville St. Laurent.

Around the same time, Peter was commissioned to write original music for a children's play that Charlotte Jones (the wife of the Record Centre owner mentioned earlier) was to act in, called *Cri-cri à l'école*. Peter played all the instruments, overdubbing them on his Sony stereo tape deck. These were the first instances of anyone in our tight musical circle to compose anything. After his Lincoln Avenue apartment was broken into by thieves, Peter started hiding his recording equipment in the oven when he went off to his research job at McGill.

The Mountain City Four worked a couple of weekends a month and had many fans who showed up religiously to hear us at the Fifth Dimension, a coffee house started by Morty Golub and Michael Nemiroff, rechristened the Fifth Amendment when Gary Eisenkraft took it over. The club was on the second floor of a building in the old garment district on Bleury above Sainte-Catherine West (this area, adjacent Place des arts, is now the Quartier des spectacles). Another place the MC4 played was Moishe Feinberg's Potpourri, a stylish bookstore-cum-coffee house on Stanley Street that had a real stage, a step up from most coffee houses, which tended to be makeshift. Bob Dylan's first Montreal show was on that stage, and my friend Michael and I were two of the five people in the audience that night. It was pretty informal so I requested "Baby Let Me Follow You Down." He was surprised that anyone knew his songs and broke right into it. When it came time to play the harmonica solo, the one that was in the rack around his neck was not in the key of the song. He played it anyway and I was struck by his nerve, and impressed that he carried it off. The Potpourri is where Kate and I met Gail Kenney, long-time friend and photographer, who was the chief cook and bottle-washer at the time. In 1975, she took the pic of the two of us for our first Warner recording.

A couple of years on, the MC4 became regulars at the Montreal Folk Workshop on Avenue du Parc. The space belonged to the Order of the Moose, a men's social/service club, and had a bar over which hung a depiction of a little boy in a nightshirt on his knees saying his evening prayers, with the caption "God Bless Mooseheart."

I never knew the significance of this until just now, when I googled it. The Order of the Moose funded a school in the US Midwest for the orphaned children of deceased Moose brethren. The orphanage was called Mooseheart.

Occasionally the MC4 would venture out of the city to the Lennoxville campus of Bishop's University in the Eastern Townships or to play a private party in the country. On one such outing our destination was Mansonville, about 130 kilometres southeast of Montreal and close to the US border. We were travelling in Jack's father's car, and Peter, Kate and I were listening to a story Jack was telling. Jack was a wonderful storyteller, but he was also the driver and oblivious to where we were headed, which in this case was in the wrong direction. We knew we had to cross a bridge and we did cross one, believing it to be the Champlain, but as I remember, it was only about one-tenth of the span of that immense structure. An hour into the trip, someone noticed a mileage sign for Toronto. We were on old Route 2 at the Ontario border. After consulting a roadmap, we went cross-country, arriving at our destination after midnight, the party ended and the hosts already in bed. I remember someone in nightclothes coming out into the driveway when they heard our car.

We didn't knowingly blow off gigs, except one (but it wasn't our fault). We were seated around a table one evening at the Sun Sun restaurant in Montreal's Chinatown when Jack, who had been reading the entertainment section of the *Gazette*, announced suddenly, "Ha! Guess who's playing the Folk Workshop tonight?"

"Who?" we asked, curious now because he seemed so enthused.

"WE are," he replied, deadpan, before breaking into his evil little laugh.

The ad ran, but the venue had failed to book us. We continued on with our meal. I suppose we could have made the gig, but we didn't have our instruments with us. Music was an avocation for the four of us; at that point none of us seriously entertained the idea of doing music as a life occupation, and that may have accounted for the MC4's collective nonchalance.

Over the next couple of years, others joined this elite little group: Chaim Tannenbaum, a very talented guitar and banjo player who was blessed with a beautiful voice; and Peter's brother Christopher and Dane Lanken, both good bass singers. For a while Dane also played electric bass. Still later, Ron Doleman would sit in on fiddle when Peter's sister, Phyllis, came along to play the piano. After Dylan went electric in the spring of 1965, we did too. Chris, who was a good craftsman, made Kate a fake-fur guitar with an amp and speaker. It was a work of art, but the big wooden tuning pegs that were soldered onto the gears started falling off and the instrument could only be tuned with a pair of pliers. Chris also designed and made himself a bass in the shape of a belt buckle. It was hollow except for the neck and the buckle frame, and was another work of art. Both these instruments belong in a museum. We never had an actual drummer other than Jack, who occasionally tapped out a beat on the back of a guitar.

The sloppy stage presence and endless tuning of the Mountain City Four, now x 2, was something Kate and I would take with us later when we started doing concerts as Kate and Anna McGarrigle. At first critics slammed us for what was perceived as a lack of professionalism, like forgetting an instrument or a capo in the dressing room and holding up the show to go backstage and get it. But over time the audiences grew to expect a certain amount of chaos. I never felt comfortable on stage, so the informality helped me relax. When we were too rehearsed, which wasn't often, both Kate and I sometimes found ourselves wishing for something to go wrong.

Kate used to tell this early story of the stage. In 1971, when she was an unknown, unsigned artist, she took a solo gig at an afternoon folk festival on Long Island. Kate was riveting in an urban coffee house setting, but she was in the suburbs now and she wasn't getting through to the audience who talked loudly throughout her set, almost as if she wasn't there at all. This is what some audiences do when they don't know who you are. The final straw came when a dog wandered up the stairs onto the stage, causing the audience to howl with laughter. She broke down in tears and had to leave the stage, but she had a good story to tell and would laugh hysterically, tears streaming from her eyes, when she got to the part about the dog.

Apart from a couple of early performances by Le Trio Canadien that our mother attended, our parents didn't come to our shows. Our father, whose musicality we inherited, didn't think there was much of a future to be had in music, or at least in show business. He thought it was a seedy business and would not have tolerated us singing in bars. Because we were performing in coffee houses, where folk audiences appeared genuinely interested in the music, he never voiced an objection. He liked and respected Jack and Peter and he and our mother allowed seventeen-year-old Kate to go off to New York with them to see Bob Dylan at Town Hall in April 1963.

I was already in New York with my friend Gail Kenney, staying with friends of hers on Gramercy Park, one of whom was an artist who was painting a big red bull's eye in the hard-edge, op-art style. I stayed out all night with his roommate and spent the dawn on Delancey Street sharing a mickey of rum with the homeless while warming our hands over the blazing fires these men had lit in big oil barrels. The scene was post-apocalyptic; in the early sixties, that part of the city was practically in ruins.

The next day, Kate and I literally bumped into each other on 42nd Street. "Guess who I ran into in New York? My sister!" We must have called my mother from NYC and found out about Grandpapa dying. He was in hospital when we left. We offered to come home immediately, but she wouldn't hear of it and told us to have a good time. We made it home for his funeral.

That night we all went to the Dylan concert at Town Hall, a show which Harold Leventhal was promoting, and Dylan's first in a real New York City concert hall.* The MC4 had met Harold Leventhal on one occasion, when he was in Montreal staying with impresario Sam Gesser. Sam hosted a showcase in his Marcil Ave.

---

* Six months later, Dylan played the larger and more prestigious Carnegie Hall. The MC4 drove down for that concert too.

living room of acts he wanted his friend Harold to see. The MC4 was one of these. After a short set, Mr. Leventhal came up to us and said something to the effect of "Come and see me when you're ready," then turned to Jack and said, "And you, big fella, take your hands out of your pockets." When Jack wasn't holding a guitar, he always kept his hands in his pockets, like Jack Benny. Jack went on for some time about how the great Harold Leventhal had deigned to speak to us. Harold Leventhal was an important figure in New York folk circles, but none of us at that time were ready to take that step, and it's probably just as well.

As Dylan sang, "The times, they are a-changin." By the end of 1963, the music of the Beatles, followed by the Rolling Stones, and all that this entailed, had arrived in North America, a sort of cultural WMD that obliterated the current North American music scene.

DEREK LAMB

(Anna)

In 1961, Derek Lamb, a British-born animator, was in Montreal working at the NFB. He wrote and designed Jeff Hale's *The Great Toy Robbery*, a spoof on England's Great Train Robbery of 1963. In it, Santa's sleigh is held up and looted on Christmas eve by a bunch of outlaws on horseback. The bad guys ride off clutching teddy bears. His follow-up film, done with Danish animator Kaj Pindal, was *I Know an Old Lady Who Swallowed a Fly*, based on Alan Mills' song about an old woman and her insatiable appetite. She died, of course, after swallowing a horse. In the evenings Derek could be found in Montreal's downtown coffee houses singing his trademark British Music Hall songs in a whispery, seductive voice. The Trio Canadien first ran into him at La Poubelle on Guy Street.

In 2005 Kate wrote:*

Every night when the sun went down
They left the Town were they did dwell
With their guitars they headed downtown
Kate and Anna and Michèle.

It was hootenanny night at La poubelle
Up stepped a bold, young British swell
With a voice so sweet, tongue in his cheek
He sang the songs of the Music Hall.

Over the years our paths would cross, both socially and professionally. After teaching film animation at Harvard and later in NYC,

---

* A couple of verses from the song Kate wrote about first hearing this talented, charming man. Derek died in 2005 and she and I sang it at his Montreal memorial.

in 1976 Derek was back in Montreal heading up the English Animation department at the NFB. John Weldon was now working there as an animator. *The Log Driver's Waltz*, a visual retelling of Wade Hemsworth's song, was completed in 1979. It was an important collaboration for all involved. John Weldon drew the nimble-footed log driver, alongside his colleague Eunice Macaulay,* Kate and I and the MC4 did the music soundtrack and Derek Lamb produced it. It was the best-known of the Canada Vignettes, a series of Canadian-themed shorts that ran on CBC TV all through the '80s.

When the drive's nearly over,
I like to go down
And watch all the lads as they work on the river.
I know that come evening
They'll be in the town,
And we all like to dance with a log driver.

In 1981, Derek and filmmaker Caroline Leaf (*The Street*, based on Mordecai Richler's story) turned the cameras on us with *Kate and Anna McGarrigle: A Portrait*.

---

* John Weldon and Eunice Macaulay won an Oscar in 1978 for *Special Delivery*.

DANE

(Anna)

October 13 was my father's birthday, and on this day in 1963 two boys on a red and white Lambretta scooter arrived unexpectedly at our place in Saint-Sauveur. They had driven up from Montreal to see our friend Nina Hinds, but she wasn't home. Her mother, thinking Nina might be with us, had directed them to our house.

Kate knew both boys from McGill. One was John Weldon, a cousin to Peter Weldon, founding member of the Mountain City Four, with whom Kate and I were now singing. At this time Kate was going out with Chris, Peter's younger brother, and they were both in engineering at McGill. The other boy was Dane Lanken, a tall guy with curly auburn hair, who owned the scooter. The two lived in Montreal West and had been friends since kindergarten. Their playful behaviour reflected this, as they constantly teased and poked each other, using their surnames to communicate the way teachers did. *Hey, Weldon! Hey, Lanken!* They were so unlike the boys I knew, who usually made a point of acting older than their years by taking up the pipe or wearing an ascot. My mother probably found them immature, but I remember our father liking them, and I was especially charmed by Dane. It was Canadian Thanksgiving weekend, because Dane remembers staying for dinner and that I wore a tuque on my head throughout the meal, to my mother's annoyance.

There's a photo from the 1930s of my father with some friends standing outside The Pub in Saint-Sauveur on a winter's day. His friends are all looking very cool, but not Daddy. He's clowning for the camera, eating a handful of snow. The woman with him (not our mother) appears to be laughing at his antics. On this day, I felt like that girl.

Dane wanted to be a filmmaker, not a "serious" avant-garde one as was in fashion then, but a comedic one along the lines of Buster

Keaton, his hero. On a subsequent visit to Saint-Sauveur he brought his father's old Bell & Howell eight-millimetre camera, and a few of us headed to the golf course along the base of the ski hills to shoot a spoof on golf starring Dane as a truly bad golfer. Golf was not the sexy sport it is today, with its youthful heroes Tiger Woods and Rory McIlroy. It was more an establishment sport played by older, conservative people in Bermuda shorts and silly white sun hats. I remember some of the golf patrons looking on disapprovingly as Dane, who was inexplicably wearing a long coat and holding the club in a prissy manner (pinkies outstretched), mocked the sport as he tried repeatedly to hit the ball.

HEARTS ARE TRUMP

(Anna)

Milton Street, one block north of Sherbrooke West, runs from Saint-Laurent to University, and there was a lot of *va-et-vient* (back and forth) on this street that connected the McGill campus to the Beaux-arts. Some of us had gone with John Weldon to watch a rehearsal of the McGill Players' Club, the university's student theatre troupe. I don't recall what the play was, but it had a quasi-dance component, so the piece must have been a recent creation, maybe even written by a student. One of the actors moving awkwardly about the stage with arms outstretched, spouting his lines and looking very self-conscious, was John's new roommate Philippe Tatartcheff. The two were sharing a basement apartment on Towers Street near Sainte-Catherine West, a gritty downtown neighbourhood between Guy and Atwater that my mother used to call the Valley of Broken Hearts.

It was a long way from Geneva, Switzerland, where Philippe was born. His family arrived in Montreal in the early fifties, eventually settling in Timmins, a gold-mining town in northern Ontario, where his father was the town doctor.

Step out on Main St. where the town and the forest meet
There's plenty of gold around, but it's four thousand feet underground.

—*from Philippe's song "Country Bar, Northern Star"*

Before coming to McGill, Philippe attended a French *collège classique* in that northern Ontario town, run by the Frères des écoles chrétiennes. I don't think his family was Catholic. Nonetheless, Philippe received a good old-fashioned religious education, just as Kate and I had. As a result, he was quite anticlerical.

By early 1968, when Kate and I shared an apartment on Côte Sainte-Catherine near Mont-Royal Avenue, we three had become good friends. There are some old black-and-white pics of a trip the three of us took downriver to Rivière-du-Loup in our mother's Peugeot 403, a car we insisted she buy after our father died but that she never really learned to drive because it was a shift. This trip was very much like the one Kate describes in her song "Matapedia," racing to catch that same ferry at Rivière-du-Loup across the St. Lawrence to Saint-Siméon on the north shore.

60 minutes 60 miles, 30 minutes 30 miles . . .
But I could not slow down, no I could not slow down.

This time, however, the three of us did stop on the way back, at the shrine of Sainte-Anne-de-Beaupré, where we lit votive lamps in the chapel before fooling around in the graveyard, covering all our bases as we taunted Death.

In the fall of 1968, the Beaux-arts suffered three labour strikes, starting with the student occupation of the school, followed by the professors and lastly the janitors walking off the job, effectively shutting down the school and mimicking the massive labour and student unrest in Paris in May 1968 that brought the French economy to its knees. By January 1969 the school was still in lockdown. I got a job soon after and never did go back to get my diploma.

Kate and Chaim Tannenbaum had worked up some Ma Rainey songs and performed them at the Yellow Door Coffee House in the McGill ghetto. Roma Baran, guitar player with Montreal folk artist Penny Lang, was at one of these performances, and a while later Kate was asked to sit in on piano with Penny's band. Chaim went off to England to continue his studies in philosophy at the University of London. Philippe went off to Paris to get a master's in French lit. In 1969 Kate and Roma took a break from school, split from Penny Lang's band, and went to New York to suss out the music scene. They were now a duo, with Kate on piano and Roma on guitar. The two became very adept country blues musicians, modelling themselves on black American blues artists Leroy Carr (piano) and Scrapper Blackwell (guitar), and referred to each other as Catherine Carr and Roma Blackwell, spiritual wives of the two blues legends. They took up the two Ma Rainey songs Kate and Chaim had done, "Oh Papa" and "Barrelhouse Blues," and were looking to add to their repertoire. The two of them were now going between Saratoga Springs and NYC.

Around this time, Kate called me in Saint-Sauveur, where I was staying with my mother while I nursed a broken heart and pondered my next move. She told me in passing that the new breed of musicians they'd seen in Greenwich Village folk clubs, namely the Gaslight and Gurdy's Folk City, were singing their own compositions. One of these new "singer-songwriters," as they were to be called, was Loudon Wainwright III. Kate was particularly impressed with his originality, his urgent vocal delivery and his unrelenting guitar strumming. Loudon had just been signed to Atlantic Records. He took inspiration from the street life of Boston, where he lived at the time, was politically incorrect and, when need be, called a spade a spade, or an Irishman a drunk.

> *Black Uncle Remus, he moans and sings*
> *His tears have rusted his banjo strings.*
> *You may call for Jesus or your mama maybe*
> *When your life's gummed up in the old tar baby.* *

Or

> *Mary Maguire and Big Frank Clark got drunk again last night*
> *I was waiting for my bus when they happened along*
> *Man, it was a beautiful sight.* **

---

* From "Black Uncle Remus" by Loudon Wainwright III, on his debut, self-titled record on Atlantic (1970).

** From "Central Square Song," also on Loudon's debut record.

The idea of writing a song intrigued me. I was alone in the house, my mother having gone off to Ma Wilkins's for a game of bridge. In the dimly lit living room, the old Steinway upright beckoned, and I sat down and wrote my first song, "A Heart Is Like a Wheel."* Being able to voice my sorrow at that time saved my life.

They say that Death is a tragedy
It comes once, and it's over.
But my only wish is for that deep dark abyss
'Cause what's the use of living with no true lover.

A couple of weeks later, Kate and Roma were in Saint-Sauveur and I played it for them. It was very rudimentary, as I never really played the piano after grade seven, but I remembered where the notes were and knew a bunch of chords. They worked it up for piano and viola da gamba before Roma moved on to the cello. The total effect was stark and eerily beautiful, and it became a signature song for them as they got better known on the east coast folk circuit. Kate and Loudon eventually hooked up and he moved to Saratoga.

After a long on-again, off-again relationship that had begun after my father's birthday in 1963, by the early seventies Dane and I were living in relative peace on the top floor of a brownstone on Sherbrooke West near Saint-Marc. He was an entertainment writer, reviewing movies and live music shows, at the Montreal *Gazette*, Montreal's English-language morning paper, where the writing of reviews and the layout of the paper was all done at night. Sometimes he wouldn't get in till 8 a.m. and we'd meet as I was leaving the apartment for my day job.

My evenings were usually free and I began co-writing songs with friends. I never liked writing lyrics, but some of the people around me were very good at it. In late spring of 1973, after the Montreal Canadiens

---

* Linda Ronstadt later shortened the title to "Heart Like a Wheel" when she covered it on her Grammy Award–winning album of the same name, released in 1974.

won the Stanley Cup, I wrote a song in French on the accordion about Henri Richard, the team's beloved captain, with Richard Baker, a young musician from BC (who would later be the guitar player in Doug and the Slugs). Henri Richard had announced his retirement in a year's time and the song was a plea to him not to leave the team: *Henri Richard, prenez pas votre retraite!* ("Don't retire, Henri Richard!") Richard Baker played it for André Perry, the Montreal producer who famously recorded John Lennon and Yoko Ono's "Give Peace a Chance" during their bed-in at the Queen Elizabeth Hotel in 1969. I should mention here that as a member of the press Dane was invited to the bed-in for World Peace. I tagged along pretending to be a photographer, but I was too star-struck to snap any pictures.*

The following winter, André proposed recording the Henri Richard song as a single. The idea was to release it in time for the 1974 hockey playoffs, but we needed another French song for the B-side and I asked Philippe, now back in Montreal, to help me write something. The song we banged out was "Complainte pour Ste-Catherine." It took us all of twenty minutes. André had a state-of-the-art studio in a former synagogue on Amherst Square, but for some reason the two songs for the single were recorded at Studio Marko, the same studio where Michèle Forest, Kate and I had done our one song demo in 1962, now expanded and in new digs on De La Gauchetière East. A ragtag bunch of friends accompanied me to the studio to play and sing on the session: Philippe, Chaim, Dane, Peter Weldon and Michèle. André called in his friend, local musician Lewis Furey, to overdub a droning Cajun-style fiddle on "Complainte."

The 45 rpm was released, but within days the Canadiens had lost in the quarter-finals, so the single didn't do much of anything, despite my deer-in-headlights appearance on a local French TV show geared to fourteen-year-olds, where I lip-synched the Henri

---

* John had always been my favourite Beatle. I owned his two little books of stories and drawings, *In His Own Write* and *A Spaniard in the Works*, as well as *En flagrant délire*, the French adaptation of *IHOW*.

Richard song while playing my red accordion. Nobody knew who I was, including me . . . Who the heck was I? Most people who go into showbiz have some idea of the persona they want to project. I had none. I loved the songwriting process, it suited my personality, but I never liked the stage. Still, the kids in the audience clapped enthusiastically on cue and I dutifully kissed a wildly popular host I'd never heard of. My friend Deborah Adler came with me to hold my hand. I joked later that she could just as easily have done it instead of me and no one would have been any the wiser. Deborah had danced with les Feux-follets and had a lot more verve and stage presence than I did. She would later inspire my song "Dancer with Bruised Knees":

For years we had been one with the stars
A pas de deux *of renown*
I'd leap and he'd catch me on the fly
But once I came crashing down.

Despite the Canadiens' loss and the song about Henri now being redundant, not all was lost. Most people who heard "Complainte pour Ste-Catherine" liked it, and when Kate and I were signed to Warner Brothers a while later, our producer, Joe Boyd, wanted us to re-record it.

Caroline Holland had gone to McGill with Kate, and she and I became close in the late sixties, taking road trips in her mother's car at the end of the school year to places such as Virginia and North Carolina. We liked the same pop songs and would sit enthralled, listening over and over to Harry Nilsson wail "Without You." Our earliest creative effort was "You Tell Me That I'm Falling Down," later covered by Linda Ronstadt. Audrey Bean was another co-writing friend. She was going out with Dane's brother Peter, and our first song was "Cool River," covered by Maria Muldaur.

I had an old upright piano, a guitar, an accordion and a Sony stereo deck with a stereo mic. It didn't have sound on sound, but you could mix down the two recorded tracks onto a Sony cassette machine and then transfer this back onto one track of the Sony deck, leaving an empty track for overdubbing harmonies. Audrey had a lovely voice, and the two of us did some nice tracks, one of which was the demo of "Cool River." Philippe and I, buoyed by our luck coming up with "Complainte pour Ste-Catherine," continued writing French songs on a regular basis with a mind to pitching them to Quebec artists of the day. The apartment at 1832 Sherbrooke West was a regular little Tin Pan Alley North.

Sometimes the inspiration came from news stories. In the daytime I worked for a community service organization called the Friends of St. Ann's (or as Jane used to call it, the Frauds of St. Ann's), and Philippe was a translator for the Protestant School Board of Montreal. The FofStAs, originally founded in Pointe-Saint-Charles, had moved to Côte-des-Neiges near Queen Mary Road, just around the corner from St. Joseph's Oratory, the massive shrine on the north side of Mount Royal where the infirm of the world flocked, hoping for a miracle cure.

This place came to be because of Brother Alfred Bessette, the humble gatekeeper of the Collège Notre-Dame, a boys' classical college. Better known as Brother André, the diminutive cleric overcame his struggle with nocturnal demons by praying to Saint Joseph.* Brother André had a special devotion to the saint and during his long stint at the college he developed the power to heal the sick. He never took credit for the miracles, always attributing them to Saint Joseph and promising to build a shrine in his honour. Construction on this monument started in the 1920s, and was well under way when Brother André died in 1937 at the age of ninety-one. By then his reputation as a miracle worker had spread far and wide. When his body lay in state in what was still just the crypt of

* Saint Joseph is the patron saint of the dying, but he's also a figure of derision in Quebec. When you say a man is a "Saint Joseph," he's usually a patient older man married to a much younger woman, henpecked, and who's not seeing any action—like Saint Joseph, husband to Mary and stepfather to Jesus, must have been.

the church, upwards of 500,000 pilgrims came from all over to pay their respects. Among them was our mother, Gaby, and three of her friends, who had been out having cocktails after work and were pretty well oiled when, on a lark, they hopped a tram over the mountain to stand for hours in the long queue that had formed at the base of the hill below the shrine. My mother remembered a circus-like atmosphere around this event. It was the place to be, like some kind of medieval Woodstock, with the faithful climbing the steep stairs to the shrine on their knees.

After Brother André's death, the money fairly poured in from people all over the world whose prayers to the saintly man had been answered, and building continued. It was a proper shrine with authentic relics: the near-saint's body in a stone tomb and his pickled heart in a jar set in a marble niche. By the late sixties, the shrine was near completion, the enormous space within the dome was finished, and a brand new Casavant five-manual pipe organ was installed. Unfortunately for organized religion generally, this occasion coincided with the new age of enlightenment in Quebec and a steep falling-off in church attendance. The original chapel in the crypt, chock full of crutches and rickety wooden wheelchairs hanging on the walls and from the ceiling, dusty old testimonials of Brother André's successes, had become a bit of an anachronism in this modern age, and maybe even an embarrassment to the emerging secular populace.

One fateful night in 1973, thieves gained access to the museum area and stole the heart of the Venerable Brother André. People had been pilfering from the shrine for years. In the late sixties, two girls I knew at the Beaux-arts turned up at school one day wearing priests' cassocks, the long black woollen robes with all the tiny buttons down the front. They had taken them from their hooks in the sacristy of St. Joseph's. There was something so funny about the girls, with their heavily made-up eyes and dressed in priests' clothes, that our drawing teacher had them model for us that day.

The theft of the heart, however, was a more serious matter. As Kate's Russian friend Slava Egoroff once said, "The heart is our antenna to God." Stealing a relic imbued with miraculous properties and holding it for ransom sounded like an art stunt, and the crime bore all the hallmarks of the 1970 FLQ kidnappings, still fresh in the collective memory of Montrealers. There were anonymous communiqués to the press, setting up clandestine midnight rendezvous for clues, and a ransom set at fifty thousand dollars for the heart's safe return.

Philippe and I were drawn to this macabre story, and because I was working just around the corner, we spent a couple of lunch hours snooping about the spooky old Oratory with the intention of writing a musical based on the missing heart, entitled *Sans coeur et sans béquille* ("Without a heart and without a crutch"). Philippe's familiarity with the Catholic arcana would stand him in good stead, as demonstrated in this sample of his lyrics:

Quiconque (a) fait un sacrifice
A droit à quelque récompense
Après cent ans d'injustice
Quelques siècles d'indulgences.
(Whosoever has made a sacrifice
Is owed some measure of recompense
After a hundred years of injustices [inflicted on us by the Church]
A few eons of indulgences [to shorten the stay in purgatory].)

During the Middle Ages, indulgences were the equivalent of "get out of jail but not quite for free" cards, which the wealthy aristocracy could buy from the Church to shorten their stay in purgatory should their souls end up there, and they were one of the bugaboos that started the Reformation. However, if you ended up in hell, indulgences would do you no good.

The search for the heart went on for over a year, and like all sensational news stories, the public's interest in it waned after a couple of months. Before long, everybody had forgotten about the missing heart. As I was writing the preceding, the big news story was the puzzling disappearance of Malaysian Airlines Flight 370. Three months on, there was nary a mention of it on those big American news channels that devoted all their resources for weeks on end to this one story.

Then, one day in late 1974, the heart turned up. It had been delivered *sub rosa* to the office of Frank Shoofey, the notorious underworld lawyer, who negotiated its return to the Oratory, minus the ransom. But by then the heart had lost its cachet. Some maintained it was never Brother André's heart to begin with, but that of a pig. This was around the time Dr. Christiaan Barnard, the South African heart surgeon, had transplanted the heart of a baboon into a human, where it beat for several days. So hearts were much in the news.

Now, with the heart safely back in the Oratory under lock and key, Philippe and I lost interest in the musical.

MONTREAL CLUBS AFTER 1965
(Anna)

By 1964, Moose Hall (the home of the Order of the Moose) was up and running, and there's a rare picture of us at that time—Kate, Jack, Anna and Peter, the four original MC4 members—taken by Brian Merrett, who had gone to hear someone else at the Wednesday night hootenanny and had one shot left on his roll and snapped it. We didn't know Brian then, but he and Dane would meet in the seventies through their mutual efforts to save many of Montreal's downtown landmarks threatened with demolition. The old cinemas fared particularly badly. Brian took many of the photos for Dane's *Montreal Movie Palaces*, published in 1993 by Penumbra Press.

Around 1967, Gary Eisenkraft opened the New Penelope on Sherbrooke West just a couple of blocks from Avenue du Parc. It was a big club with a real stage and sound system and lights, and was for "big" out-of-town acts like the Mothers of Invention, so not strictly a folk club. Next door to the Swiss Hut on Sherbrooke was the Country Palace, where bluegrass legend Bill Monroe once played. The MC4 never played either of these clubs. We were strictly amateur and performed in smaller venues.

Across the street from the Penelope was the Association espagnole, a more French-oriented club where Dane and I once saw fiddling legend Philippe Gagnon and his young disciple Dominique Tremblay playing twin stainless steel fiddles made by a Tremblay relative who owned a sheet metal factory. Our uncle Austin owned the Noorduyn factory that refurbished old Norsemans, but its main business was making stainless steel kitchen galley equipment and carts for Air Canada. I remember mentioning the steel fiddles to him and may have proposed he make a steel guitar in his factory, like the National. It could have been called the Norseman.

Love is a steel-guitar
Love is a battle-scar.

—from "Love Is" by Anna, Jane and Kate McGarrigle

COAST TO COAST

(Jane)

And it's on to South Bend, Indiana,
Flat out on the western plain
Rise up over the Rockies and down on into California
Out to where but the rocks remain . . .

The Gold Rush. The Movies. Jack London. John Steinbeck. What an aura California had, and what a powerful pull it exerted on us. Once Dave got the green light from UC Berkeley, we never looked back, never doubted the decision to walk away from our stable, secure life to try our luck in the Golden State. We were young, we had skills, times were good. Excitement mounted by the day.

The first step was US residency. We had a warm welcome from the American vice-consul in Saint John, who offered us the choice of temporary visas at fifty dollars each or permanent visas at a hundred dollars per. After about one minute's thought we splurged on permanent visas, a good call, as it turns out. The civil rights movement was gearing up in the United States, and in line with its ideals, the Hart–Celler Act was passed a year later by Congress to rebalance immigration quotas. The new system accepted more immigrants from Asia and Africa into the United States, thus fewer from Canada and Western Europe. By 1968, the green card that had been virtually assured to Canadians and Brits became as scarce a commodity to a Canadian as it had previously been to a Korean.

In early May 1964, we packed a few belongings, some clothes, books and records, and left them to be shipped once we had a permanent address. We tidied up our affairs in New Brunswick, said goodbye to our friends, and jumped into the MGA for the first lap of the trip, Fredericton to Montreal, where we stayed with Dave's folks until our official departure. We said goodbye to the Dows, then

Gaby and Kate and Anna and a few friends at Sherwood Crescent. We took a quick run up to Saint-Sauveur to say a last goodbye to my father and a few more friends who had gathered at the house. As we were walking out to the car, Daddy pressed a small packet into my hand, a folded and refolded twenty-dollar bill, his habit whenever he gave us paper money. "Take Davey out to dinner somewhere nice," he said. Then he gave me a hug. "Ah, Janie darling, I wish I was going with you."

He half meant it. A month before, he had said in a letter, "Janie Dear, How I envy you and Davey and your proposed California odyssey—'Youth will be served.'" He went on to tell me about his grand-uncle John McGahey, who prospered in California and, after not being heard from for fifty years, started sending cheques for a thousand dollars at a time to Grandmother McGarrigle. No wonder Daddy was high on the place. There was another grand-uncle on Daddy's side, Philip Conway, who went to California as a "forty-niner" during the 1849 gold rush and left behind a tinted photo taken in a San Francisco studio but, alas, no history of windfalls for Grandmother McGarrigle.

"Come and see us," we urged my father.

"We'll see," he said.

We had an open, leisurely itinerary at the front end of the trip. We stopped by the Parliament Buildings in Ottawa, where we said goodbye to Jim Regan, a friend from New Brunswick who was now working in the office of Prime Minister Lester Pearson. At the time, Canada was about to get its own flag and many designs had been under consideration, now narrowed down to a few prototypes that were in a safe in Pearson's office pending a final choice. Jim showed us photos, signalling which version he favoured. Dave's parting advice: "Run it up the flagpole and see who salutes."

We detoured up to Georgian Bay for more goodbyes and enjoyed a few days of cottage life in Muskoka, then on to London, where we stopped overnight. We officially crossed into the United States at Port Huron, Michigan, and were issued our landed immigrant papers with instructions to report our whereabouts to the Department of Justice every January from then on. Only a few days after previewing the new Canadian flag, we were cruising under the Stars and Stripes.

Our route took us through Flint, Michigan, home of GM's Buick and Chevrolet factories during the glory days of the American car industry, a hard, gritty place that feels just like its name. We hit it during the early afternoon, and I was taken aback by the amount of traffic around us. I'd never seen so many cars in one place, and the noise was terrible. Surrounded on all sides by GM's behemoths, our little British sports car felt like a rowboat in a fleet of navy destroyers.

There may have been a softer aspect to Flint, but we didn't linger to find out, pressing on to Benton Harbor for a night, then along the shore of Lake Michigan to Chicago, where we treated ourselves to a nice dinner with Daddy's twenty bucks and stayed a few days to enjoy the beautiful Midwestern city.

After racing across Iowa and Nebraska, with a stop in Denver, we drove Highway 6's steep, twisty ascent to Loveland Pass, where we crossed the Rockies at twelve thousand feet, with a stop at the observation point that marks the Continental Divide. As you look to the west, the rupture in the earth is an awe-inducing sight, and in retrospect this was a hugely symbolic moment for the two pilgrims who had made their own breakaway to the Pacific. But we just took in the vast beauty of it all and continued on our journey, inching down the western side of the pass, seven thousand feet of steep hairpin turns, through a raging snowstorm—it was the fifth of June—till we reached Vail, Colorado. We pushed on to Salt Lake City for a visit to the Mormon Temple, thence to Reno, our last stop before the San Francisco Bay Area. At the time, Reno was known to the outside world as a quickie divorce capital for glamorous movie stars, and a gambling paradise. We wanted to try our luck at the tables, and looked for an elegant casino where a tuxedoed James Bond type might be playing *chemin de fer* nearby. But we found only seedy gaming joints and sad-faced losers wandering South Virginia

Street, the main drag, folks who had literally lost their last nickel and had no way of getting home.

Sitting in a coffee shop having breakfast the next day, we overheard the owner telling a customer how one of his regulars wouldn't be in that morning; he had been shot the night before in a bar down the street. It was like travelling back in time to the Old West, good preparation for our visit to Virginia City, Nevada, a ghost town that had been a thriving centre at the time of the Comstock Lode. The office of the *Territorial Enterprise*, a newspaper Mark Twain wrote for in the 1860s, is now a historical site open to visitors, as is Boot Hill, made famous in Western movies as the final resting place of desperadoes who died "with their boots on." I had always credited Boot Hill to Hollywood screenwriters, but there are many Boot Hills scattered around ghost towns in that part of the country.

We had crossed the Rocky Mountains and the great Salt Lake Desert, and we would finally cross the Sierra Nevadas at seven thousand feet, then "down on into California," as Kate's song goes. The interstate took us through Donner Pass, named for the Donner Party, who left Independence, Missouri, in April 1846 in a wagon train bound for California. They would have had to cross the Sierras before winter set in, and for a multitude of reasons they didn't make it in time. More than half of the original party perished, frozen or starved to death, on the wrong side of the ten-thousand-foot peaks, the survivors being rescued late in the winter of 1847.

But our thoughts were not with those ill-fated pioneers. We were light-hearted and enjoying the gradual descent to the gold country of the Sierra foothills. About twenty miles west of the Nevada state line, we stopped at the California Agricultural Inspection Station, where agents in booths confiscated fresh fruits and vegetables from out-of-state cars to head off out-of-state pests. We turned over a few oranges to the agent.

"Where are you folks from?" he asked.

"Montreal, Canada," we told him.

"Welcome to California," he said, and waved us on. We were in!

A hundred miles later, we had bypassed Sacramento and were within range of Berkeley. For the last eighty miles, the interstate median was landscaped with flowering pink and white oleanders, and on either side of the freeway, acre after acre was planted with orchards and crops of all kinds. As promised, our new land was lush and bountiful.

Because Dave would be going to UC Berkeley, we thought we'd want to live in the East Bay. We were ready to get off the road, so we committed to the first place we saw. It was a small apartment adjoining the owners' home on College Avenue in Oakland, just over the Berkeley city limits. It was adequate, a bit on the gloomy side, with heavy drapes and dark velour furniture and crocheted doilies everywhere, but the price was right. Too late, we realized that the elderly couple who owned it were passing strange. They both wore green plastic eyeshades, and smelled of "old"—not unclean, but musty. They carped at each other as they came and went with sheets and blankets, and barked at us to be careful with their things. We had a furtive consultation and decided we could hack it for a month, since we'd already paid and had nowhere else to go and no jobs.

We went into San Francisco the next day and started the search. Dave got hired on right away at Bechtel Engineering, but I held out through several interviews for a good fit. I learned that Canadians and Brits were prized in San Francisco for being smart and hard-working, so I could afford to be selective. I answered a promising ad in the *San Francisco Chronicle* for a girl Friday in a small firm of real estate developers. I had a good feeling about the place when I met Barbara Sutton, the girl I would be replacing, and it got even better when I saw how deferential the partners were to Barbara. Working conditions in Bill Duffie's office had spoiled me a bit, but it looked as though Barton Development would meet that standard. One of the partners, Peter Salz, saw from my resumé that I spoke French and chatted with me for a bit in French, then gave Barbara the thumbs-up. French wasn't in any way needed for the job, but Peter was a European by birth and a cosmopolitan type who liked the idea of having someone around he could speak French with. My new office was on the twenty-third floor of the Russ Building on Montgomery Street, the swankiest address in San Francisco's financial district. I started work the next day.

Our living situation quickly became a bit of a nightmare. During the day, in our absence, Mrs. Y, the landlady, was in and out of the apartment, and quite brazen about it, commenting about the bed not being made or the dishes left in the sink. At night, through the walls, we could hear the old geezers fighting with each other till all hours. We came home one evening to find Mrs. Y waiting in our apartment to let us know she had sent a piece of our mail to the FBI. We asked her why in the world she would do such a thing, and her explanation was that the envelope's return address was a PO box in Sacramento, the state capital, and had instructions not to forward. From that, she deduced that we were Canadian spies. She added, darkly and ominously, that she'd never forgotten the Rosenbergs, not exactly on point, unless she was hinting that we were Jewish, a mistake that, for some reason, many other people made when we first lived in San Francisco.

We dreaded going home after work and did everything we could to postpone it. We made new friends daily and met them for drinks after work at places that served complimentary food during happy hour. One night it might be spaghetti, another night hot dogs. Often we landed at Paoli's for the fried zucchini sticks and meatballs. There was a bar called the Admiral Duncan that served fifteen-cent vodka martinis along with a cheese and cold cut buffet, and we went there at least two nights a week. We went out for proper dinners too, anything to avoid going home, but sooner or later we had to get on the bridge to the East Bay.

We arrived back at the flat on the late side one night to find Mr. and Mrs. Y in our apartment taking a floor heater apart. They were both in their green eyeshades, the old guy on his knees reaching down under the floor, his missus crouched over him giving him unwanted advice. He snarled at her, "Shut up, you old bitch. What do you know about it, anyway?" She yelled something back at him.

The next day we went back for another look at a one-bedroom flat on Nob Hill at 1457 Jones Street, between Washington and Jackson. The living room window had a sliver of a view of San Francisco Bay, or so we convinced ourselves. It was a bit more than we had planned on paying but a great location and with a landlord who seemed sane, so we signed up and moved in shortly thereafter.

Meantime, I expected every day to hear from the FBI, grim deportation scenarios playing out in my head. I confided in Peter Salz, my new employer. He had been a US intelligence officer during World War II, and knew somebody he could call at the regional FBI office. Peter's friend told him we could relax, they were used to hearing from cranks. Good news, and eventually we received the mail Mrs. Y had intercepted: it was from the California Department of Motor Vehicles and contained our new driver's licences.

Dave left his job at Bechtel and started the fall term at Berkeley, specializing in computer science. A month later, Mario Savio launched the Free Speech Movement, and all hell broke loose on the Berkeley campus. Dave was aware of the movement that was going on around him but not involved in it. We held liberal political views but were not activists, beyond stating our opposition to the war in Vietnam, a position that sometimes landed us in hot water with the new people we were meeting. Many of them were quite invested in the military, having already done their national service, or were still in the army, serving out their draft duty at the San Francisco Presidio or Fort Ord in Monterey. A few times we heard, "Why don't you go back to where you came from if that's how you feel?" As required, Dave had reported to his draft board as soon as we arrived, and received a deferment; he was both a student and married, and was classified 1-Y.

Within days, we felt like established San Franciscans, which is generally the experience of people who move there. Though it dates back to the 1770s, the city did not come into being in any real way until the time of the gold rush, and has always opened its arms to newcomers of all stripes. San Fransisco has a history of tolerance and acceptance, and it's not an accident that the gay movement took hold there, or that it was the epicentre of the rock movement and other cultural phenomena of the 1960s.

I found the mobility between social strata and ethnic groups a refreshing change from Canadian cities, which tended to be a bit stuffy about their old families and whether your work was white-collar or blue-collar, not to mention the language divide that was particular to Montreal. My boss Peter Salz, and his wife, Elise, were wealthy secular Jews who could have schooled their kids anywhere, but they sent their oldest son to Gonzaga University in Spokane, Washington, a Jesuit institution, so he could learn to think, said Peter. That was an eye-opener. Jewish people in Montreal did not send their children to Catholic universities.

Memorial Day weekend in 1965 marked the first anniversary of our move to the United States, and on the holiday Monday, May 31, we were out sailing on San Francisco Bay with friends. We had chartered a Rhodes 19 and sailed it to Sam's, a dockside restaurant in Marin County where you could tie up for a few hours and have a Ramos Fizz and some brunch.

We left Sam's and were tacking back and forth toward the city, enjoying the view of its many hills rising up as the fog burned off. Searching out our apartment with binoculars, we could see smoke where our building should have been, so we cut the day short to get home and check things out. Thankfully, our building was safe, but there was a note from my co-worker Don Zimmerman pinned to the door of our apartment. It read, "Jane, please call your sister Kate right away." The news would have to be very bad for Don to make the long trip back and forth across the Golden Gate Bridge on a holiday.

It was as bad as it could be. My poor father's lungs had finally given out and he had drawn the last of the precious breath he'd fought so long and so hard to keep.

It hit me very hard. He had written to me shortly before we left Fredericton, mentioning that he'd caught cold working outside in

Saint-Sauveur "with not a lot on in the way of clothes." I think that was a marker in the general decline that started when we moved to Sherwood Crescent. I remembered the letter while I was packing for his funeral, and wept bitter tears for not having paid more attention, for having gone away and left him.

I flew home alone, leaving Dave to write his final exams, and wept from airport to airport. Uncle Lorne met my flight and drove me to Sherwood Crescent, where Kate and Anna and Gaby were waiting, along with a few friends who were there to prop us up. I took some tranquilizers that a friend was offering and had an extreme reaction, crying hysterically one minute, laughing maniacally the next.

Most of that week is a blur except for two clear recollections. On my first day home, I spent about an hour alone in the room at the funeral parlour where my father was laid out while everyone else went for a bite to eat. It was unquiet and disturbing in the room, and I felt a prickly sensory discomfort all through my body. I had to fight down the urge to run out of the room. I wondered if it was his restless soul not yet settled in its place in eternity. I remained by my father's side, but was immensely relieved when someone came an hour later to spell me.

The other memory is of an evening after the funeral when Gaby and Kate and Anna and I went up to Saint-Sauveur together. Auntie Anna came up on her own the next day to stay for a bit. Some people dropped by that evening, perhaps Uncle Austin, who lived in Saint-Sauveur, perhaps a few neighbours, and we were all in the living room listening to Auntie Anna play the piano. We were singing along with her and the phone closest to the living room started to ring with its loud, insistent peal. Gaby asked Aunt Anna to stop the music, as she feared the caller would find us disrespectful to Frank, having music when we were supposed to be in deep mourning. That started a brief, heated argument about what Frank would have wanted or what he would have done in the circumstances, all this time the phone still ringing off the wall. We did finally stop the music and someone answered, but I knew Frank would have kept playing and singing. Death would not have trumped music.

It was a long time before I could think about my father without crying, and even now, fifty years later, certain memories of him fill my eyes with tears. Kate and Anna and I are so much his daughters, carrying our emotions and irrational superstitions right at the surface, so easily transported by dreams and fantasy. He was the master dreamer who had big dreams for us, and it is unutterably sad that he didn't live to see how far Kate and Anna took music, his great passion. As for me, I didn't become a concert pianist or diplomat, which he'd hoped I would, but I married well, something of great importance to him when it came to the females of his tribe, and got myself to California to start a new branch of the family.

IN THE UN-MERRY MONTH OF MAY
(Anna)

In mid-April 1965, Kate went off to Survey School, a month-long course that McGill's second-year engineering students attended at the end of their school year to familiarize themselves with the tools and techniques of surveying. The students didn't choose their particular engineering specialty until the third year, and surveying would be useful to someone taking up civil engineering or architecture. The Survey School was off-campus in the Laurentian town of Saint-Gabriel-de-Brandon, an hour and a half's drive northeast of Montreal. There the predominantly male students were housed in motels, two to a room. Kate and her roommate were two of only six girls in second year.

On McGill's downtown campus, the engineering students dressed like the young professionals they were soon to be. With their slide rules and T-squares poking out of their bookbags, they appeared to have a greater sense of purpose than, say, the shaggier arts students clutching their dog-eared books of poetry. Survey School was a place where the young engineers could let down their hair as they tromped about in jeans and cut-offs, in sun or rain, with plumb bobs, transits and theodolites.

Kate had taken her guitar along, and when she wasn't working on surveying assignments, she would have shown off the Joseph Spence pieces she had taught herself to play by listening to a Folkways recording of this Bahamian guitarist. For many years the only person besides Kate whom I had heard play these intricate tunes in that syncopated picking style was American guitar virtuoso Ry Cooder. Many Canadians are familiar with Cooder's adaptation of Spence's "Happy Meeting in Glory," the catchy theme to Stuart McLean's popular *Vinyl Café* on CBC Radio in Canada and NPR in the United States.

By the time Survey School was out in mid-May, Kate and fellow student Caroline Holland had become good friends. It was Caroline who dropped Kate in Saint-Sauveur that weekend on their return from Saint-Gabriel. She was headed to her family's lake house on Lac-des-Seize-Îles, about a half-hour's drive from our place. While they off-loaded Kate's stuff, it was discovered that one of them had ended up by mistake with a hairpiece belonging to one of the other girls in engineering, the one girl who did not see Survey School as an opportunity to dress down and who instead dressed up for her fieldwork in tight pants and heels, with the hairpiece to augment an already elaborate hairdo. It was a light moment, and my parents were very happy to have Kate home again.

I had recently completed my first year as a full-time student at the Beaux-arts and was already working as a temp for the summer. Now Kate was looking for summer employment, and she began riding the morning train downtown with me to check out the job prospects that McGill posted on campus for its students.

On May 30, in the evening, our father drove from Saint-Sauveur to Montreal. We were all a little surprised to see him. This was his busy summer rental season, but he hadn't been feeling well and was probably seeking out the warmth and security of his family. He retired to the bed in the small alcove off the living room, and apart from getting him a cup of tea and keeping the noise level down, I don't remember any of us paying much attention to him. Looking back, I recall that his face was greyer, but he displayed no outward signs of distress.

The following morning, when Kate and I went to kiss him good-bye before leaving for the train, he handed us five dollars and asked us to get him a mickey of Demerara rum while we were downtown. "It's what keeps me alive." And he was out of the stuff. Our mother would have been at home with him until she left for her half-day job at Marconi just after lunch.

Kate met me when I got off work at 5 p.m., and after picking up his rum at a downtown liquor store, we headed for Central Station, taking the shortcut through Eaton's across the main floor. While we were there, the bottle of rum that Kate was carrying slipped out the bottom of the brown paper bag and broke on the floor. There wasn't time for us to go back to the Commission des Liqueurs or we would miss our train.

When we got home, there was a note on our apartment door telling us to ring the neighbour's bell. The woman who lived across the hall told us that our father had phoned our mother at work, asking her to come home immediately. An ambulance was called, and because our father couldn't breathe in the reclining position, he rode in the seat up front beside the driver, leaving no place for our mother. The attendants told her she would have to take a cab to the Queen Mary's Veterans Hospital on Queen Mary Road just west of Côte-des-Neiges, where my father was an outpatient. We would later learn that our mother had difficulty getting a cab and this delayed her arrival at emergency. Once there, she at first didn't recognize the unconscious figure slumped over in a wheelchair as her husband. An admitting clerk was attempting to get information from him. She was frantic. "Can't you see the man is dying?" she pleaded with the clerk. Our father had no identification on him, and without a name they couldn't find his file. The poor man died right there in the chair.

Back at the apartment, the two of us waited anxiously for word from our mother. It was some time before we heard the familiar sound of the heavy door in the lobby clicking shut. Kate and I were born optimists, and neither of us was prepared for what we were about to hear. We ran out to the landing and saw our poor mother clutching the railing, sobbing, as she climbed the stairs to our first-floor apartment. Our uncle Lorne had gone to the hospital to help out and he was at her side. She looked straight at us through thick tears and said dramatically, *"C'est fini."* The words were delivered as if this was the last scene in a sad film.

If he had had his rum, would it have kept him alive as he always claimed it did, at least for a little while longer? Did Daddy's spirit leave his body at precisely the moment the bottle of rum hit the floor, releasing its own sweet, life-giving spirits? Later, Kate and I would convince ourselves of that paranormal possibility.

It was a long time before our mother forgave herself, suffering "a remorse of conscience," as she called it, for treating our father's illness too lightly. I think we all felt a certain amount of guilt when it came to our father and his poor health, especially over the last few years, as Kate and I began slowly drifting from the family unit to make lives for ourselves, lives that didn't include our parents.

Our mother didn't like to be the bearer of bad news and charged Kate with calling Jane in San Francisco. We were now in the unenviable position of having to call an undertaker. Our mother remembered that the brother-in-law of our father's best friend worked for a funeral home. He knew our family and this brought us some comfort. Back then, undertakers were religion- and language-specific, like parish churches. His outfit catered to Irish Catholics, which our father was. My mother had me pick out the clothes he would be buried in. We were having a warm spring, but in 1965 death was still a sombre affair, the swinging sixties notwithstanding, and the deceased in a light-coloured suit would not have done. Because he was dressing for eternity, I chose an old-fashioned navy with a grey pinstripe and a double-breasted jacket I thought made him look dignified, like Sir Anthony Eden, if out of style.

In death the foot points downward like a dead bird's. Could ballet have been inspired by dead swans, which ballerinas so often portray? In any case, our father did not require shoes. The undertaker came by the apartment the next morning to collect the clothes and told us our father would be ready for viewing that evening. All those bad dreams of Daddy dying had come true.

Jane flew in from San Francisco that evening. Friends, boyfriends old and current, and family came to support us and we got through it. The makeup artist saw fit to comb some brown dye through our father's white hair to make him look younger, eliciting positive comments from some ladies as to how well he looked. I was very touched when my old boss with hair the colour of money and the switchboard lady from the stock brokerage firm arrived to pay their respects. She was wearing the little black hat with the veil over her face. I hadn't seen them in more than a year.

Our father's funeral took place at the English Catholic church we attended in TMR, the one we all found a tad bland. We asked the organist to play his favourite song, a ditty about a little brown bird singing that he used to play on the piano at night, and that we listened to from "the small beds of our childhood, counting stars through the wavy glass of the old storm windows."*

For practical reasons, he was buried in the Côté family plot in Cimetière Notre-Dame-des-Neiges, where Gaby's maternal grandparents Édouard Côté and Catherine Bannon were buried, along with their eldest daughter, Dora Côté Vaillancourt, who died in childbirth at seventeen. Our mother and her sisters had access to the plot through matrilineal succession and Gaby had often told us that when her time came, that's where she wanted to go. It made sense for Frank to be there too.

For a long time after his death I had a recurring dream. I was walking along a busy street, maybe St. James Street, and I could see him up ahead of me in a grey overcoat but hatless, which was strange because our father always wore a hat, even in the house. I would call out, "Daddy," and he'd turn around and wait for me. Looking into his red-rimmed hazel eyes, I asked hopefully, "You didn't die after all?" He never answered, just stared back at me with his crooked, enigmatic smile. I always woke with a sad, hollow feeling.

The Brown Bird Song

All through the night there's a little brown bird singing,
Singing in the hush of the darkness and the dew,
Sweeter songs of love than the brown bird ever knew.
Would that the song of my heart could go a-winging,
Could go a-winging to you, to you.

---

* From "Counting Stars," lyrics by Ian Vincent Dow, Jane's son, on *The McGarrigle Christmas Hour* (2005).

BOB DYLAN

(Anna)

In the summer of 1965, Dane and I went to Newport, Rhode Island, by scooter to see Bob Dylan. John Weldon and Bruce MacKay, another Mo' West boy who also drove a Lambretta, came with us. Dane took the eight-millimetre camera along to document our trip, leaving a few feet of unexposed film to capture Dylan. The atmosphere at the festival grounds was charged as we rolled up on the scooters. Mike Bloomfield was on stage and Dylan would be next up; we had to hurry. People were desperate to get their hands on tickets. Dane had an extra two that he'd bought for friends who couldn't make it. A guy at the gate pleaded with him and Dane sold them to him at face value. But when we got to our seats, the person sitting next to us was not the guy Dane had so kindly sold the tickets to—he'd sold them to a scalper.

After a few solo acoustic numbers, Dylan picked up an electric guitar and brought out his band. The crowd was on its feet or standing on chairs and Dane had to lift me up so I could see the stage. We were among those who were thrilled to hear his songs awash in electric guitars, with the added punch of bass and drums. Those who only liked their Dylan dry and straight-up were said to have booed him, though neither of us remembers hearing any booing. We were too far away to get any decent footage, but Dane captured a few frames of BD returning for his encore, a tiny black figure coming up a staircase onto the stage which was bathed in a red wash, and looking very much like the Devil himself rising from hell. I'm sure his angrier fans would concur with this description.

By early 1967, Dane had acquired an old Bolex sixteen-millimetre to shoot a film he would enter in a competition for young filmmakers held later that summer at Montreal's Man and His World, Expo 67. The film was entitled *Athlone and Aspidistra*, and was listed as an

Athlone Stinson production. Athlone Stinson was Dane's pseudonym, taken from an exit on the Métrolitaine where you got off for the National Film Board and for the Town of Mount Royal. The film, a love story, starred Dane and me in a series of outdoor scenes, including a picnic in a field of daisies. While Dane and I beat off the June blackflies, Kate and John Weldon operated the camera. The post-production was done in Dane's brother's bedroom in Montreal West; Peter was away studying architecture in Edinburgh. While Dane spliced film—there were hundreds of strips of the black-and-white emulsion hanging from the floor-to-ceiling bookshelves—I drew quasi–art nouveau designs on the title cards containing the dialogue, which were then filmed, developed and inserted between the live-action sequences. It was a silent film, but it was around the time that Procol Harum's "A Whiter Shade of Pale" was being played non-stop on the radio, so I will always associate this psychedelic hit with *Athlone and Aspidistra*.

The film was delivered on time, and though it didn't win first or even second prize, it did receive an honourable mention and as I remember was the only film that got any laughs at the public screening late that summer. Oddly enough, it was John Weldon who became a filmmaker, an animator famous for the NFB's *Log Driver's Waltz*, for which Kate and I and the Mountain City Four did the soundtrack. It was one of the NFB's Canadian Vignettes that aired all through the 1980s on CBC TV, and may be the most popular film the NFB ever produced. Dane went on to become a journalist, an entertainment writer for the *Gazette* for ten years, later a feature writer for *Canadian Geographic* magazine.

GOOD ART
(Jane)

Life goes on. I went back to San Francisco. Dave finished up his master's degree and was recruited on campus by IBM. We moved to Russian Hill, to an apartment tucked away at the end of a little cobblestoned lane off Hyde Street, where the cable car line runs from Powell Street to Fisherman's Wharf. It had a spare room for company, a fireplace in the living room and a parking space for our new Mustang convertible.

There were changes where I worked, an amicable parting in the company, and Peter Salz took me with him to an eight-storey office building on Sansome Street that he had acquired with different partners. Don Zimmerman and his secretary Lee Cieski followed us and shared space in our office. Peter made me the assistant manager of the building and gave me an expense account. He put me in charge of tenant relations—his least favourite part of property management—and taught me how to keep books and read a balance sheet. He began renovating and redecorating the building, and sometimes took me to interior design shops in nearby Jackson Square, where we sifted through carpet samples and books of wallpaper. My help wasn't needed with aesthetic choices, but Peter was a sociable man and liked company on these jaunts. We often ended our morning at India House for a Pimm's cup and some curry.

Elise Salz was very knowledgeable about art and spent a day a week babysitting a Union Street gallery that belonged to a friend who was a society proctologist (very profitable, from what I could understand). Once in a while we dropped in on her and got her take on the paintings that were showing at the gallery.

Dave and I entertained Elise and Peter one evening not long after we moved to 22 Delgado, trying to reciprocate in some small way for the sailing trips on their beautiful yacht, the use of their place at Tahoe Tavern and other graciousness that went beyond good employee relations.

At the time, we had paintings of all sorts on the walls, and Elise went around and looked carefully at everything, not commenting much, except for one piece she thought was dreadful—"Jane, you have to take that down"—and another—"Now, that's good art." The good art was titled *Preparation for a Reindeer Bouillabaisse*, a thirty-by-forty-inch mixed media work on Masonite, bright reds and yellows and blues, with four small reindeer glued to it and painted over. The painter was Anna McGarrigle; the reindeer were from Chas. Hill Co., a florist shop owned by Dane Lanken's parents and where the artist helped out during the holidays.

FLOWER SHOP
(Anna)

Dane and his brother Peter were brought up on the family's twenty-five-acre farm on western Côte-Saint-Luc Road where their father, Uffe, grew chrysanthemums in long glass greenhouses to supply the Montreal floral trade. By the mid-1950s the city of Côte-Saint-Luc began expanding westward and their agricultural property and others like it were rezoned for multiple dwellings. The Lankens sold their farm in 1958 and the family moved to a split-level on a small lot in neighbouring Montreal West. To the two boys and their parents, Côte-Saint-Luc had been an Eden, a place that held so many fond early memories. Uffe was an amateur photographer, and there are photos of the little boys smiling as they posed beside big mum pots or astride their father's Farmall tractor. Dane, who was about thirteen at the time of the move, was particularly marked by this sudden change and the disappearance of his childhood home. Ten years later, he would talk his father into buying a 250-acre property in Eastern Ontario, a ninety-minute drive from downtown Montreal. The land was stony and dirt cheap and it was unlikely anyone would expropriate it soon.

After a short stint manufacturing Danish furniture, Dane's father returned to more familiar work. He bought a flower shop on Sherbrooke West at Prince Albert in Westmount and he and his wife, Gudda, had it for roughly fifteen years. The store had a regular staff of about seven people, but at Christmas and Easter, both peak times for florists, Dane and his brother were expected to help out. This was the case when they were still in school and later when they were working at other jobs. From the mid-sixties on, I became a regular, and Kate, Judy Hinds and Ron Doleman all worked there at some point. If you dropped into the shop to say hello to the Lankens, and they knew you had a driver's licence, Gudda might hand you the keys to one of their cars and ask you to take a rush funeral arrangement to some out-of-the-way place that wasn't on their driver's route. Funeral flowers are the bread-and-butter of the floral business and florists hate to see "Please omit flowers" in an obituary. But nothing annoyed them more than the green grocers who also sold cut flowers, these for a fraction of what the flower store would normally charge.

One very cold Christmas Eve, Dane and I took a carload of plants to the south shore, a vast suburban area that stretches for miles in all directions. Normally, every address was checked in the big Montreal Lovell street directory before a plant left the shop, but this was off-island. It was close to midnight when we got to Saint-Bruno, where the last poinsettia was going. One of the women at the shop, a sweet older lady, was famous for writing the addresses down wrong, often omitting a number, as in 145 instead of 1415. The writing on the label was in her hand. We were now at the top of Mont Saint-Bruno (one of the Monteregian Hills) and there was no such address. Dane, whose green thumb and love of plants is legendary, finally snapped. "FUCKING Miss B.," he said, and lowering the window of the VW Beetle, he threw the plant out into the snowbank. I felt badly for the plant but it sure felt good to be rid of that thing.

Miss B. had grown up on a horse farm. Her father bred race-horses and she had always played the ponies. I remember her sneaking out the door to meet her bookie on the street and handing him her picks for the day's races with a big wad of cash. I don't think she ever wrote down the wrong numbers for the horses. That kind of betting was illegal, but nobody in the store cared. In fact, I and others often joined her in the betting, but I never had her luck.

At the back of the shop, in her small, chaotic office, Gudda organized the orders for the day with Blackie, their old dog, lying at her feet under her desk. She might drink up to twelve cups of coffee over the course of the day (we used to count them), but her pulse never went above sixty beats per minute. There were coffee stains on everything and half-empty Styrofoam cups on all the surfaces in the office. Dane's father, Uffe, did all the heavy work, unpacking large boxes of flowers, de-thorning the roses, filling large cans of water to put them in and then carrying these to the display fridges at the front of the shop. He also made most of the big funeral arrangements, which could be composed of gladiolas, giant mums, carnations, various coloured pompoms and roses, eucalyptus, asparagus and leatherleaf ferns. The poor man had his hands in cold water a lot of the time, soaking the blocks of "oasis," a green foam that went in the bottom of the white papier mâché containers to hold the stems in place. He used to say his fingers felt like carrots, they were so stiff. I remember him telling us about a work dream he'd had. In it, he had to make a last-minute arrangement (for a funeral, of course) but with big floppy fish that he couldn't get to stand upright in the container. Uffe regularly made his own pickled herrings. His brain must have cut and pasted the wrong bits together that time.

The store came before everything else. A couple of times on Christmas Eve when they were all still working in the shop, Gudda sent me home to their house in Mo' West to put the turkey in the oven. They were Danes, and like most northern Europeans, they celebrated on the twenty-fourth. They were going to have that turkey no matter what, even if it was 2 a.m. when they sat down to eat, and everybody in a bad mood. The Christmas season was always an insane time of year at the flower shop, and it was hard to sustain a childlike appreciation for the feast.

Dane could always borrow one of his parents' cars on the condition that he return it to the shop before it opened in the morning. The parking was behind the shop and there were places for three vehicles. This was around the time the Front de libération du Québec (FLQ) was putting bombs in mailboxes or near post offices; the FLQ targeted federal property. The Westmount Post Office at Sherbrooke West and Prince Albert was right up against the shop to the east. Very late one night in December 1971, Dane returned his mother's Mustang to its spot behind the shop. Less than an hour later, a bomb exploded in the lane and blew out the back door and window of the shop. The car was shot full of holes, windshield and windows blown out.

There are other stories from the shop that can't be told in polite company and that usually involved the younger staff.

After selling the flower shop in 1974, the Lankens took it easy. They were both excellent cooks and there was lots of time now to go all out at Christmas and generally. After Kate moved back to Montreal with the kids, Gudda and Uffe behaved almost as de facto grandparents to both Rufus and Martha, whom they knew before Dane and I presented them with Sylvan in 1977 and Lily in 1979. The Lankens loved little children and gave them free rein in their house. Their living room was always strewn with building blocks and toy furniture that Uffe had made in his basement woodworking shop. It gave me great peace of mind to know that Sylvan and Lily were safe with Dane's parents when I had to work and Dane had come with me.

MY FIRST APARTMENT
(Anna)

In the summer of 1966, a year after my father died, I moved out of the family's apartment in TMR. I was twenty-one and had just completed my second year at the École des beaux-arts. My mother was furious with me for breaking up our family unit of three, now reduced to just Kate and Gaby. The family bonds had weakened with my father's death, and I took advantage and escaped into the world. As youth is said to be cruel, I felt little remorse. I wish now I hadn't been so insensitive. My mother always gave the impression of being independent, but I think this was because she was too proud to beg. I took it for granted she would get on with her life, just as I was doing with mine. I was too self-absorbed to see that she was alone, without a mate, and facing an uncertain future.

I thought if I told my mother where my new apartment was, this might placate her, maybe even interest her. Instead, she reacted with disgust. "Evans Street? You're not going down there. We couldn't wait to get out of that place!" I thought I'd discovered a charming, out-of-the-way corner of Montreal, but as fate would have it, my new place was less than a block from where the fabled Latrémouille home had stood on Ontario Street West, just east of Saint-Urbain, the setting for so many of the stories I had heard over the years. Turns out I hadn't escaped at all, but I did jog my mother's memory with the mention of Evans Street, and as she regained her composure she said wistfully, making the best of the situation, "I wonder if Dora Masson still lives in Evans Lane?" Here was a name I hadn't heard, but as usual my mother found it inconceivable that I wouldn't know whom she was talking about. "Oh, come on, Anna! You know, Dora, I went to school with her!" She said it louder. "Dora Masson! She lived there with her father. Her mother was dead." She added, laughing, "And there was a dirty old man who used to hide in the lane. We were always running to get away from him." Laugh laugh! My mother was probably about eleven or twelve when she had played in this lane with Dora, and they already knew about perverts!

By the late 1960s, most of the flats on the block-long street were taken up by students from the École des beaux-arts just up on Sherbrooke West at Saint-Urbain.* It was unlikely though not impossible that fifty years on, in 1966, Gaby's friend Dora still lived in the lane. But I had better things to do than go chasing after a spectre from my mother's past. I suspect she felt badly about not staying in touch with her inner-city friend after the Latrémouille family left the gritty downtown for the greener pastures of Westmount. If my mother hadn't boycotted my new place, she could have come to look for Dora herself. I don't know why, but I'm haunted by visions of little Dora. It's 1915 in Evans Lane. A small girl with dark braids, dressed in a pale grey smock of the day and long black stockings and slippers, is running away from someone.

I shared the sixty-dollar-a-month apartment with Klara Horne, a friend studying at McGill. Apart from it being cockroach-infested, which I discovered only after I had moved in, it was a cute corner three-and-a-half with vaulted windows and looked like an artist's studio. We had just been lectured at school by Albert Dumouchel, the godfather of Quebec printmakers, about how it was the role of the artist to work and, if need be, starve in a garret, not to concern himself with getting degrees and diplomas, which he saw as bourgeois trappings. He may have even advocated dropping out of school, the rationale being that the sooner you did this, the sooner you'd find your true artist self. I wasn't the only one scratching my head and wondering what the heck I was doing at school.

But the École des beaux-arts was an interesting place to be in the sixties, with the overlapping of artistic styles, abstract expressionism hanging on tenaciously as it was being nudged aside by pop

* The École des beaux-arts building is now home to the Office de la langue française, which is much mocked, at least by Montreal's disgruntled anglo minority.

art, op art and conceptual art. As mentioned, this was the era of the FLQ and the mailbox bombs, and the school's largely French student body not surprisingly embraced the separatist cause. The small Beaux-arts campus included the École d'architecture, whose entrance was on Saint-Urbain, and an old coach house that had been converted into a sculpture studio.

Midway between the McGill and École des beaux-arts campuses on Sherbrooke West stood the Swiss Hut, a resto-bar frequented by students from both schools. Back then McGill was left-wing, not the Ivy League American-style college it advertises itself as today, with many more radical, alternative types on campus than there are now. The Hut, as its name suggests, was rustic, with log walls and big banquettes that sat up to six or seven, all in very dark varnished natural wood, and getting darker with every cigarette smoked. It was Montreal's Cedar Tavern, that famous artists' bar in New York City. Coat racks in the form of huge stylized hands stood between the banquettes, with jackets hung on the big square fingers. The place had two rooms, an inside one where the French mostly sat and the outer one where the bar was and where the English sat, so the two solitudes analogy applied here as well. The waitresses were efficient, hard-boiled and middle-aged. The unsmiling Madeleine with her deeply scarred face was the favourite, a banged-up Jeanne Moreau. She served the food and drink and moderated arguments, many of them political, with "*Aye c't'assez là!*" ("Cut it out!"), making sure these didn't escalate to fisticuffs. My feisty roommate Klara, who liked a good argument, got herself banned from the place, at least temporarily.

One evening a sculpture student and committed separatist whom Kate and I used to hang around with told us, after far too many Labatt 50s, "If it comes down to a fight in the streets where I'm on one side and you're on the other, I would be obliged to shoot you!" He delivered this with an impish grin and we laughed it off, but I never forgot that moment, and every time there's an election in Quebec—as there is right now as I write—his words come back to haunt me.

My mother was so angry with me for leaving home that she rented out my room so I couldn't ever come back. A forty-something gentleman, recently divorced and working nearby, answered her ad in the TMR *Weekly Post*. During the interview, my mother inquired, in passing, if he and his ex-wife had any children. No, there were no children. His former wife hadn't wanted a family, he confided, adding that he'd undergone a vasectomy. I'm not sure why the new roomer needed to share this intimate detail of his sex life with my mother, but my mother seemed satisfied. A deal was struck and he moved in. Some time later, at a family gathering, she was telling her brothers and sisters-in-law about how she had rented out my old room to a single man, a virtual stranger. They were alarmed to hear this. Wasn't she concerned for Kate's and her safety? Not at all. Her new tenant was castrated.

Aside from the usual youthful shenanigans that happen in a first apartment, on at least one occasion the place was a hive of creativity.

In '66, both Kate and Dane had been in Vancouver. They hadn't travelled together, but they were part of the annual mass exodus of kids to the west coast. To get there, you either hitchhiked or took a "drive-away" car with two or three friends, which is what they had done. There were always more cars in the east and it was cheaper for a dealer to send a used car to another dealer by driving it than to pay to transport it on a train. After five thousand kilometres of pedal-to-the-metal driving, the cars delivered in this fashion were usually in need of transmission jobs.

That fall, the two intrepid travellers were back in Montreal and raving about something called a "light show," a west coast phenomenon, and they talked of putting one on in Montreal. Another friend, Brian Nation, already living in Vancouver but back in Montreal for a visit, was also on board. They commandeered Klara and me and our friend Carla Marcus, an artist, to help out. The three of us hadn't actually seen a light show, so we took our orders from those in the know.

The McGill Student Union was booked for the show. Klara was the only McGill student in good standing at this point, both Dane and Kate having flunked out (Kate temporarily), so she negotiated the rental of the hall. Visual projections were key for this multimedia spectacle. Overhead projectors were borrowed from McGill's audiovisual department, and baby oil and food colouring would be mixed on the glass and manipulated to the mood of the music. Kate would operate one of these that night and clean it up later. Dane located a strobe light and black lights.

Then the six of us—Klara, Kate, Dane, Brian, Carla and I—spent weeks around the rickety drop-leaf table in the apartment, making a couple of hundred hand-painted slides to slot into Kodak carousels. These would be projected onto the walls and the moving mass of people we were expecting to fill the big hall of the Union. The popular local band Sidetrack, fronted by Allan and Christopher Brown, two brothers from TMR, would provide the music with Dane on bass. Carla and I sewed minidresses out of thick silver crepe wrapping paper from Eaton's gift wrapping department for the two girlfriends chosen for their go-go-dancing abilities, who would be positioned on platforms on either side of the stage.

On the night prior to the show, we had a dry run of the finished slides, projecting them onto the wall of the building across the street from the apartment, to the puzzlement or perhaps delight of passersby. If Dora was still living in the lane, she may have seen this wild display.

Today, there is nothing left of Evans Street as I knew it then. The small corner building Klara and I were in, 146 Evans, was razed thirty years ago to expand the original Bell Telephone exchange that had gone up in the late 1920s and for which my mother's family home on Ontario Street West was expropriated and torn down. Makes one wonder about serendipity, or in this case reverse serendipity. Ma Bell both giveth and taketh away. Gaby's and Janie's first jobs, along with those of countless other young Canadian women, were on Bell Tel switchboards. This telecommunications behemoth was following us around, wiping out our pasts with its elephantine foot, but it couldn't take away our stories. Our stuff was safe in the ether—or at least we thought it was, until Edward Snowden's 2013 revelations about the extent of the cyber-snooping that's been going on.

"SISTERS McGARRIGLE"

(by Derek Lamb)

When first I heard the sisters sing
They were shy girls in their teens
And I was a young man in Montreal
Fresh from England, green.
Their voices in harmony sang a gentle lullaby
To entice the birds right off the bush
And spread love across the sky
Spread love across the sky.

And the first time I was invited
To play music at their home
They played piano,
Sang "Wayfaring Stranger,"
And I sang "Molly Malone."
Their mother was a fine lady
And I took a shine to their dad
He said to me, "Son, you sing so sweet,
Sure you're not an Irish lad?
Sure you're not an Irish lad?"
That was the finest compliment
Remembered to this day.
These are fond memories that do not fade away.
I found an old photograph
And I dusted off the frame
And in my mind the piano played
And the sisters sang again,
The sisters sang.

I'm just a poor, wayfarin' stranger
A-travellin' through this land of woe.
There's no sickness, toil or danger
In that great world to where I go.
I'm going home to see my mother,
I'm going there no more to roam.
I'm just a-goin' over Jordan
I'm just a-goin' to my home.

And now I wish for old times' sake,
In a reminiscing manner,
To be invited once again to sing with Kate and Anna.
Hear their voices in harmony sing a gentle lullaby
To entice the birds right off the bush
And spread love across the sky
Spread love across the sky.

PEACE AND LOVE
(Jane)

That we had rolled the dice and fallen into a feather bed was due in no small part to an accident of birth. Dave and I were born in 1939 and 1941 respectively, when so many men were overseas fighting in World War II and not at home starting families. When we came of age, there was less competition for everything we went after: entry to the United States, acceptance at a top school, good jobs, affordable housing in a jewel of a city.

After finishing his degree in June 1965, Dave began commuting to Silicon Valley, as it's now known, to work out of IBM's Palo Alto office. Working as a sales rep, he called on the Stanford Linear Accelerator Center (an atom smashing facility), Stanford Research Institute and Stanford Hospital, clients that would benefit from the scientific applications of IBM's new 360 mainframe computer. He took lots of ribbing about working for IBM, a conservative company known for its strict employee dress code—dark suit, white shirt, plain dark tie and matching socks—but the work was stimulating and he enjoyed his customers. They were mainly physicists and academics, a little more "out there" than run-of-the-mill corporate clients.

I walked or rode the Muni bus downtown to my job at 500 Sansome Street. I showed office space, drafted leases, collected rents, paid bills, prepared financial statements, supervised the day-to-day operations of the building and of course attended to the all-important tenant relations. The two buttons that were always lighting up on my dash were janitorial service and ambient temperatures. This is when my expense account went to work. For example, Tenant: "The cleaners skipped the mailroom again last night." Me: "You don't say! We'd better go out for a martini and talk about it." Or, Tenant: "Fred's office is too warm, mine is too cold. Can't you regulate it?" Me: "Yes, of course. Let me take you to lunch and we'll figure it out." The solution to the latter problem was to have "personal" thermostats installed in their offices; the thermostats were dummies but surprisingly effective. I wasn't exactly saving humanity, but I enjoyed the easy affluence of the 500 Sansome crowd and the bon vivant perks of the job.

Not long after he joined IBM, Dave was sent to Los Angeles to attend one of their charm schools, as those month-long indoctrination sessions were laughingly called. He flew one way and returned at the end of the course on a motorcycle he'd bought to get around LA for the month. It was a Yamaha Big Bear Scrambler, a sort of hybrid off-road/on-road machine. He could abuse it on his own in the dirt, and I could ride with him on the freeway or around town— brilliant. I loved the bike. Once in a while we rented me a little Honda 50 with a push-button starter and I putt-putted behind Dave through city streets and on back roads, but I mostly rode on the back of the Scrambler.

Unknowingly, we had arrived in San Francisco at a key moment in its history. While we were going about our Young Establishment lives, a powerful social movement was emerging, and in no time at all it had achieved critical mass. A trifecta of rock music, anti-war protests and psychedelic drugs coalesced to make San Francisco the seat of the 1960s zeitgeist. There were echoes of the fifties Beat generation in its lingo and customs, and in the venerable presence of Beat poet Allen Ginsberg and late-era Beat Ken Kesey. They became the elders of the hippie movement and were surely the spiritual godparents of the flower children who chased it all the way to San Francisco. Whether you liked the counterculture or not, it was impossible to ignore it, and it did provide context and climate for a re-examination of values.

Over at 500 Sansome there was a brilliant young lawyer named J. Tony Serra who had signed up for a small suite of offices and was building a practice defending drug violators—users and dealers— and draft resisters. Tony and his social philosophy are effectively portrayed in the 1989 film *True Believer* with James Woods playing the lead role. From Tony, a crusader for his personal belief system, I received enlightenment of sorts about drugs (and a few other things) that caused me to reverse my anti-marijuana position, though this was more theoretical than practical since I had no interest in actually smoking the stuff.

As to draft resisting, President Lyndon Johnson had stepped up the Vietnam War after the Gulf of Tonkin Resolution, and the troop buildup was relentless. IBM secured an "essential skills" deferment for Dave, so we were able to breathe easy for a year, but the net was tightening and not everyone was that lucky. I remember Peter Salz going to the airport to pick up his son's skis that had been shipped home from Spokane, and coming back to the office in a very sombre frame of mind. He had retrieved the skis himself from the cargo area, where they waited for pickup along with dozens of stacked coffins, bodies of young men killed in action being returned to their families for burial. The difference made by social circumstances could not have been starker.

The cultural scene in San Francisco was growing more intense and exciting every week. Local bands were breaking out and playing all over the city. We got around on the Scrambler to the many indoor and outdoor venues where we could see Country Joe and the Fish, the Paul Butterfield Blues Band, Sopwith Camel, Canned Heat, Moby Grape, Big Brother and the Holding Company, all local bands; and to the Matrix in Cow Hollow, where Janis Joplin made regular appearances, as did Grace Slick and the Jefferson Airplane. Marty Balin of the Airplane operated the Matrix, but we didn't know that then, and probably wouldn't have believed that hippie musicians could run a business.

Golden Gate Park became the venue for benefit concerts and "happenings," which were big in San Francisco in the mid-sixties. The biggest happening of all would take place in January 1967 when the Human Be-In drew tens of thousands of disaffected young people eager to reject their parents' social and moral values in favour of a more enlightened path. Frauds that we were, we shed our straight clothes for these events and dressed in bell-bottomed jeans, flowered shirts and fringed vests. We rolled in on the Scrambler, dug the scene, and kidded ourselves that we were "passing."

I was receiving regular letters from home, many of which I stashed in a box and kept with me through all the moves that eventually brought me back to Montreal. Gaby's letters cross-referenced with those of Kate and Anna written at the same time make for great reading all these years later. Gaby had inherited my father's little cottage rental business and had a hard time in the year following his death. Pipes froze in the deep cold of the Laurentian winter, tenants behaved badly, tradesmen cheated her (or so she thought). Uncle Austin makes many appearances in her letters, sending men from his factory to repair or rebuild, driving her around, sharing a few Scotches with her of an evening.

My poor mother agonized about Kate and Anna. "Why won't Kate settle down to her job?" This would cross a letter from Kate saying she had decided not to go into work at the Norgate Shopping Centre Royal Bank, where she was a teller, and had instead taken the bus to Saint-Sauveur to visit a friend.

"Why do your sisters reject society? Is it that they can't stand to be around squares?" (Gaby had put her finger right on it.) This would cross a letter from Anna saying she had moved back up to Saint-Sauveur hoping to get some songs written but was finding it hard to concentrate with "someone" always nagging at her to get a job. I wish I could have written to Gaby from the future: "Don't worry, Ma, Kate and Anna are right on track."

In every letter, Gaby mentions a chat with a realtor about selling the property in Saint-Sauveur. Should she or shouldn't she? What did I think? What did Dave think? What did Peter Salz think? In any event, she never did sell it, for which we're very grateful. The old homestead is a great family treasure, even though it's a bit of a nosebleed to keep up sometimes.

In August 1966, I received a letter from Kate, datelined Vancouver, describing how she and a couple of boys had gone out west in a drive-away car, Kerouac-style, to check out a Trips Festival. The next thing I knew, she was at my door. She'd caught a ride south with friends who were headed back to Buffalo and had done a 1,500-mile dogleg to be in San Francisco for a few days. Her travelling companions were Bobby Hogg, Kitty Katz and a magnificent blue Bedlington terrier. They were all delightful and we sat in the living room for the next few hours drinking tea. Bobby Hogg taught at SUNY in Buffalo, and gave me a copy of *Connexions*, a book of his poetry that I still have as a memento of that long-ago afternoon.

Kate kipped with us and was left to her own devices while Dave and I went to our jobs. I came home one afternoon to find her sitting quietly in an armchair in my living room, staring down at the steeple she'd made of her hands. She looked a little off and I asked her if she was all right. She looked up at me, all dreamy and spacey, and said, "Are you cool?" She had hitchhiked to Marin County and smoked some grass, then caught a ride back to town. I was cool, but in the very early stages of coolness, and I didn't know what to make of this development. I knew for a fact that my neighbour across the hall was definitely not cool, and if he thought for a moment there was a drug fiend in the building he would have the cops on us. I was mentally dialling Tony Serra's number while Kate extolled the virtues of marijuana and reassured me that it was perfectly harmless. She eventually came down, and as far as I know didn't smoke pot more than a couple of dozen times again in her life.

Her friends picked her up a few days later and they drove back to New York. As a hostess gift, Kate gave me a piece she'd picked up at the Trips Festival. The artist had taken the innards out of a vintage box camera, papered the walls and back of it with an intricate pattern print, and made a vitrine by closing the front with amber glass. Above the amber glass was a half-circle of faux emeralds in a sunburst setting (probably an old brooch), and behind the amber glass a polished stone dangled from a golden chain. It was a stoner's dream. I carried it around for years till it was stolen in a burglary in the 1980s. I keep hoping it'll turn up on *Antiques Roadshow*.

There were two grocery stores near where we lived on Delgado. The Searchlight Market was on the northeast corner of Hyde and Union, and run by a guy we called the Pirate because he bootlegged frozen orange juice on Sunday morning at a 200 percent markup. The other store was a long, deep space with a narrow front on the west side of Hyde, facing our lane, and was run by a young guy named Jimmy. We liked Jimmy and made a point of buying our milk there, and anything else we ran out of, unless it was Sunday, when he was closed and we were forced to deal with the Pirate. Sometimes Dave rode his motorcycle right into Jimmy's store, just for the hell of it, and visited with Jimmy.

One night Dave came home with something that wasn't on my list, a baggie of grass. It seems our Jimmy was dealing more than milk and cans of soup. Of course, I had to try it, and found the sensation very strange and a little disturbing. It's not something I really took to, though I was glad to have it demystified at last.

HITCHHIKING TO THE WEST COAST

(Anna)

Dane and I made a plan to hitchhike to the west coast in late August 1967 after we had saved enough money from our summer jobs. I was an office temp and Dane was helping his parents in their Westmount flower shop. We would return three weeks later in time for me to start the fall term at the Beaux-arts. Dane would begin work as an entertainment writer at the Montreal *Gazette* around the same time.

When the day of our departure was finally upon us, I had lost all enthusiasm for the long trip, and as usual when doing stuff with Dane, we got a late start. We took a taxi with our bags to the west-bound 2 and 20 in Lachine and positioned ourselves with thumbs out beside this busy roadway. The sun was setting in the west and we were headed for it.

Our first ride was with a travelling salesman who took us to Ottawa. He was spending the night in the village of Aylmer on the Quebec side of the Ottawa River and continuing on to North Bay in the morning. We would all stay in the same hotel to get an early start. It was a dreary-looking place, what my mother used to call a commercial hotel, and straight out of an Alexander MacLeod story. The rooms were off a dimly lit corridor that reeked of stale tobacco and old latrines where tired old-lady wallpaper met manly dark-stained wainscotting. We moved the old brown metal bed-stead to the centre of the room, away from the walls that were crawling with big black bugs, and turned off the lights. It was going to be a long trip.

Flash-forward, and Dane and I are standing in front of the Big Nickel in Sudbury, Ontario, the home of Falconbridge Nickel Mines Limited. At this time the place was a hell of sorts, a moon-scape where nothing grew, and yet people managed to live there amid the stench and particulates that poured from the smelter's stack. "It's the smell of prosperity," Dane would say. A town was dead when it stopped smelling. (Stompin' Tom Connors's "Sudbury Saturday Night" was not yet known, but it was an accurate portrayal of the place at that time.)

I'd always liked the name Falconbridge since first hearing it at the stockbroker's. "Falconbridge is down a quarter point!" (It was a blue-chip nickel stock.) The word evokes the days of yore, of falconers with hooded raptors perched on gloved hands, and kings and queens in crowns of hammered gold parading around in drafty stone castles plotting the murder of a rival. In the late eighties, when Rufus was into Dungeons and Dragons, Kate took inspiration from this pastime and wrote "Mother Mother Oh Help Me":

Get for me a bird of prey
Starve it night and day
Set it loose where tyrants dwell
And make a Heaven from this Hell.

Northern Ontario is a land of superlatives: the Big Nickel, Lake Superior, the Big Goose in the town of Wawa, a word that comes from the Ojibwa for goose. We theorized that some Indian words were in fact French words to begin with, and imagined the first voyageurs in canoes hugging Lake Superior's northern shore and pointing skyward saying, "Oie, oie," the onomatopoeic French word for goose.

Before we left Montreal, my mother had said to us, "Don't forget to call your uncle Duncan when you get to Winnipeg." My uncle had been widowed a few months earlier when his wife, Myrtle, my mother's younger sister, died of a bad heart, despite an intervention at the Mayo Clinic. I remembered Myrt as a demon housekeeper who sometimes babysat us as small children when our mother had things to do in Montreal. After Uncle Austin had dropped us in Cartierville, we would board the 17 streetcar and ride it to the Garland terminus in Snowdon, where Myrt lived. Kate and I would kneel on the rattan seats beside our seated mother and stare out the window at the open fields of Ville Saint-Laurent, home to Canadair, and a rapidly growing suburb. As we approached the city, the narrow backyards of duplexes drew us in, where clotheslines fluttered in the breeze like Buddhist prayer flags.

Myrt and Dunc had no children of their own, and maybe because of this she seemed excessively strict. A pet canary called Cornelius completed their lives, and to amuse us Myrt would let the bird out of its cage to fly around their small art deco kitchen on Clanranald Avenue. Dunc worked for James Richardson, the wheat broker, and in the late fifties he took a transfer to the head office in Winnipeg. After this move my mother worried constantly about poor Myrt, with her bad heart and blue lips, having to contend with Winnipeg's hard winters.

Duncan was six foot six, very thin, bespectacled and with a long rectangular head. He chain-smoked and was a proud Shriner. When he donned his velvet fez, he was over seven feet tall, and with the ceremonial sword slung about his hips, he cut an imposing figure. But his wife's brothers found him silly and made fun of him.

Now, at the eastern outskirts of the windy city at the confluence of the Assiniboine and the Red, we looked for a phone booth. It was a Saturday, and as I dialled my uncle's number I imagined him at home alone, mourning my aunt. I was dreading the visit, but he'd be happy to hear from me. (Ring ring . . .) There was no answer. As Jane would say, "We dodged a bullet." Now there was no reason to hang around Winnipeg and we could press on to Vancouver, Canada's glittering jewel, still 2,400 kilometres away.

We hailed a taxi to take us across town. As we approached Portage and Main, the traffic thickened. It was a Shriners convention, of all things! Spectators lined the streets throwing coins at men in maroon fezzes driving around recklessly in little toy cars and on tiny motorbikes to raise money for their charity hospitals. The Shriners in fact do wonderful work for hospitals and sick children, and are set to open a new children's hospital in Montreal. But at the time, all I could think was that if a flying saucer full of spacemen had landed at that moment, what would they have made of the spectacle? I looked for Dunc, as he would have stood out, but I didn't see him.

We were picked up west of the Peg by a couple of off-duty truck drivers who were headed by car to Virden, almost three hundred kilometres away. Partway into the trip they began drinking gin, occasionally passing the bottle back to us. For the sake of camaraderie we drank from it too. But as time passed and more gin was consumed, they began to get a little too familiar. Would the two of us be interested in joining in their swinging sex parties when they were next in Montreal? Apparently Montreal was a tough town to get something happening in. Next, a veiled threat was uttered. I was terrified. The car was a two-door coupe and we were trapped in the back. Dane ordered them to stop, we were getting out.

They let us off at a rail yard near their hometown and we were relieved to see the last of them. Our plan was to hop a freight, but it's not as easy as Buster Keaton makes it look and we ended up spending what was left of the night on the railway platform. The next morning our "friends" pulled up to see if we were still there. They looked as if they had been up all night. They apologized for scaring us, but we were wary now.

Another ride I remember was with a man delivering a brand new yellow school bus to some outlying community. Seemed pretty innocuous, a ride in a school bus. Atom Egoyan's *The Sweet Hereafter*, a film I really like, was decades in the future. I was twenty-two and had never been on a school bus, but the novelty of it soon wore off. It was slow and noisy and cornered like a caboose, and the ride went on for several hundred kilometres. The driver was happy for the company, but all three of us had to yell back and forth the whole time to be heard over the din. Our only divertissement was to change seats every so often to get a new slant on the scenery, which had a certain sameness about it.

We somehow got to Saskatoon, where Peter Weldon was attending a seminar at the University of Saskatchewan, and spent the night in his dorm. Then on to Edmonton, where I bought myself a beaded leather jacket and a pair of Inuit-style mukluks for Kate. In Jasper we met an American student who had just come down the Alaska Highway, and the three of us slept in an empty train car before hitching our way to Banff. From there, Dane and I went west. It was dark when we arrived in Golden, BC, and we were advised by locals who saw us standing there with our thumbs out not to stay outdoors because of the bears. As if by a miracle, a slow-moving passenger train appeared. It was headed for Vancouver. I don't remember the railway office being open or even if Golden was a scheduled stop. I like to think it was angels that flagged it down for us.

In Vancouver, we stayed with colleagues of Peter Weldon, two young research scientists at UBC, Yoav Privis and Carol Moss, who had a nice apartment overlooking English Bay. The Beatles' *Sgt. Pepper's Lonely Hearts Club Band* had just come out and a certain amount of time was spent smoking dope and listening to it on headphones while we tripped through its many sound layers and said, "Wow! Wow!" a lot. Dr. Paul Spong, the neuroscientist-cetologist famous for studying how killer whales and dolphins communicate, was a friend of theirs. Late one night when we were all pleasantly stoned, he snuck us into the aquarium in Vancouver's lush Stanley Park, where he worked. With the help of a bucket of live fish, he put the killer whale and its two dolphin pool-mates through their paces. We worried for the safety of the smaller dolphins as the killer whale chased them back and forth across the tank. I remember him saying that the dolphins together could ram the killer whale to death. The mental image I retain of this young long-haired hippie scientist attempting to communicate with our brother mammals from the deep epitomizes the hopefulness of west coast culture in the 1960s. I can't imagine anyone today getting a grant to talk to fish; you would need to extract something from the fish that could be commercialized.

We made a quick trip to Victoria and rented a scooter to go to a nearby beach, a long, desolate stretch of sand littered with velvety green seaweed and big pieces of driftwood. This was my first view of the open Pacific. All the time we were growing up, our mother never bought fish products that originated in this ocean because of the atomic bombs the United States had dropped on Hiroshima and Nagasaki at the end of World War II.

Time was a-wastin'. From Victoria we took the ferry to Seattle, where we boarded a bus that travelled down the coast to San Francisco. This city is laid out on a grid, with streets criss-crossing its seven or so very steep hills. I imagine it was the US Army Corps of Engineers that did this and not the Spanish, the previous occupants. Jane and Dave's place was on Russian Hill close to the Hyde Street trolley. They both worked, and their place was quite grown-up and had dark green walls. Dane and I visited the Haight, where the Summer of Love was winding down, and saw the Byrds at the Fillmore. Jane introduced us to Cost Plus, maybe one of the first import stores to sell inexpensive home decor items made in Asia. We stocked up on those round rice paper lampshades. They took us out to the Berkeley campus, that shrine to sixties radicalism. Dane and I were peaceniks. Back home we would march to protest the war in Vietnam, climbing Côte-des-Neiges with thousands of other demonstrators, chanting in French, "JOHNSON ASSASSIN! JOHNSON ASSASSIN!" as we made our way to the US consulate. Young people are agents of change, and their expressions of outrage are important to a healthy society, however naive or misguided they may sound to some.

A couple of summers ago, Montreal students protested a proposed rise in their tuition fees by wearing red squares and staging impromptu demonstrations called "casseroles" where people banged on pots with wooden spoons. Rufus had a show during the summer Jazz Festival that year. To show his solidarity with the students, he came onstage wearing a red square, a gesture that got him a big round of applause. He told the audience that he always sided with the underdog.

At Half Moon Bay, an hour south of San Francisco, Jane gave me her bikini. She was pregnant with her daughter Anna and wouldn't be needing it anytime soon. Some people were getting on with their lives. It was time for Dane and me to return to Montreal.

Dane and I are very different travellers. When he's behind the wheel, he likes to take his time, visiting local museums and stopping to read every historical plaque. The more regional and obscure the information on the plaque, the better. He so loves historical plaques that when the Eastern Ontario township we live in was commemorating its bicentennial, he undertook to write and erect a dozen or so plaques to impart a little local history to people travelling through. In one spot, at a deserted crossroads, there are only rocks and trees. Not a trace is left of the busy cheese factory that once stood there. We have to take his word for it.

I find it hard being a passenger; the word itself suggests passivity. I remember one trip made in the early seventies to the Shelburne Fiddle Championship northwest of Toronto in Dane's white VW Beetle. He was writing a story on Johnny Mooring, a Nova Scotia fiddler he had once heard play in a local bar and who had won the top fiddling prize at Shelburne a number of times. This itinerant musician was well known in Glengarry County, Ontario, and used to stay with neighbours. Dane had been struck by the fiddler's wizardry and onstage charm. He had intended to write a piece on Mooring, but before he had a chance to interview him, the poor man was beaten to death in the parking lot of a Quebec roadhouse where he had just given a performance. The assailants thought the musician was making eyes at the woman they were with. Even if he had been, was that a good-enough reason to kill him?

During the fiddle competition, I had used a small portable Sony tape deck to record a number of performances as a musical reference to listen to on the return trip. An intricate waltz by a Quebec fiddler called Lucien Ranger appealed to me. On the way home I proceeded to teach myself to play it on the button accordion I had with me in the front passenger seat. Over and over, I started and stopped the tape as I learned each passage. This antisocial behaviour went on for hundreds of kilometres and Dane never once told me to stop. By the time we got home, I could play it perfectly.

Singing is another good way to make the time pass on road trips. Our kids were encouraged to sing on long drives. I'm reminded of a time when Kate, Dane, the four kids and I were leaving the Mariposa Festival grounds after a performance in the 1980s, back in the days when it was held near Barrie, Ontario. It was dark. Rufus was teaching his sister and cousins the "Alabama Song" by Bertolt Brecht and Kurt Weill, when Dane stopped to pick up a couple of young hitchhikers who were coming from the festival. The two squeezed into the back of the rented van with the kids. Now the kids had an audience, a captive one, and the volume of the singing went up a few notches. Led by a very strident Rufus, the four of them tormented the poor hitchhikers by their screaming of "Show me the way to the next whisky bar. Oh, don't ask why. Oh, don't ask why. For if we don't find the next whisky bar, I tell you we must die. I tell you we must die." Over and over. This could have been my inspiration for "Why Must We Die?," a song on our *Matapedia*. To answer my own question: we die because we can't find the next whisky bar.

ALTAMONT

(Jane)

When Anna and Dane hitchhiked out to see us in late summer 1967, I was pregnant with our first baby, who was due on Valentine's Day 1968. I had almost lost the baby on a sailing trip a few weeks before. The skipper was a rookie and had taken us out in his new Coronado 25 to get some experience, with old salt Dave looking over his shoulder. He had set a course for Paradise Cove in Marin County, and when a storm blew up, he wouldn't turn back. This was the same idiot who lived across the hall and was such a hard-liner about pot. I can still hear him yelling over my objections, "Janie, we're going to Paradise Cove." We ended up having to push off boats that were crashing into us when we did have to dock, and I started bleeding that night. I stayed in bed for a week and the bleeding stopped, but I was still taking it easy when Anna and Dane came to visit.

There were no further complications except that the blessed event was almost three weeks late and my beautiful Anna Catherine was born on March 4, 1968, rather than Valentine's Day. Peter Salz had thrown his own version of a baby shower for me early in the new year, an elegant catered lunch in our conference room attended by about a dozen people I did business with. A few of the guests were partners in the building and represented huge local financial interests, the Levi-Strauss family among them. On the other side of the table were Tony Serra and another lawyer from his office, who represented a different slice of the community. San Francisco being the kind of town it is, everyone was congenial and bonhomie reigned, though I imagine Tony got in his share of digs at the high rollers. It was a typically quirky/classy Peter event, and I went home with some very nice gifts.

After Anna and I had been home from the hospital for about a month, I needed to keep a follow-up appointment with my OB/GYN. I scheduled it for Friday, April 5, the day my cleaning lady would be coming in, so that she could keep an eye on Anna while I was out. Mattie, my cleaner, was a tall black woman, all bone and sinew, a little on the sullen side, but conscientious and thorough. She had good references and had been coming to me every Friday for about three months.

That morning, while I was getting ready to leave the house for the first time since Anna's birth, I heard on the radio that Martin Luther King had been shot in Memphis the night before. At that point in our lives, we knew exactly six black people. There was Charlie, the custodian of 500 Sansome; Dorothy, a young woman who worked in the mailroom of Van Nostrand Publishing down the hall; and Curtis, an IBM colleague of Dave's who was from the South, and had been an army officer before going to work for IBM. There was a couple, Lonnie and Gloria, whom we knew slightly. Lonnie worked in high-tech, and Gloria was a high school principal. And there was Mattie. Not once had we ever discussed with any of them the civil rights movement, or the role of Dr. King as its leader. They never brought it up and neither did we. I think it was just an uncomfortable subject for everybody.

So that morning, while I certainly registered the horror of the assassination and its impact on civil rights, I wasn't thinking about how personally it might affect people of colour. My mind was more taken up with my medical issue, a spot of postpartum depression, than it was with Dr. King's assassination.

When Mattie turned up for work half an hour late, and in a worse mood than usual, I was a little sharp with her. I left her instructions and flew out the door to catch a cab to my doctor's office on California Street in Presidio Heights, some distance away. I tried calling the house from the doctor's office, but there was no answer—drowned out by the vacuum cleaner, I thought. I rushed home. When I arrived at the apartment, I found Mattie sprawled out in an armchair, all gangly arms and legs, and mumbling to herself, something like, "He's gone, he's gone. They done killed him." The house hadn't been touched, except for the liquor cabinet, and she was completely hammered. My heart pounding, I ran to check Anna's crib; she was howling but otherwise fine. I gave Mattie her money and shepherded her down the lane to Hyde Street, where I tried to hail a cab. A couple of cars slowed down but kept going when they saw her. I didn't know what I was going to do with her, and Dave wasn't due home for hours. Finally a driver agreed to take her. I gave him enough money to get her home and that was the end of it. We never spoke again.

I put together that the incident had to do with MLK's murder, but I thought of him as a politician and still didn't appreciate what Dr. King represented to black people: their hope, their salvation, the chance of other possibilities in life besides cleaning up after people like me, or at least having the choice. In time, I understood how personally demoralizing his murder was. I hope Mattie lived long enough to see Barack and Michelle Obama and their two little girls in the White House. It certainly didn't seem like a possibility in 1968.

Our apartment lease had a restriction against children, but although we knew we would have to give it up, we had not counted on having our hand forced by a neighbour. Our friend across the hall, of anti-pot and wayward boat fame, let us know he would complain to the landlord if we didn't give notice ourselves. The couple upstairs added their voices. They didn't want a crying baby around. It was time to move.

We started looking for a house on the Peninsula to cut Dave's driving time, and settled on one in San Carlos, about a fifteen-minute commute to Palo Alto. We had recently stayed with friends who had a home in Mandeville Canyon, in the Brentwood neighbourhood of Los Angeles, and it had really made an impression on me. It felt like the country: no sidewalks, just dirt shoulders on either side of a narrow road, and mailboxes outside each house. I described my dream neighbourhood to our realtor, who led us straight to a house for sale on Dover Court in San Carlos. Not quite as spiffy as Mandeville Canyon, but very nice, with the rural look and feel that we wanted.

The quarter-acre lot was a downward slope from the street, the house and front yard shaded and hidden by a giant California oak. The original structure, a one-storey artist's cottage, sat under a second floor that had been added after the fact, one huge room with a big fireplace, and windows on three sides that looked out over miles of wild terrain, which turned out to be part of the San Andreas Fault. The original ground-floor family room opened onto a terraced garden with a brick path that led to the potting shed at the end of the yard. The long-time owner and her mother had done most of the landscaping themselves, and done it with loving care. There was a house just north of us (with a grape arbour between our yards!) and a horse corral and barn south of us, and three other houses on the court, all but one tucked way back like ours. And if the property itself wasn't attractive enough, the street name was the same as that of Dave's family home, Dover Road in Montreal—too good an omen to ignore. Our offer was accepted, we gave notice on Delgado, and we moved in a month or so later, at the beginning of September as I remember. I started making our new home comfortable for its three occupants— and, as it turned out, a fourth who would be arriving the next year.

The Anna pregnancy had come with morning sickness, the frightening sailing incident, a very late arrival, a long labour, and a hard forceps delivery when she finally made her appearance. On July 11, 1969, after an easy pregnancy, Vinnie did most of the work getting himself born. When I felt the twinges, I called Dave, who raced home from work to find me washing the kitchen floor, my nesting instinct gone amok. We dropped Anna with a friend, Laura Vitlacil, and drove to the small private hospital in Redwood City used by my doctor for his procedures. A nurse checked me and, after getting the doctor's instructions by phone, gave me a med, probably oxytocin, to move things along. The process suddenly went into overdrive and there was no time for anything but to let the birth happen. There were no staff doctors at the hospital, and Ian Vincent Russell Dow was delivered by a nurse who'd been a midwife in Ireland. I wasn't prepared for natural childbirth, but after some hurried instructions about breathing and pushing (much like rocking a car back and forth to get it out of a snowbank), Vinnie surfaced. He was already in his incubator when the anaesthetist raced in, fresh off the links in a green and white golf dress, and went through the motions of giving me oxygen. The doctor was right behind her, just in time to catch the placenta. Neither Vinnie nor I were the worse for wear; in fact, I felt great. I could have gone home and washed the rest of the floors, but the hospital kept me in for almost a week, as they did back then.

Now that we were living in a suburb with two little ones, we didn't get around as much, but we were re-inspired to bust out on the Scrambler after seeing *Easy Rider*. We hired a babysitter and dug out our fringed vests to attend the Rolling Stones' free outdoor concert, scheduled for December 6. There were other great bands on the bill, and the Woodstock of the West, as it was being described, promised to be the happening to end all happenings. All that was needed was a place to stage it.

The Altamont Speedway was an eleventh-hour choice, being the only venue available on such short notice after Golden Gate Park bowed out, and was confirmed only two days before the scheduled date. It was not known how many young people would trek to Tracy, the Speedway's location sixty miles southeast of San Francisco, but the gig had been widely publicized and was highly anticipated. The great Human Be-In had drawn an estimated thirty thousand people to Golden Gate Park, and it was thought at least that many would show up at Altamont. One wild estimate put the number at a hundred thousand. Neither the Stones' organization nor the Speedway's owner arranged for facilities or security, so there was nothing in place when some *three hundred thousand* people converged there on December 6, 1969.

Somehow, the California Hells Angels were drafted to provide security for the stage area, an idea that might seem counterintuitive now but made perfect counterculture sense at the time. Ken Kesey was known to associate with the Angels, as documented in Tom Wolfe's book *The Electric Kool-Aid Acid Test*, and after the Summer of Love and all the consciousness-raising in its wake, people were more open, less risk-averse, more accepting of the "other," even courting the "other." For their part, the Angels had gone on a charm offensive, helping old ladies across the street and stopping on the freeway to rescue stalled motorists. Tales abounded of stranded car owners one minute begging for mercy, the next offering a prayer of thanks when the hairy outlaw biker on a Harley turned out to be a Good Samaritan.

When Dave and I arrived at the Speedway on the bike, passing hundreds of cars abandoned by the side of the road and thousands of people on foot, it looked as though capacity had long been exceeded and we would most likely be turned back. Right then a few dozen Hells Angels rode up behind us, waved us into their pack and escorted us through the entrance gate. Once inside, they peeled off to their preferential seating and we were left on our own to find a spot amidst the waves of humanity in the fields beyond the stage area.

We ended up on a far-off hillock where there were other motor-cycles and people picnicking. We were too far away from the action to enjoy it as a concert, and were unaware of the violent disorder going on in the immediate stage area, but we had a couple of freaky incidents of our own.

Not long after we settled in, a crew of drunken bikers staggered through the crowd toward us holding up their buddy, a deranged man wearing a vest "decorated" with unsheathed hunting knives and flailing wildly with a knife in each hand. We sat absolutely still and stared at the ground, hoping they would just keep going, and didn't move a muscle till they were well past us.

Hours later, after our picnic, Dave approached a fellow motor-cyclist who was only a few feet away from us. I think he wanted to ask for a light. The guy was in a crouch with his back to us, fiddling with his bike. He turned around very slowly, still in a crouch, his face hidden behind a hideous Joker mask and his penis on full dis-play (nothing to write home about, either). Jayzus. Forget the match. We packed our stuff into my rucksack and moved to another spot. There were no further incidents, and we didn't learn of the murder and mayhem till the next day's news. The calamitous event figures prominently in the 1970 Rolling Stones film *Gimme Shelter*.

CAFFÈ LENA

(Anna)

The overnight Greyhound from Montreal to New York City in the late sixties and early seventies made a halfway stop around 3:30 a.m. in the town of Saratoga Springs. Most riders associated Saratoga with the inside of the Spa City Diner, the greasy spoon where the bus discharged its passengers so they could use the washrooms and get a sandwich to go. In the harsh neon light of the stainless steel diner, the thin, unsmiling man behind the counter, with pockmarked olive skin and wearing a stained white cook's smock and soda-jerk hat, somehow managed to take all our orders and make the food in the thirty minutes we were there. Nobody gave a second thought to the town of Saratoga Springs and what lay in the dark beyond the diner's parking lot; Manhattan was our destination.

There was a lot more to the place, as I was to find out on my first real visit to Saratoga Springs, in late 1969 or early 1970, when I went to see Kate and Roma Baran. Saratoga is said to be an Iroquoian word that Kate once told me translated in English as "scum on the water." Although this unflattering translation isn't mentioned in the Wikipedia entry for Saratoga there are a few other suggestions as to the origins of the word but they are all disputed. The town is famous because of its mineral springs, so "scum on the water" sounds like a good bet.

Beginning in the 1860s it became a popular summering spot for the very rich. The summer houses that the wealthy built for themselves were huge and opulent and in a vast variety of architectural styles, each one trying to outdo the next. The famous Saratoga Springs horse track was built around this time and it is said to have been the first large sports facility in the US. As you drive into the town from the east on route 9P, miles of white horse fencing, stables and paddocks line the road on either side of a spectacular grandstand.

In 1970 the downtown of Saratoga Springs was in a state of decay. Abandoned grocery carts were everywhere—lying on their sides in parks, poking out of hedges—a sure sign the place was on the skids.

Kate and Roma were staying in an unfinished shed at the back of the Caffè Lena on Phila Street, named for Lena Spencer, the actor who owned and operated it. It was a folk venue and magnet for the many travelling folk artists who found themselves in its vicinity, as Kate and Roma did then. When I first visited, it was the dead of winter and their digs were very cold, almost like living outside. A wall separated the shed from the Caffè proper, a large room with a clutter of round tables and bentwood chairs that focused on a small stage with an upright piano. Off to the left as you came up the stairs from the street was a separate room with bleacher seating that behaved as a theatre. This is where Lena put on her plays. The Caffè Lena was renowned for both its music and its theatre but also for its delicious desserts. When Kate and Roma had business in NYC, they would pick up Lena's weekly order of cannoli shells from a certain *pasticceria* in Little Italy. In the kitchen behind a partition, Lena filled the cannoli shells with her homemade custard and baked the hazelnut cakes the Caffè was famous for serving. Aside from tony Skidmore College, then still in the town proper, there were a number of other private and community colleges in the area and an unlimited supply of young people Lena could call upon to wait tables or take the door.

Saratoga was host of the Saratoga Cup, the fourth most important race in the United States after the Derby, Preakness and Belmont. One of Lena's good friends was an older gentleman called Tom, a tall and dignified Irish-American with a rude manner, who had spent his life working out the betting odds in horse racing before the arrival of the parimutuel machines, and who was now retired in Saratoga. Tom had a key to the Caffè and stopped in every morning to sit and read his paper, including the racing form, in the quiet of the empty space. Kate told me that, from their shed, she and Roma could hear old Tom come in, cursing audibly as he climbed the steep stairs from the street. Once seated, he'd take a shot of hooch from a bottle he kept hidden in the Caffè and his mood would instantly improve. "Helloooo pussycat," he affectionately addressed one of Lena's many cats, this one a resident of the Caffè.

Lena didn't live in the Caffè but over a Main Street storefront in a rambling two-storey tenement, the walls of which were covered in floral wallpaper, all of it peeling. Though she owned a bed, she had the peculiar habit of sleeping bolt upright in a chair with her legs and feet stretched out on another chair. As she settled in for the night, one by one the cats jumped up on her until the small round woman was completely covered in them. Maybe the upright position was a precaution against getting smothered by her feline friends. I was seriously allergic and couldn't be in her place for more than a few minutes or I'd have an asthma attack.

Along with cats, the hospitable Lena collected people, folksingers who'd made their way from the west coast and decided to stick around. One summer the Idaho poet-singer Rosalie Sorrels arrived for a gig with several of her children. Lena put them all up, and by the fall they still hadn't left, so the kids were enrolled in Saratoga schools.

I see on the Caffè's Wikipedia site that it is described as "smoke and alcohol free." It certainly wasn't always this way. Lena was a heavy smoker, Pall Malls as I remember, but she wasn't a drinker and the Caffè did not serve alcohol. But the Executive Bar and Restaurant right next door did, and that's where most of the visiting acts headed between sets to get oiled up for the next one. If you were a frequent performer at the Caffè and a habitué of the Executive, the owners, a pleasant young couple, might name a sandwich after you.

While Kate lived there, she wrote the "Saratoga Summer Song," a composition celebrating the freedoms of the place. One of Saratoga's many bars, the Tin and Lint Pub on Caroline Street, run by two good-looking guys called Fred and Dennis, was a place where you might finish off an all-nighter before heading down to the Four Sons deli for an early breakfast before hitting the hay. "We danced and played some tennis, made love with Fred or Dennis," went Kate's song.

Another musician who settled for a while in Saratoga with his family was Frank Wakefield, the Southern virtuoso mandolin player and former member of the Greenbriar Boys. Lena liked him a lot, but she didn't like it when he drank, making sure there was no booze around when he had to perform. Kate told me about a time Lena rented some studio space in the next town over so Frank could record some of his mandolin oeuvres, all of which seemed to be entitled "Jesus Loves This Mandolin-Player" and were numbered 1 to 158, the same system Bach used. Wakefield was hugely prolific. Lena had warned Frank beforehand there would be no drinking during the recording session—he was there to work. According to Kate, this mandolin player so beloved by Jesus arrived that morning at the studio wearing a large sombrero and his signature clench-toothed smile. As the day wore on, Frank appeared to be getting drunker with every take. It was then that Lena, finally putting two and two together, yanked the sombrero off his head, whereupon the bottle of gin, now pretty much empty, tumbled onto the floor. If you were a woman and Frank liked you, he called you his "ol' nigger lady," a term of endearment. Lena was his No. 1 ol' nigger lady.

Another colourful personality who lived in this historic, broken-down town was the Welsh-born stage actor John Wynne-Evans. He must have been in his late forties when I first laid disbelieving eyes on him, an eccentric creature with long, peroxided blond locks who went around in a floor-length robe of black crushed velvet and a face fully made up, ready for the stage. This gloriously faded old town was his stage, and the action followed him around as he plied his way up and down the side streets of a midsummer's eve. He had a curious smell about him, a mixture of sweet boozy sweat and mothballs, that was not unpleasant, and I found him utterly charming.

Lena had started the Caffè with her husband, a professor at Skidmore College, the prestigious girls' school in the town. By the time Kate and Roma showed up, the Spencers were divorced, the husband having run off with a student. "Skidmore girls come back to town/All the freaks head underground."

I remember Lena saying that in 1961, when Bob Dylan auditioned to play the Caffè, she didn't think he had any talent. Her husband liked the baby-faced troubadour and booked him. She showed us the photo her husband snapped of Dylan and his then girlfriend Suze Rotolo, seated at a round table in the Caffè backlit by a window. Maybe because Lena had missed the boat with Bob, she found herself a protegé, Bruce, a tall, sweet, skinny, working-class kid with red hair who hailed from nearby Schenectady, home to General Electric, which Kurt Vonnegut mined so brilliantly in his novels set in and around the fictional town of Ilium. Bruce played guitar and wrote songs, and Lena thought he was a diamond in the rough. He was the son she never had, and she found opportunities for him to display his talents, opening for all the acts that came through town. I should mention that Lena did "get" Don McLean, another musician originally from the Tri-City, who had played the Caffè and in a year's time was to have a huge hit with "The Day the Music Died" (a.k.a. "Bye Bye, Miss American Pie").

In July, Balanchine's NYC Ballet took up summer residence in Saratoga, performing at the Arts Centre. "And the New York City Ballet dancers/Danced while all the neighbourhood cancers/Celebrated their birthdays in the sun," wrote Kate. In August, the horses arrived with the huge retinue that follows these fleet-footed creatures. Anybody who has ever been to Saratoga has remarked how vast and elegant are the track and grandstand, paddocks and stables. A black woman, a former maid in one of the big houses, owned a small house abutting the racetrack, and ran a select bar out of her living room for the track's wealthy patrons. She had recently acquired a piano and had told Lena she was looking to hire someone to play the standards. Kate went to audition for the job, which was to be paid in tips. By way of enticing her, the woman said, "If you play 'Raindrops Keep Fallin' on My Head' when Mr. Whitney walks in, he'll give you five dollars!" Kate played great barrelhouse piano, the music that would have been heard in Southern black bordellos and blind pigs of the 1920s. I seem to remember Kate giving the woman a sampling of her style, but it was deemed a little rough for her genteel establishment and Kate ended up not taking the gig. Could she have played "Raindrops" with a straight face? Or did she see herself in a dead-end music-biz scenario doing covers, the music biz as our father had imagined it to be, a grasshopper serenading the ants, like Alan the lost boy-accordionist whose accordion was still in our cupboard in Saint-Sauveur?

That seductive summer in the town of Saratoga Springs, with all its freedoms, began to lose its appeal. Just being free wasn't the end goal. "This crazy summer is past now/Sunrise to sunset is fading fast now/And we who are free swing like the rope on that tree."

But she wasn't ready to leave just yet. By the summer of 1970, Kate was living with Loudon in an apartment at 4 Franklin Square, a dilapidated Greek Revival building with very tall Doric columns and at the time threatened with demolition. It was in this apartment that Loudon smashed his red Gibson guitar (a Hummingbird, as I remember), burning it in the living room's graceful marble fireplace and then writing a song about it. "It burned until all that was left was six pegs and six strings/Kate she said, *You are a fool, you've done a foolish thing.*" Damn the consequences. It didn't matter what you did, or how reprehensibly you behaved, as long as you got a good song out of it. It's one of my favourites.

The mansion at 4 Franklin Square fared better than the red Gibson. It became a listed property in 1972 and in time was restored to its former glory.

Saratoga Summer Song

We were nice young adults
We proved ourselves, we showed results
Like cats and dogs who'd undergone a fix
Fashionably cynical
And love to us was clinical
Long ago we gave up getting our kicks

But the summer sun came down on all
And it was fun to feel and fun to fall
Into a sloppy teenage scene
Gossiping and having crushes
Dimming lights to hide the blushes
My God, I thought I was sixteen

All those happy hours
Turned green buds into flowers

This crazy summer is over
No more bees, no more clover
And the rope at the swimming hole swings by the weight of the wind
Skidmore girls come back to town
All the freaks head underground
And we who are free swing like the rope from that tree

We danced and played some tennis
Made love with Fred or Dennis
We drank lots of beer and ate a whole lot of food
We put our bodies to the sun
For God to see and everyone
We swam dressed and we swam nude

And the New York City Ballet dancers
Danced while all the neighbourhood Cancers
Celebrated their birthdays in the sun
And all that sun brought dope and lust
We weren't too smart, and we had a bust
But nobody slept alone

Night turned into day
And summer went away

This crazy summer is past now
Sunrise to sunset is fading fast now
And all I want is to see the rope on that tree
So bring back the bagels, bring back the lox
Let's have another vernal equinox
Bring back the laughs, bring back the tears,
Bring back the beers, bring back the dope and the rope.

—lyrics by Kate McGarrigle

ROMA

(Jane)

On the east coast, Kate and Roma had based themselves at the Caffè Lena and were working the folk circuit around New York and as far afield as Ann Arbor and Denver. I got a very funny letter from Kate, datelined "St. Sauveur—Saturday night," no day, month or year, but it would have been spring 1970. She's happily anticipating the Philadelphia Folk Festival and an audience of twenty-five thousand people, and credits her friend Bruce Phillips (U. Utah Phillips, the Golden Voice of the Great Southwest) with getting them the gig. She writes: "He and I were playing poker last winter in Lena's kitchen in front of about 8 or 10 people when we both ran out of money. Next of course to go were things like belts, boots, etc. We were playing 7-card no peek, a very high stakes game. Needless to say, we both lost within two hands, i.e. our clothes, while everybody drank coffee and looked on in disbelief." She quotes the director of the festival—"Anybody who can play strip-poker with Utah deserves to play the Phila Festival"—and goes on to say he gave Roma and Kate one of the best spots.

A few months later, Roma turned up in San Francisco and called me. The duo had been offered a deal by Vanguard Records that Roma wanted to take and Kate didn't. They parted company on less than good terms. Anna thinks Kate was holding out for a better offer, having seen what Atlantic had put on the table for Loudon. Kate later told me she thought Joan Baez, Vanguard's lead artist, would get all the label's attention. Whatever Kate's reasoning, Roma was very unhappy and I could understand her point of view; they'd worked hard toward getting a record deal and Kate had quashed it.

I knew Roma by reputation but met her for the first time only after she arrived in San Francisco. She's a great person, and I enjoyed getting to know her independently of the scene back east. I remember that she was volunteering at a service that placed abandoned pets with older people who lived alone. I went with her one day to pick up a dog that we delivered to its new owner. It was an old dog going to an old lady, and they seemed to get on very well.

Roma eventually returned to New York. She would later produce Laurie Anderson's hit "O Superman." Still later she went to law school and became a criminal defence lawyer working to reverse the sentences of death row inmates. To quote Roma, "I work with the most dangerous people in society and I've seen more humanity on death row than I ever saw in the music business."

KATE AND LOUDON'S WEDDING

JANE: Kate and Loudon tied the knot in January 1971 at his parents' home in Bedford Village, New York. I flew back east with daughter Anna and drove with Dane, sister Anna, little Anna and Gaby to the Wainwrights', who were putting us up. We were warmly received by Loudon *père* and mother Martha, and bonded with his sisters Teddy and Sloan and brother Andrew.

The wedding was a small affair, family and close friends. I remember that Loudon was married in a suit he borrowed from his best man. Kate was beautiful in a high-style brown and black designer dress. Anna had put an outfit together, a black fitted sweater and a gathered skirt that she'd made out of a dark, silky material with a coloured print. We ate and drank, sang and danced. I can still see Anna in her black stockings and patterned skirt doing some mystical little dance of her own devising. Kate and Loudon sang us "Oh Poppa," Kate on piano and Loudon on guitar. It was a lovely time and we relived the highlights over breakfast the next day before heading off to Montreal.

ANNA: Kate was expecting a baby, and she and Loudon were living in a cottage nearby. I remember that their guest accommodation was a grey metal hospital bed from an earlier era that Loudon had recently acquired. At the time, I associated this cold steel furnishing with Loudon's song "Hospital Lady," written about his mother's sojourn in hospital, from his first recording released in 1970 on Atlantic. Looking back now, this grim, inanimate object turned out to be an omen.

Within a couple of months they had decamped for London, living first in a flat in Kennington then on Holland Park Road near Notting Hill. There they hooked up with Chaim Tannenbaum, who was studying for a postgrad degree in philosophy at the University of London. The three of them used to busk down on the Portobello Road. I always found it funny that Loudon, an up-and-coming artist signed to a major label, was singing in the streets by choice.

That spring, Kate made a short trip back to Saint-Sauveur to see Gaby. She was radiant in a new lavender wool knit dress with a natural suede trim down the buttoned front and on the cuffs, and she was a little over five months pregnant and "showing." Kate presented our mother with a pink linen dress and a black straw hat with a wide brim she had bought for her at Harrods. Easter was coming up and Gaby was thrilled with the gift. As she modelled the hat for us, she went through her head and hand gestures for the show tune "Alice Blue Gown," making us laugh. "I was both proud and shy, as I felt every eye/And in every shop window I primped passing by."

Within a couple of weeks of Kate's return to London, she went into labour prematurely and gave birth to a baby boy who sadly lived but a few hours. The Irish Catholic nurse at the small private hospital where she was being cared for asked if she might baptize the child, otherwise he'd spend eternity in limbo. This act of kindness meant a lot to Kate. James was the name she and Loudon chose, and Kate told me how poor Loudon had to go buy a coffin for the infant.

Bizarrely, in November 2009, when Kate was only two months away from her own death, Martha gave birth prematurely to her first son, Arcangelo, while she and her husband, Brad, were in London touring her Piaf tribute *Sans fusils, ni souliers, à Paris*. Hers had an immeasurably happier outcome, due in large part to the excellent care she received at London's University College Women's Hospital.

JANE: Towards the beginning of summer 1971, I received a letter from Kate in London, just after she'd lost the baby at five and a half months. The infant boy had made a little squawk then been whisked away. She never really saw him. The tone of the letter was sad but resigned, a heartbreaking contrast to the letter that had immediately preceded it, reporting on a good medical checkup, "perfect health" and the new maternity dress she'd bought. She was exactly five and a half months pregnant at the time of the exam. Reading this now, forty-four years later, Anna and I wonder if the doctor missed something, or even perturbed the baby in some way that would cause a premature birth. We'll never know. Kate and Loudon separated and left London.

On our end, things weren't cheery either. Dave's little sister Debbie had contracted some weird illness while trekking in the Himalayas, at first thought to be hepatitis. She flew home to Montreal, where she was diagnosed with Hodgkin's disease, by that time quite far along.

ANNA: It was Loudon's choice to split up after the unhappy event in London, and Kate was devastated. My sister never liked being the bearer of bad news, so when something of an unpleasant nature had to be imparted to someone, she used to say to me, "Anna, can you do it? You're the older, more responsible one."* The lyrics to "Tell My Sister," composed at that time, were a nod to that dynamic in our relationship: "Tell my sister to tell my mother/I'm coming home, home alone."

She returned to Gaby in Saint-Sauveur and spent the early part of the summer of 1971 recuperating by resting in the sun and knitting. But when her condition didn't improve, our mother took her to see a doctor, who diagnosed peritonitis and prescribed a course of antibiotics. A follow-up X-ray revealed that her Fallopian tubes were blocked, a result of the infection, and the doctor took my mother and me aside to tell us she would probably never have children, before telling her himself. We left his office in tears. At least the peritonitis and the accompanying fever she had been running around with for months were gone, and she began to get her strength back.

---

* I was older by a year but I certainly wasn't more responsible.

FIDDLE

(Anna)

Loudon had given Kate the Volvo wagon he'd bought when they were first married, a kind of consolation prize, and it wasn't long before Kate was on the move again. During their short time together, Loudon had also given her a Vega Tu-ba-Phone banjo, which she taught herself to frail (a.k.a. clawhammer style) using Pete Seeger's instruction book, and a very nice old fiddle. She took these with her when she returned to Saratoga in the state of old New York and the familiarity of the Caffè Lena scene. Roma was still in the United States, going between Saratoga and New York City, and Kate addressed her in "Come a Long Way."

> *Oh we come a long way since we last shook hands*
> *Still got a long way to go.*
> *Couldn't see the flowers when we last shook hands*
> *Couldn't see the flowers on account of the snow.*
> *…*
> *All my life I wanted to roam*
> *To go to the ends of the Earth*
> *But the Earth really ends where you started to roam*
> *And you and I know what a circle is worth.*

One of the people staying with Lena in the early fall of 1971 was George "Smoke" Dawson, a fiddler and bagpipe player based on the west coast. He and Kate hooked up and so began a mutually advantageous relationship. His home was in Mendocino, California, where he worked as a fisherman, and he had to get back for the fishing season. She had the car.

> *And the trees grow high in New York State*
> *And they shine like gold in autumn.*

Never had the blues from whence I came
But in New York State I caught 'em.
Talk to me of Mendocino
Closing my eyes I hear the sea.
Must I wait? Must I follow?
Won't you say, "Come with me?"

Kate played Gaby's violin to Roma's cello when the two were still together, the same fiddle our mother sawed away on in the Bell Tel Orchestra. Smoke helped her develop a rudimentary but very effective accompanying style of fiddle, detuning certain strings to get a drone effect when double-stopping. Folk fiddler Alan Stowell, who was also living in Saratoga, would have given her pointers too.* She held the instrument up to her chest instead of under the chin. This way she could see the neck to position her fingers more accurately on it, and the rustic stance suited her better.

---

* I remember her loosening the hair on the bow and slipping the neck of the fiddle between the hair and the wood so that the hair was now lying across the strings and the wood bow was under the neck. With the fiddle in an open tuning it was another way to get a drone effect similar to a type of Swedish fiddling.

KATE AND LOUDON
(Jane)

October 26, 1971, found Kate sitting in a café in Mendocino, penning me a letter. She wrote of travelling across the country with Smoke Dawson and mentioned they were planning a trip to San Francisco at some point.

They turned up at our place in San Carlos about a week later and took over the guest quarters for an indefinite stay. The plan was to float around the Bay Area, do some gigs and connect with friends. The next thing I knew, Smoke was being bounced out of the guest quarters to make room for Loudon, whose arrival was imminent. We packed up poor old Smoke's stuff and drove him back to Mendocino. He wasn't very happy about it but took it like a soldier.

I barely had time to change the sheets on the guest bed before Loudon was at the door. Together again, Kate and Loudon settled into the guest room, but my sense was that things were still choppy.

For reasons that are no longer clear to me, we hatched a mad Christmas plan that had Dave flying to Montreal with Vinnie while Kate, little Anna and I attempted to drive there. We were travelling with skis, a dozen musical instruments in cases, and lots of bags. Little Anna was in her car seat with colouring books and other diversions as we rolled through blizzards across a couple of mountain ranges in a drafty Oldsmobile convertible. We gave it up in Denver, dumped the car on a friend and flew the rest of the way. We hadn't budgeted this change, but I had a plan.

In 1971, I was thirty years old, Kate was twenty-five and little Anna was almost four. I made a copy of Kate's baptismal certificate that she travelled with as proof of age when she was carded, and changed the date of birth to 1950. Now she was a minor and travelled half fare. I had done the same thing for Anna when she and Dane visited me in San Francisco in 1967. We told the passenger agent that little Anna was two years old and didn't need a ticket. She was bundled up in a blanket to hide her long legs and sucking her thumb as instructed. Next hurdle was the baggage allowance, which we exceeded by at least ten pieces. Kate launched into a story of some kind to the agent, who was already very tired of us, and he just tagged everything at no extra charge and sent us on our way, end of story. Ah, the golden age of travel.

Loudon stayed on in San Carlos for a few weeks, eventually returning to New York and a reconciliation with Kate. Rufus was born on July 22, 1973, Kate's infertility a happy misdiagnosis.

MOVING PAINS
(Jane)

Dave and I were house hunting again. The house next door had been sold by the Hammond family, wonderful neighbours, to a young couple who were decidedly not wonderful. They drove their Corvette too fast, played their high-end stereo too loud, let their skittish Doberman wander off leash. The Doberman liked our carport and would stand between me and my car, growl and bare his teeth. I had to take the children back into the house and wait until he wandered off. The couple mocked me when I complained. "Oh yeah? Killer's been over there bothering you again?" We were driven out.

I hated to leave Dover Court. We had put a lot into the house, adding a beautiful deck that looked out over the canyon, a new kitchen, a guest room and bath. It held memories of the greater family and extended family who had visited us. We had received a lot of people in San Carlos at one time or another, sometimes to enjoy a California vacation, sometimes for a respite from troubles at home. Everyone loved the place and we were urged not to sell it, but we didn't have the stomach for a range war with the goons next door and started looking for another home.

We found a house we liked in Woodside Hills, closer still to Dave's office in Palo Alto, and moved in a couple of days before Christmas 1974. It was a California ranch-style home on an acre landscaped with fruit trees, and had a forty-by-twenty-foot swimming pool. The house was built in a U shape around the pool patio area, with sliding glass doors opening onto it on three sides. A family of three kingsnakes lived in the pampas grass on the far side of the patio and came out once in a while to sun themselves or coil up under the apple trees out back. California kingsnakes are constrictors and natural predators of rattlesnakes, and thus make desirable "pets." They're big creatures, you can't miss them when they slither out of the pampas grass, but we appreciated (if didn't exactly enjoy) their presence and tried not to bother them.

The sellers were late getting out of the house, and our buyers were chafing to get into their new quarters and started moving in before we were really out. We took possession of 1790 Fernside Road on December 21 and pushed to make a decent Christmas for Anna and Vinnie. Getting a tree up before we were even unpacked, trying to persuade stores not to slam the door on me on Christmas Eve so I could pick up a few things, organizing a Christmas dinner . . . it was all exhausting, but we were in our new home and happy to be there. There was a smaller patio off the kitchen that I hadn't noticed first time around, and it was a delight to make its discovery. It was on the north side of the house and had some neglected citrus trees and a blooming wisteria vine along the fence. I started feeding and reviving the fruit trees in the first week after our move. We looked forward to our own oranges, lemons and kumquats.

At home in Montreal, Debbie's condition grew steadily worse and caused her parents great anguish; Don's own health started going downhill, in fact, this strongest, most stoic of men was falling apart. When Debbie was admitted to hospital at Easter time, Don suffered a series of small strokes and was admitted to hospital himself. The two hospitals were across town from each other, exacerbating the hardship for Irene and Joan, who were spending as much time as they could with the patients. Debbie never left the hospital and succumbed on May 22, 1975. Dave went home for her funeral and returned to California a week later. He hadn't yet unpacked when we received word that his father had died, killed by the illness and death of his baby. Dave made another trip home for his father's funeral and to help out with family affairs. I stayed behind with the children, who were now in school. Irene and Joan came and stayed with us for a couple of weeks to get away from the sorrowful realities at home and be with what was left of their family.

"WORK SONG"

ANNA: In 1973, things began to move quickly, at least for Kate. Rufus was born in July of that year, proving the doctor wrong, and Maria Muldaur had recorded Kate's "The Work Song" for her first solo Warner release, the same album that had the offbeat radio hit "Midnight at the Oasis," written by David Nichtern. The gospel-influenced "Work Song," with the verbal hook "You couldn't call it soul, you had to call it heart," had been suggested to Maria by her friend Greg Prestopino, who was helping her find original material. Greg had met Kate in 1971 when she and Loudon were living in Boston. He invited her over one evening to play his piano and fell under her spell listening to her songs. It was Peter Weldon who introduced us to Maria's work when she was the coquette girl singer and occasional fiddler in the Jim Kweskin Jug Band, a group her husband, guitarist Geoff Muldaur, was also a part of. Geoff was a good friend of producer Joe Boyd. Kate was new to the music biz, but it was starting to look as though it was all about who you knew.

By the spring of 1974, Maria was preparing a follow-up album entitled *Waitress in a Donut Shop*. Again Greg came to Kate for material, and she sent off a cassette of songs to him in LA. Joe Boyd, who was producing the record with Warner VP and producer Lenny Waronker, called Kate to tell her they were doing another one of her songs and could she fly out immediately to work on it. When she got there and heard the song, she said, "I didn't write this, my sister did." On the cassette Kate had sent Greg was "Cool River," the song I had written with my friend Audrey Bean. Now I was being summoned.

It did occur to me that Kate had somehow planned it all. In any case, I was feeling optimistic about this turn of events, so I quit my job at the Friends of St Anne's and left for LA the following day, taking my red accordion. The US immigration officer at the Detroit airport smiled and asked, "Can you play that thing?" I obliged him with a tune and he waved me in. I was walking on air.

Now, in the LA studio, Spooner Oldham, famous for playing the organ on Percy Sledge's "When a Man Loves a Woman," was seated at the piano playing my song. His thin, trembling hands extended over the notes, and between two fingers of his right hand he held a cigarette with a long ash. The song had a lot of chords, a couple of them coming out of left field; I still have trouble getting through it. But he didn't once hesitate. Kate and I sang harmonies to Maria's lead, and David Grisman would overdub a mandolin.

Greg, a musician and songwriter who had moved to LA permanently, begged Lenny for studio time to do a demo with the two of us while we were still in LA. It was this demo that got us a deal with Warners.

JANE: In 1974, Kate and Anna were in Los Angeles making a demo tape for Warner Brothers. They were staying at the Chateau Marmont, and invited me to join them. I made some arrangements for Anna and Vinnie and set out on the 101 South. I've always loved that the 101 has local names for some of its stretches, Bayshore in the Bay Area, Ventura Freeway in southern California; I rolled into West Hollywood on the Hollywood Freeway.

At the time, the Chateau Marmont was not the glamour palace it is now, but it had a special cachet in spite of its reasonable prices and slightly rundown rooms. The building is beautiful, on Sunset near La Cienaga, discreetly tucked up a lane; its guests were mainly musicians or actors, "show people" as my father would have said. There were a few permanent guests, Maximilian Schell being one I sometimes used to see in the shadows of the underground garage. The hotel had one- and two-bedroom suites and full kitchens, and Kate and Anna each had a suite of their own for their stay there. I moved in with Anna.

When K&A were finished with the demo, we jumped into my car, another Oldsmobile convertible, and headed toward Malibu to drop Kate off with her friend Libby Titus. The Band had a compound there and Libby was married to Levon Helm at the time. He made an appearance, as did Rick Danko, and we were late getting on the road again for northern California. It was Saturday, May 25, Memorial Day weekend; we intended to drive to San Carlos in a straight shot and hadn't arranged any accommodations. There was a lot of traffic and we were looking at about six hours on the road.

A couple of hours later, north of Santa Barbara, we were both flagging and decided we should stop for the night after all. I thought we could get a room around San Luis Obispo, and sure enough, up on a hill, the Madonna Inn was all lit up and beckoning us, but they were completely booked. The desk clerk called around for us, but there were no vacancies near or far. We considered approaching local law enforcement to see if they would give us a nice safe cell to stay in but discarded the idea. We bought some coffee to go and got back into the car.

We drove till my eyes were shutting and we had to stop, at least for a nap. I took the next exit, San Ardo, and headed in the direction of the coast till we found a little clearing with nothing at all around it. Anna scrunched into the back seat and I curled up in the front. We were exhausted but fearful of the situation we were in, and not without reason. We were in the middle of nowhere, on the fringes of Los Padres National Forest. California had experienced a wave of random killings in the 1960s and '70s; indeed, we learned a few days later that a family had been brutally murdered by some marauding lunatic in a campground not very far from where we had laid our heads down.

But we did fall asleep and survived the night. We woke up, shivering, to sunshine and tweeting birds. We stretched. Anna did her customary early-morning-out-in-a-field headstand and then went around to the trunk; absent a good cup of coffee, she pulled out a bottle of Jack Daniel's. We took big swigs and hit the road. The bourbon put us in a holiday mood and we took the scenic route to the beach.

Following a secondary road through the national forest to the Coast Highway, we came upon Mission San Antonio de Padua, a historical site, and stopped for a visit. There was a large pot in the middle of the courtyard and Anna had me take a picture of her standing inside it. Mission accomplished. We continued to Highway 1 and turned north to Carmel. We spent a few hours on the beach, had a swim, a nap, and arrived home refreshed. Anna stayed a few days and returned to Montreal.

ANNA: In 1974 Kate and Loudon were living in an apartment on 115th Street at Broadway directly across from the entrance gate to Columbia University. While Kate and I recorded at the A&R Studios in Midtown, little Rufus was mostly babysat by the building superintendent, a large woman in her early seventies named Anna Krauck. Of German stock, Anna was a Brunhilde type who always had on one of those cotton housedresses that buttoned up the front that women don't wear anymore. She lived in a ground-floor apartment next door to Kate and Loudon with her two large German shepherds and her batty older sister Nancy. The two women wore woollen tuques, even when inside. The handy thing about Anna was that she was available on short notice. She mostly took care of Rufus in Kate's apartment but sometimes she had to take him over to her place. Sam, the more aggressive of the two dogs, wore a leather muzzle when Anna took him out on the street because he bit people. "Get out of the way! I'm coming through with Sam!" she warned as she came through the lobby with the angry dog. There was a deep concrete trench around the building that Sam patrolled at night and a high iron fence just beyond it. From inside Kate and Loudon's apartment you could hear the big dog dragging his dry, cracked paws across the rough cement as he circled the building. Anna would say if anyone were dumb enough to come over the fence Sam would take him apart.

Kate and Loudon expressed their concern to her about having Rufus in her apartment with the dog. She assured them that Sam was as gentle as could be with eighteen-month-old Rufus; why he had even had his little hand in the dog's big mouth! Maybe it was all just inner-city bluster. Sam certainly never bit Rufus. Big Anna was fierce but completely trustworthy.

We began recording in New York City in late 1974 and finished nine months later in LA, with Joe and Greg co-producing.

JANE: When the folks at Warner Brothers heard Kate and Anna's demo, they lost no time in signing them and put them in the studio soon after to begin the recording process; some of the sessions would be done in New York, some in LA. Anna called me up one day while they were working on the west coast to ask if I would come to LA for a few days and play the organ on "Heart Like a Wheel." I had never done studio work and was a little nervous but looked forward to spending some time with my sisters and playing on their record. They were staying in their old digs at the Chateau Marmont, and I checked into Anna's suite for the duration. The gig turned out to be a little more daunting than I had at first thought; the organ was the basic track that voices and other instruments could be overdubbed on later, and the take had to be completely accurate from start to finish, no dropping in and out to correct mistakes. It was nerve-racking, with the meter running at $150 an hour and the engineer not used to amateurs, but we eventually got a satisfactory track—after twenty-six takes, if I remember correctly. Anna added a couple of ethereal banjo tracks in an unconventional tuning and Kate put down a guitar track to tie things together. K&A traded off on lead vocals and we all sang in harmony on the chorus. There have been some beautiful versions of the song, notably Linda Ronstadt's cover that was the B-side of her big hit "You're No Good," but our version will always be the definitive one to me.

Kate had written "Go, Leave" during one of her on-again, off-again periods with Loudon, but it was recorded in that group of sessions, when things between them were relatively stable. Even so, it must have evoked some painful memories, because she was fighting back tears toward the end of the song, a few drops falling onto her guitar. It was a very moving performance for the audience on the other side of the glass, Anna and I, and the production team, Greg Prestopino, Joe Boyd and John Wood, who perfectly captured it.

ANNA: In preparation for the tour to support our new record, which was due out in January 1976, Kate and I began rehearsals with a band in NYC. The musicians had been hand-picked by Greg Prestopino and they were all excellent players. Then it was off to Boston to do two weeks' worth of gigs in a Somerville bar called the Inn-Square Men's Bar. By day, the bar was a blue collar hangout. It opened around 8 a.m. for the convenience of men working the night shift who wanted a couple of pints before retiring. At night it was a music venue attracting many of its patrons from neighbouring Cambridge, home to Harvard. Playing this club would give us experience before an audience and the time to work out any kinks.

With twenty-four-track machines in the recording studios, the tendency was to layer all kinds of stuff onto a song. Our five musicians were proficient on more than one instrument and also sang back-up harmonies. This variety would allow us to sound in concert the way we did on the recording. The public expected this; at least, back then they did. It was the opposite of the "unplugged" fad of the nineties, itself a direct result of overproduction.

A dresser was also hired to make us presentable. She suggested long skirts and frilly blouses. We opted for less formal attire. During the day, this tall, blond ex-model would go off to the shops in Harvard Square and bring back items for us to try on. I remember us looking pretty nice. The whole entourage, including our lawyer Judy Berger and Jane, was living in a Cambridge hotel.

Peter Weldon and Chaim arrived at the club one evening in a dishevelled state after a marathon drive from Montreal. There were parties every night in the rooms. Warners was footing the bill for all of this, to be charged back to us against future royalties. When Greg went back to LA, his friend Bill Elliot replaced him as the band's music overseer. Bill recorded the last couple of shows we had done at the Inn-Square Men's Bar and we made a date to listen to the tapes after the Christmas holidays.

In January 1976, Bill brought the tape to Kate's apartment on 115th St. He was very excited to play it for us, he thought we sounded great with the band. But after listening to it, Kate and I weren't convinced. Compared to our smooth new record, which we had heard a lot over the holidays, the bar performances sounded raw.

We wondered whether going on the road sounding like this would do us more harm than good. Kate, who was six months pregnant, was sitting with her feet up, ankles swollen.

JANE: There would be a tour to follow the record's release in January 1976, and the record company had assembled a team around Kate and Anna to prepare for it. This was happening in Boston, and I got another call from my sisters inviting me to meet up with them; in fact, they sent me a plane ticket. I packed some winter clothes and flew back east for a week and checked into their hotel.

I had been teaching myself to play the banjo during the gas crisis of 1974, when it could take an hour or longer to buy a few dollars' worth of gas. Dave called on customers all over the Bay Area and it was my job to keep both our gas guzzlers in fuel. I had been fooling around with a borrowed Vega Whyte Laydie banjo and started taking it with me on my gas runs. With the kids strapped into their car seats in back, and Pete Seeger's *How to Play the 5-String Banjo* open on my lap (a tip from Kate), I taught myself "Old Joe Clark" and other simple banjo tunes, stopping every few minutes to move the car forward a couple of feet. I later treated myself to a banjo of my own, a Vega Tu-ba-Phone, and decided at the last minute to bring it with me to Boston, thinking there might be some jams going on after official rehearsals, but that was a pipe dream—the players were completely focused on the shows. I did spend a few hours with Peter Weldon, an expert player who endured my beginner's efforts and gave me a few tips.

There's always time to shop when the McGarrigle girls get together, and we found a Marimekko store nearby, where I loaded up on the Finnish designer's rugs and bedspreads and had them shipped home. We also bought ourselves some clothes (without the help of the hired dresser) and I came away with a bright red Norma

Kamali shirt and some wool slacks that I wore to the show.

Kate and Anna made their official debut with the newly hired band, under the direction of Greg Prestopino. I remember that Greg was cracking the whip pretty hard and people were on edge. To me, a stone fan, they sounded very good in the club, but K&A were unhappy with the exercise and fired the band.

I went back to California and prepared for a more relaxed Christmas than the previous year now that we were properly settled into the house and the family crises were behind us.

"KITTY COME HOME"

ANNA: The record was released on time and the tour was to begin six weeks later. Kate, who was pregnant with Martha, due in early May '76, had begun to suffer from edema and her doctor told her to stay off her feet. Cold feet and swollen ankles. We cancelled the tour and thereby committed career suicide.

Kate and I did fulfill some of our obligations to the company, agreeing to do all the east coast press and radio the label had set up. Gaby came along on these press trips to look after Rufus, as did our friend Deborah Adler, a.k.a. the Dancer with Bruised Knees. But with the tour cancelled, the record languished in the warehouses.

Martha was born on May 8 when Kate and Loudon were living in Waccabuc, Westchester County, New York. I babysat Rufus while Kate was in hospital nearby. I don't remember us giving much thought to "the record." Life was going on regardless. In early summer of '76, Kate heard from her friend Peter Philbin at rival label Columbia that our record was getting good press in the UK (London's *Melody Maker* declared it to be the best pop record of 1976). This, combined with the fact that the one French song on the record, "Complainte pour Ste-Catherine," was already on the hit parade in Holland and getting airplay in northern Europe, warranted us making a short tour in those territories. The record business is a business like any other; you go where people want you. After leaving baby Martha and Rufus in Saint-Sauveur with Gaby and a couple of young women who helped her, Kate and I set off to the UK and Holland with a small group of musicians. Chaim, who was back in London, joined the band.

JANE: In the months following, Kate and I spoke often by phone. We called each other to talk recipes, and for a while we did the *New York*

Times Sunday crossword on the phone. So when she called me on Thanksgiving Day 1976, I wasn't expecting her to be in tears. "Well, Wainwright's gone," she said. "I have a turkey in the oven, but he's walked out and he's not coming back." She was shattered.

ANNA: By the fall of 1976, Loudon and Kate had split up again. Loudon stayed on in the bright country house in Waccabuc where Kate had moved the Yamaha grand she'd bought with her advance from Warners. There would be no reconciliation—he was already in a relationship with Suzzy Roche. Kate retreated to the dark New York City apartment with the children. She considered moving to LA and she wanted me to go too. My mother talked her into coming back to Montreal, at least temporarily, and she and I drove to New York to collect Kate and the kids. Shortly after, I wrote "Kitty Come Home."

> *The birds in the trees call your name,*
> *Nothing's changed, all's the same*
> *Home, come home, home, Kitty come home.*

We helped her find an apartment at De Maisonneuve and Clarke in Westmount a couple of blocks from where Dane and I were living. It was a new beginning for her. For all of us, really.

EPILOGUE

In writing this family memoir, we feel like the character of Hoichi the Earless, a figure in Japanese mythology who has been dramatized in numerous stories, plays and books, including Lafcadio Hearn's *Kwaidan: Stories and Studies of Strange Things*. Hoichi the blind singer has a habit of playing his lute-like *biwa* in a local graveyard. There, the ghosts request the saga of their own once-glorious clan, a piece Hoichi knows very well. He doesn't realize he's playing the *biwa* for ghosts when he tells his guardian, a priest in the temple where he lives, about the very appreciative audience he's been performing for of late. He is blind, after all.

The temple priest, curious to know who Hoichi's audience is, watches as the *biwa* player goes into the graveyard. Fearing the spirits have begun to possess Hoichi, the priest, in an elaborate ceremony, inscribes the *biwa* player's entire body with sacred texts, making him invisible to the ghosts. Unfortunately, in his haste to ghost-proof Hoichi, the priest has forgotten to cover his ears with the ghost-proofing text. When Hoichi returns to the graveyard the following evening a ghastly samurai in the employ of the long-deceased and now angry clan, denied their storyteller, slices Hoichi's ears off.

We can only hope that by writing down the family stories, we will be provided with enough protection from our own ghosts.

ACKNOWLEDGEMENTS

For Kate, who was not afraid.

Thanks to the folks at Random House Canada, in particular Louise Dennys and Anne Collins, and to our ever-forbearing editor, Amanda Lewis, for pulling us over the finish line.

ANNA: For my family, Dane, Sylvan and Lily, and Kate's family, Rufus, Martha, Arcangelo, Viva and Francis Valentine. I thank you all, big and small.

Special thank yous to Kathleen Weldon, for her lovely drawing of Gardencourt; Dane Lanken and Gail Kenney, for their priceless photos that adorn this book; Brian Merrett for the 1964 photo of the Mountain City Four; Randy Saharuni, for the cover photo—I knew we'd use it someday; Vanessa Bonneau, for her word sense; Jörn Weisbrodt, for getting the ball rolling; Brad Albetta, for feeding a hungry writer; Deborah Adler, for her help with the Kate Fund; Caroline Holland, for opera tickets and legal advice; Campbell Hendery and GCT™, for transporting me on many levels; Michael Ondaatje and Tom Mennier, for their illuminations.

A special thank you to Janie, my sis and good friend. I will miss those winter writing sessions by the warmth of your cosy Jøtul stove, our weekly lunches at Lester's on rue Bernard and the trips to Jean Coutu to buy lipstick.

JANE: Thanks to my darling children, Anna Catherine and Ian Vincent Dow, and their partners, Bob McMillan and Kathleen Weldon, for their loving support and encouragement; to Dave Dow, for his near total recall of our shared memories, joyously revisited; to Peter Weldon, my faithful reader, for his valuable advice, so tactfully dispensed; to Caroline Holland, for guidance and support in this endeavour and many others over the years; to my friend and former colleague André Béraud who, on hearing my stories about growing up in Saint-Sauveur, encouraged me to commit them to paper, and to Tara Johns for her mentoring in the early days of this tale.

Special thanks to our cousins Claudette Latrémouille, Patricia Burns Latrémouille, Earl Latrémouille and Jules Fauteux; to Joan Carmichael, Ronnie Booth, Dean Booth and Joan Green Ortiz for their recollections and research done on our behalf; to Sylvan Lanken for tech wizardry and all-around support, to Renaissance woman Lily Lanken for pulling our family photos together; to Kate's children, Rufus and Martha Wainwright, always a source of inspiration and family pride.

Most importantly, thanks to my sister Anna for inviting me into this project. It was a blast, reliving the ups and downs of our life and the joys and sorrows of our clan. In that spirit, this book is dedicated to my granddaughters, Gabrielle and Islay McMillan.

IMAGE CREDITS

All images courtesy of the McGarrigle family, unless otherwise indicated.

Daddy at home in Saint-Sauveur, 1962. Credit: Jack Nissenson.

Anna near St. Paul Street, 1962. Credit: Gail Kenney.

Projections during a light show in November 1966 in the ballroom of the McGill Student Union building. Credit: Uffe Lanken.

A rare photo of The Mountain City Four performing at Moose Hall, Montreal, in 1964. Credit: Brian Merrett.

Anna between rides during hitchhiking trip with Dane to the West Coast in 1967. Credit: Dane Lanken.

Anna peering out of the Birmingham Apartments. Credit: Philippe Tatartcheff.

Anna with Audrey Bean in Montreal, off to a game of pick-up hockey. Credit: Dane Lanken.

Kate and Roma Baran. Credit: Dane Lanken.

Uffe and Gudda Lanken. Credit: Dane Lanken.

Kate and Loudon in 1973. Credit: Dane Lanken.

Dane and Anna at the farm in Alexandria, Ontario, early 1970s. Credit: John Fretz.

Rufus Wainwright with his G-Pa, Loudon Wainwright Jr., *circa* 1978. Credit: G-Ma Martha Wainwright.

Gaby with baby Martha at Anna and Dane's apartment. Credit: Dane Lanken.

Gaby and Sylvan with the Gardencourt sign our mother hated so much. Credit: Dane Lanken.

Rufus, Sylvan, Lily and Martha in Venise-en-Quebec. Credit: Randy Saharuni.

Sylvan and Lily Lanken skating on the pond at the farm in Alexandria in the 1980s. Credit: Dane Lanken.

Kate, Gaby and Anna backstage at Mariposa Folk Festival, Toronto Island, 1975. Credit: Gail Kenney.

Kate and Anna, Mariposa Folk Festival, Toronto Island, 1975. Credit: Gail Kenney.

Deborah Adler, a.k.a. Dancer with Bruised Knees, with Kate, Anna and Andrew Cowan at the ticket counter. Credit: Dane Lanken.

Gardencourt. Credit: Kathleen Weldon.

TEXT CREDITS

ANNA McGARRIGLE was one half of the acclaimed, award-winning folk music duo Kate and Anna McGarrigle. She continues to write music and perform in family concerts.

JANE McGARRIGLE managed her younger sisters' music careers from the late 1970s to the mid-1990s. During this time she co-wrote several songs with the duo and performed with them in the studio and on tours of Canada, the United States, Europe and Australia. She continues to be active in music publishing and copyright advocacy.

www.mcgarrigles.com